Relocating to Washington, D.C., and Surrounding Areas

Relocating to
WASHINGTON, D.C.,
and Surrounding Areas

Everything You Need to Know Before You Move

and After You Get There!

ED MCFADDEN

PRIMA PUBLISHING
3000 Lava Ridge Court • Roseville, California 95661
(800) 632-8676 • www.primalifestyles.com

The RELOCATING series is a trademark of Prima Communications Inc. PRIMA PUBLISHING and colophon are trademarks of Prima Communications Inc., registered with the United States Patent and Trademark Office.

Section 2 © 2000 by Monstermoving.com

All products mentioned are trademarks of their respective companies.

Every effort has been made to make this book complete and accurate as of the date of publication. In a time of rapid change, however, it is difficult to ensure that all information is entirely up-to-date. Although the publisher and author cannot be liable for any inaccuracies or omissions in this book, they are always grateful for corrections and suggestions for improvement.

Library of Congress Cataloging-in-Publication Data
McFadden, Ed.
     Relocating to Washington, D.C., and surrounding areas : everything you need to know before you move and after you get there! / Ed McFadden.
          p. cm.
     Includes index.
     ISBN 0-7615-2569-6
     1. Washington Region—Guidebooks. 3. Washington Region—Handbooks, manuals, etc. 3. Moving, Household—Washington Region—Guidebooks. I. Title.

F192.3 .M35 2000
975.3'042—dc21

00-042096

00 01 02 03 04 05 HH 10 9 8 7 6 5 4 3 2 1
Printed in the United States of America

HOW TO ORDER:

Single copies may be ordered from Prima Publishing, 3000 Lava Ridge Court, Roseville, CA 95661; telephone (800) 632-8676, ext. 4444. Quantity discounts are also available. On your letterhead, include information concerning the intended use of the books and the number of books you wish to purchase.

Visit us online at www.primalifestyles.com

To my parents, who exhibited faith in my abilities when evidence indicated perhaps they shouldn't.

And for Beth, Sam, and William, who make everything I undertake worthwhile.

CONTENTS

ACKNOWLEDGMENTS

Until you take on an assignment such as this book, you never appreciate the energy, time, and effort so many people invest to make such projects possible. And since one never knows how many opportunities he'll have to create something that will be published, this may be the only chance to thank people who have helped along the way.

My colleagues probably wondered why I was always yawning at meetings after pulling late night and weekend research and writing marathons to pull this book together. Thanks especially to William Beaman and Gary Sledge for their patience and understanding.

Andrew Ferguson, Wladyslaw Pleszczynski, and William Schulz are three of the most talented writers and editors a person could ever know, and I have been fortunate to have them as mentors, colleagues, and, most important, friends. They taught me everything I know about reporting, writing, and editing. So if anyone is to blame for what you now hold in your hands, it is them. Greg Gutfeld did absolutely nothing to help me with this book, but since he mentioned me in his book, rules of acknowledgement require that I return the favor.

For data and background information, special thanks to the Washington, D.C., Board of Trade, Washington Metro, the economic development offices of Arlington County and Fairfax County in Virginia, Montgomery County and Prince Georges County in Maryland, the U.S. Department of Commerce, and the Bureau of Labor Statistics. Also MonsterData.com for statistical and demographic data of the area.

David Richardson and Andrew Vallas at Prima Publishing exhibited herculean patience throughout the project with this rookie. They were always there to make sure the deadlines were finally met and the problems were finally resolved. I appreciate this opportunity they gave me. Special thanks go to Max Schulz, a talented writer and editor in his own right, who brought me into Prima's orbit and assisted in bringing this project to fruition.

INTRODUCTION

One of the most awe-inspiring views of Washington, D.C., is from the seat of a plane taking the Potomac River landing approach to Ronald Reagan National Airport. The jets swoop down from the northeast, following the river's path.

Looking out your window, you first see the foliage of the Cabin John Parkway, then the gothic spires of Georgetown University. Off in the distance, high on a hill, the distinctive bell tower of the National Cathedral is visible. Below, you see the Key Bridge, then the Roosevelt and Memorial Bridges, which connect Virginia to the District.

Because of building height restrictions, the downtown has a uniform skyline, unaccented by dramatic skyscrapers. But from this vantage point, the city's crisp grid of intersecting streets broken up by the hubs and spokes of traffic circles—an urban plan that was first laid down by Pierre L'Enfant back in 1791—is perfectly clear.

The plane banks to the right on its final approach. To your right are the twin *USA Today* towers in Arlington, Virginia, and out on the left, Washington's memorials come into view, first the Washington, then the Lincoln and the Jefferson; stark, white marble turned pink and warm in the sunset. Finally, your line of sight draws you up Constitution Avenue to the shimmering white dome on Capitol Hill.

In a matter of three minutes your eyes have taken in all of Washington, from its borders along Maryland and Virginia, to the Potomac and Anacostia Rivers. In this brief moment, you've seen a true overview of the capital: its past symbolized by the stately monuments, its present embodied in the buildings of our nation's government—and in all of it, your future.

Whether you're moving to Washington to attend one of the many universities or graduate schools; beginning a career in law, journalism, or government; or simply opening a new chapter in your life, this city will suit your needs.

Don't Believe What You Hear

Given what people have written about Washington, D.C., over the more than 200 years of its existence, it's a wonder that people want to live here at all.

Historians, pundits, and anyone with a flair for turning a phrase have disparaged "D.C." (the most popular shorthand reference). People from Thomas Jefferson to Mark Twain to Alistair Cooke have derisively referred to Washington as nothing more than prettified swampland. President John Kennedy called D.C. a "city with Southern efficiency and Northern charm." Perhaps the most devastating and most often-cited description of the District was published in the 1950s book *Washington Confidential*. Washington, the authors said, was a "made-to-order architectural paradise with the political status of an Indian reservation, inhabited by . . . economic parasites; no industries but one—government—and the tradesmen and servants and loafers and scum" who feed on it.

If you've read this far and still want to move to Washington or one of its surrounding suburban communities, good for you—you will be amply rewarded for your perseverance. Because while D.C. often is the brunt of jokes, virulent commentary, and attacks, it is still one of the most charming, most accessible, and most livable areas in the United States.

This was true even 10 to 15 years ago, when the city's crime rates were the highest per capita in the country, you seemingly couldn't drive a block without hitting a swimming-pool-size pothole, and neighborhoods that once were showcases of federal architecture and graceful Southern charm were decaying. And it's true today, when crime and joblessness are down, and neighborhoods seemingly lost forever now thrive with a strong pulse of commerce and cultural diversity. As for the potholes, well, you will just have to grow accustomed to their quirky, auto-suspension-jolting charms.

Washington's Evolution

Back in 1951—indeed up until the late 1980s—Washington's economy and population were almost entirely dependent on the government bureaucracy. But in 1989 the local economy that was driven by the business of government and real estate development took a hit, and in the past 10 years the Washington area has seen an economic diversification and expansion the region had not seen since the Industrial Revolution.

In the area that makes up the Washington, D.C., metropolitan area (D.C., parts of Northern Virginia, and suburban Maryland), more people work for computer and high-tech firms than anywhere else in the United States other than Silicon Valley. America Online, Qwest, COMSAT, and Hughes Satellite have headquarters here, as do national corporations such as MCI, Sprint, Mobil Oil, General Dynamics, and the Marriott Corp.

Washington tends to have a more stable employment market than other parts of the country, thanks to the jobs generated by government contracts (the federal government spends more than $48 billion a year on private contracts in the area) and the large number of civil service and corporate jobs available here. Part of the region's attraction to corporate America is its young and well-educated pool of potential hires. You won't find a deeper concentration of institutions of higher education anywhere in the country: In a 20-mile radius you will find Georgetown University, George Washington University, George Mason University, American University, Howard University, Gallaudet University, Catholic University, and the University of the District of Columbia. And only a few miles farther away are the University of Maryland—College Park and Johns Hopkins University.

As a result, more than 70 percent of all jobs are "white collar," and the average starting salary for an entry-level, private-sector job is $27,000. But don't get the wrong idea. Washington may be a white collar town, but it's not necessarily a *starched* white collar. In fact, regardless of your taste in clothing, there is a community, a job, and a life for you in Washington that will fit you comfortably now and for many years to come.

Lay of the Land

Washington is divided into four quadrants, the center of which is the U.S. Capitol building. They are called, imaginatively enough, Northwest, Northeast, Southeast, and Southwest. Three of the four quadrants contain neighborhoods that are unique, highly livable, and affordable.

While Washington has for many years been identified as a high-crime city, many of the problems are focused in inner-city, low-income areas. And while violence and crime does fan out at times across the city, most residents find Washington to be a safe place to live. It is common to see couples or families out for an evening stroll in many neighborhoods, including downtown or on Capitol Hill, which are not strangers to crime.

This book will highlight the 15 most popular and most accessible neighborhoods in Washington, D.C. Because Washington's public transportation system is so efficient and convenient, we will also highlight several communities in Northern Virginia and Maryland that are easily accessible via Metrorail trains.

In the chapters that follow, I will provide you with detailed information for each of the recommended neighborhoods, as well as additional resources for finding housing, roommates, a job, schools, and all the other things you'll need in your new life in the nation's capital.

But it won't take you long to learn just how accessible Washington can be. At its best, D.C. can be the quintessential sleepy Southern town, much as it was 150 years ago. On weekends in the late fall, winter, and early spring, when tourism is practically nonexistent and the weekday warriors and bureaucrats have left for the 'burbs, Washington is at its most appealing. The downtown streets are less full. Restaurants and coffeehouses have lots of seats. Bookstores and newsstands have room to spread out and browse. The city's pace—which during the week is palpably high-speed—slows.

At such times Washington doesn't feel so much like the epicenter of power for the free world. At such times you can casually walk along Georgetown's M Street, into Rock Creek Park, and down along the Potomac, past the Kennedy Center, the Washington Memorial, and the Jefferson Memorial and its tranquil tidal basin. As you make your way, sipping your cup of coffee or a soda, you can take in the natural and architectural beauty that surrounds you. And you can recall that only months before you had gazed upon these very things from an airplane going into Reagan National. At such times you realize you aren't just in Washington, D.C., anymore. You're home.

STATISTICS FOR WHOLE CITY

Average Temperature by Season

	Hi	Low
January	48°	35°
February	48°	30°
March	55°	39°
April	68°	48°
May	75°	60°
June	85°	68°
July	89°	70°
August	85°	70°
September	75°	60°
October	70°	55°
November	55°	40°
December	45°	35°

Population
City population: 528,964
Washington regional population: 3,329,607

Population by Ethnicity
White: 154,603
Black: 340,837
Asian: 16,046
Hispanic: 37,705

Population by Gender
Male: 282,970
Female: 323,930

Population by Age

Under 5 years:	*37,351*
5 to 17 years:	*79,741*
18 to 20 years:	*35,291*
21 to 24 years:	*47,267*
25 to 44 years:	*216,472*
45 to 54 years:	*62,031*
55 to 59 years:	*25,441*
60 to 64 years:	*25,459*
65 to 74 years:	*44,553*
75 to 84 years:	*25,447*
85 years and over:	*7,847*

Income

Per capita income:	*$24,500*

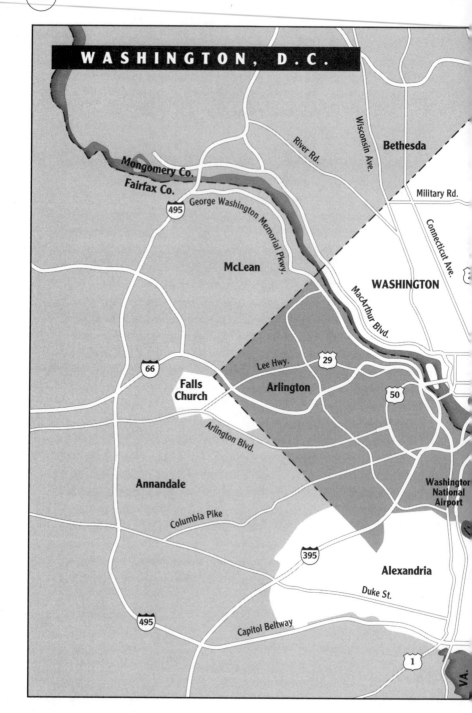

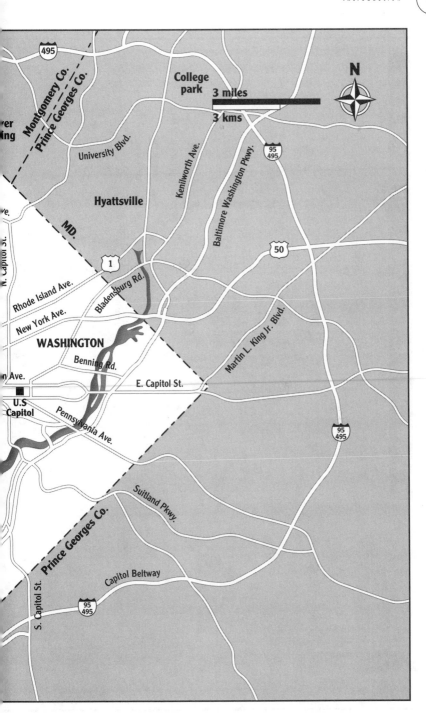

WASHINGTON, D.C., METRORAIL

N

Red Line

Shady Grove
Rockville
Twinbrook
White Flint
Grosvenor-Strathmore
Medical Center
Bethesda
Friendship Heights
Tenleytown-AU
Van Ness-UDC
Cleveland Park
Woodley Park-Zoo/Adams Morgan
Dupont Circle
Farragut North

Glenmont
Wheaton
Forest Glen
Silver Spring
Takoma

Capitol Beltway

Montgomery County
Prince George's County

Green Line

Greenbelt
College Park-U. of Md.
Prince George's Plaza
West Hyattsville
Fort Totten
Brookland-CUA
Rhode Island Ave.

New Carrollton
Landover
Cheverly

Georgia Ave-Petworth
Columbia Heights
U St./African-Amer. Civil War Memorial/Cardozo
Shaw-Howard U.
Mt. Vernon Sq./7th St. Convention
McPherson Sq.
Gallery Pl. Chinatown

Fairfax-CMU
ring-Merrifield
lls Church-VTA/UVA

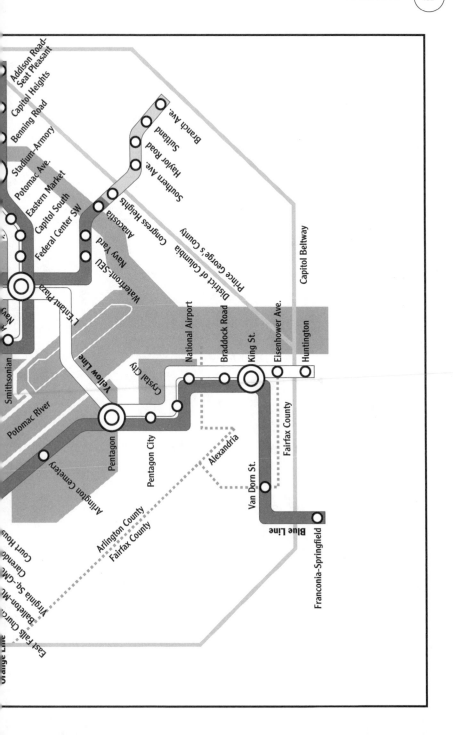

Places to Live

CHAPTER 1

Neighborhood Descriptions

Several roommates who lived in a group house in suburban Northern Virginia decided they needed to move into Washington, D.C., to be closer to their jobs and to improve their social lives, which they found lacking 15 miles from the city. One worked on Capitol Hill; two others worked in Bethesda, Maryland, another suburb of Washington. A fourth was a full-time student in D.C., a fact that had to be taken into consideration when the group's rent budget was calculated.

The young men contacted a D.C. rental agency, which showed them a home on a quiet street behind Catholic University, in a neighborhood called Brookland. For their budget, about $1,200 a month, the house seemed to be the best they could hope for. But there were problems: only one bathroom for four men, bedrooms that really weren't bedrooms at all, and an antiquated kitchen. And then there were the late-night drive-by shootings.

"It was a classic D.C. rental for young people who might be students or on a tight budget," says one of the former roommates. "There are probably hundreds of places like these with similar problems around Washington. And they have probably broken up thousands of friendships." (He should know—he hasn't spoken to two of his three former roommates in eight years.) "The house just wasn't a good idea. If we'd had more time, taken greater care, things might be different," he adds.

I know of what he speaks; I was one of those roommates, and we were poster children for a book like the one you are currently holding.

The house itself had its drawbacks. But the biggest problem for us was the neighborhood we'd selected. By day, it all appeared to be your run-of-the-mill middle- to lower-middle-class community. By night, well, it was a nightmare in the making. Our housing situation was an unmitigated disaster, and, in the end, we had only ourselves to blame. Had we been students at Catholic University—a 15-minute walk from our house—the Brookland neighborhood might have been great. But we hadn't done our research and we locked ourselves into a yearlong lease.

In thinking of D.C. as a cookie-cutter community whose neighborhoods are more or less alike, we fell into a trap that many newcomers do. While Washington, D.C., is a city full of history, it is not a giant, well-kept museum. As with any city, neighborhoods improve and slowly fall into disrepair.

Yet it's easy to see why people view the District as one giant Smithsonian Institution. Just consider the number of museums (more than 60) and monuments and statuary (more than 125 in the city alone) that are essentially your neighbors in almost every neighborhood.

The man who helped shape Washington was Pierre L'Enfant, who designed Washington, D.C., in 1792. It's unclear how much of the city he envisioned for residential purposes, as for many years much of D.C. proper remained undeveloped farmland. (The traffic circles that can be found in the city are among the few remnants of L'Enfant's Frenchified vision of America's capital. So if your car gets dinged as you try to merge on Logan Circle or Washington Circle, curse the French and feel better.)

With the exception of parkland (sometimes found in those traffic circles), there is little undeveloped land in our nation's capital. And out of the morass of federal office buildings, downtown high-rises, and university campuses, at least eight diverse and unique residential neighborhoods have formed.

As my Brookland experience bears out, not all of these areas will meet your tastes and needs. For example, a friend who had quickly relocated from Los Angeles to Washington noted that while he enjoyed his apartment on Dupont Circle, he was disappointed that the social life around him, while colorful and plentiful, was also heavily gay. Had he checked out the neighborhood before signing his lease, he might have determined that his building was smack in the middle of what is generally considered ground zero for the gay community in Washington.

In addition to cultural issues, there are safety and economic issues you need to take into account. After many years of marginal munici-pal-government leadership, many D.C. neighborhoods simply aren't desirable places to live. In some neighborhoods entire city blocks are uninhabitable and unsafe to walk through. So it's important that you gain a sense of D.C.'s communities before you try to settle on one—and sign a long-term lease.

D.C. AREA GEOGRAPHY

Washington is divided into four distinct quadrants: Northwest, Northeast, Southwest, and Southeast. The Southwest quadrant fea-tures much of the Mall, that wide open space downtown where the Washington, Jefferson, Lincoln, and Vietnam memorials are con-structed, as well as many of the Smithsonian buildings and federal agency headquarters.

The Southeast sector lies on the House of Representatives' side of Capitol Hill and includes extensive residential neighborhoods, although most feature primarily low-income housing. In the past 20 years, many individual neighborhoods in Southeast have seen gentri-fication, while others have fallen on hard times. The reality is that some of the poorest and most crime-ridden areas of D.C. are in Southeast. Later, as we examine each sector in more depth, I will dis-cuss which areas are desirable—and safe—in this particular quadrant of the city.

Northeast is on the other side of Capitol Hill and includes large residential areas out near Catholic University, Howard University, and Galludet University. Because of the large student population, some neighborhoods of Northeast offer affordable housing, especially in the form of houses for rent.

Finally, there is Northwest, the area that covers much of down-town Washington as well as the high-profile neighborhoods of

Georgetown and the Wisconsin Avenue and Connecticut Avenue corridors.

Many of D.C.'s more desirable areas—with the exception of two or three—are in the Northwest quadrant. There are a few other interesting residential pockets elsewhere in the city as well.

The areas covered in this chapter are:

In the District
- Georgetown
- Capitol Hill
- Foggy Bottom
- Woodley Park/Cleveland Park
- Cathedral Heights/Tenleytown
- Friendship Heights/Chevy Chase
- Dupont Circle
- Adams Morgan/Kalorama

Other Neighborhoods to Consider
- Catholic University/Brookland
- Shaw and U Streets
- 16th Street Corridor
- The Palisades

Virginia
- Arlington
- Alexandria
- Crystal City/Pentagon City

Fairfax County
- Falls Church
- Annandale
- Fairfax City
- Vienna
- Tysons Corner
- McLean
- Reston/Herndon

Maryland

Montgomery County

- Bethesda/Chevy Chase
- Silver Spring
- Takoma Park
- Rockville
- Germantown/Gaithersburg

Prince Georges County

- College Park
- Hyattsville/Riverdale
- Greenbelt
- Landover/New Carrollton

Outside the Area

- Virginia
- Maryland

In the District

Long-time residents of Washington, D.C., say the city still has the feel of a small Southern town. While that may be true occasionally in spirit, the fact remains that D.C. is a community of about 60 square miles. What follows is a quick overview of the main neighborhoods you will most likely consider when looking for a home.

GEORGETOWN

It's fitting that we start with D.C.'s oldest and most storied community. With all due respect to Capitol Hill, Georgetown is the best known, most identifiable, and most desirable neighborhood for people who fantasize about living the "Washington, D.C.," lifestyle. It is also one of

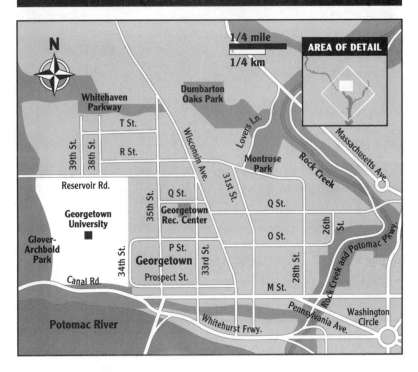

the most expensive areas to live in, both in terms of house prices and rental rates.

Georgetown lies west of downtown D.C. in the Northwest quadrant, and its borders are clearly defined. Rock Creek Park runs along its eastern side, Georgetown University on the west, the Potomac River along the south. Its northern border is Massachusetts Avenue, or "Massav" (say it as one word, like the locals).

Georgetown's main streets—Wisconsin Avenue and M Street—are lined with restaurants, bars, nightclubs, and specialty stores. Want to grab a bite to eat after 11 P.M.? No problem, Georgetown is hopping at midnight. How about a glass of wine and a bowl of cassoulet at all-night French bistro Au Pied de Cochon, or beer and Buffalo wings at Champions bar, or pasta at Paolo's? All are within just a two-block walk of Wisconsin Avenue. You can catch a set at Blues Alley or a night of theater at the Kennedy Center up the road. Other highlights of the neighborhood include Georgetown University; Georgetown Harbour, a condo and shopping development on the Potomac River; and Key Bridge, a walkway to Virginia that offers a majestic view of Washington.

On the narrow side streets that run throughout the area, quaint colonial brick walk-ups, clapboard farmhouses, and narrow World War II–era townhouses that have been converted into apartments add variety to blocks that are filled with historic mansions. On these streets, Capitol Hill policymakers mix with graduate students from Georgetown, and doctors and lawyers mingle with computer programmers with the cash to buy into the neighborhood. Some of those streets still are lined with cobblestone and the rails from a now-defunct trolley line that once ran through the city.

On Friday and Saturday nights, the regions' young professionals gather in Georgetown to party and enjoy city life. The traffic, noise, and crowded streets on a Saturday night at about 11 P.M. are reminiscent of Bourbon Street in New Orleans or Broadway on New Year's Eve. And there is usually a police presence to match.

Many people find the weekend partying a huge drawback to living in Georgetown. Traffic is troublesome; late-night revelers walking along the side streets after the bars close can be boisterous at best and vandals at worst. Crime in the area at times like this can be a problem as well.

But make no mistake about it: Georgetown is an exclusive, highly sought-after neighborhood. There are opportunities for newcomers looking to rent or purchase a home here—but you will pay dearly for the Georgetown address.

There are few large apartment buildings in Georgetown; if you are looking for an apartment, you most likely will be shown a house converted into smaller rentals. The results can be both charming and, at times, confounding. You'll find bathrooms where closets used to be, and kitchens with barely any room to eat. Dining rooms converted into bedrooms aren't prevalent, but they're not unheard of either.

Group homes, especially around the Georgetown campus and neighboring George Washington University, are fairly common, and sometimes turn over in the summer when many students leave town.

This is especially true of the neighborhoods above and behind the Georgetown campus. This area—known to its residents as Glover Park—has many small two-bedroom houses with full basements that are used as rental property. These homes can comfortably fit three people. Expect to pay $400 to $500 per person for such a house.

There are also lots of basement-level garden apartments, and many larger homes have carriage houses that are used as rental properties as well. The garden apartments—usually with private entrances—can be dark and small. The carriage houses are generally airy, one- or two-bedroom mini-homes and are among the most desirable types of rental housing in the city. As a result, few are on the rental market at any given time.

This is a driver's or a walker's neighborhood. There is no Metro stop in Georgetown, although there is bus service. Depending on where you live in the area, downtown Washington (Pennsylvania Avenue, K Street office buildings, etc.) is within walking distance.

If you do bring a car, make sure you register it with the city and get a Georgetown parking permit. It allows you to take advantage of strict on-street parking rules during the week and on weekend nights, when traffic from suburban visitors looking for a night on the town can become heavy.

While some of the negatives might stand out here, don't be fooled. One walk around Georgetown and you'll be sold. You're not just getting a room to lay your head, you're buying or renting into a lifestyle.

Neighborhood Statistical Profile

4-bedroom house $900,000-$1,000,000

3-bedroom house $750,000

2-bedroom house $400,000

Average Housing Costs

2-bedroom house:	*$400,000*
3-bedroom house:	*$750,000*
4-bedroom house:	*$900,000*
	to $1 million

Average Rental Costs

Studio:	*$700 to $800*
1-bedroom:	*$895 to $1,200*
2-bedroom:	*$1,500 to $2,500*
3-bedroom:	*$1,500 to $2,500*

Other Statistics

Average annual income:	*$70,000*
Average crime risk:	*More than five times the national average for robbery, burglary, and assault.*
Estimated commuting times:	*20 minutes to anywhere in Washington.*

Important Places Nearby

Grocery Stores

Dean and Deluca
3276 M Street NW
(202) 342-2500

Safeway
1885 Wisconsin Boulevard NW
(202) 333-3223

Pharmacies

CVS
1403 Wisconsin Avenue
(202) 337-0876

Banks

First Union
1501 M Street NW
(202) 637-2502

Riggs Bank
1201 Wisconsin Boulevard
(202) 887-6000

Bank of America Banking Center
1339 Wisconsin Avenue NW
(202) 624-4465

Hardware Stores

W.T. Weaver
1208 Wisconsin Boulevard NW
(202) 333-4200

Hospitals/Emergency Rooms

Georgetown Hospital
3800 Reservoir Road NW
(202) 687-2000

Sibley Memorial Hospital
5255 Loughboro Road NW
(202) 537-4000

CAPITOL HILL

After Georgetown, Capitol Hill is probably the oldest neighborhood in the District. When you consider how little residential property lies behind the Capitol building, the Capitol Hill "neighborhood" we will discuss is comparatively small—about 20 to 25 square blocks.

For our purposes, the boundaries for Capitol Hill run along Massachusetts Avenue to the north, 11th Street to the east, Virginia Avenue SE to the south, and the Capitol itself to the west. But in this limited area, you are likely to find extensive living options. There are few large apartment buildings, but many smaller single-family dwellings that have been transformed into rental properties or two or three small apartments.

It isn't uncommon to rent a street level apartment and find that you have a congressman living above you. Many younger House members choose to rent small apartments on the Hill, while their families stay home in their districts. The Hill also is chock-full of House and Senate staffers, policy wonks from the broad range of think tanks that dot the Hill area, as well as any number of reporters who cover politics in the Capitol.

If you are younger and looking for a group house opportunity, the Hill may be your best bet. With salaries for low-level Hill staffers beginning in the high teens to mid-20s, there are plenty of young people looking to split rents three or four ways.

During the week the Hill reeks of politics, which, after all, is what goes on up here. Day and night, Hill staffers, lobbyists, and government officials roam the area for a quiet seat at a coffee house to discuss whatever is roiling the halls of power on a given day. In close proximity to the Senate and House office buildings you will find a number of enjoyable bars and restaurants, some high-end and a few suitable for an intern's tight budget.

CAPITOL HILL

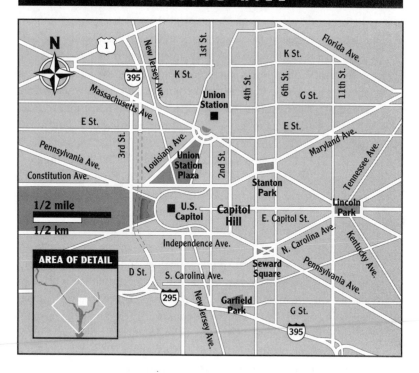

On a Sunday afternoon, though, the tree-lined streets are quiet, and the only bustle to be found is at the restaurants along Constitution Avenue that serve a hearty brunch.

Anchoring the neighborhood is the Eastern Market (7th Street and North Carolina Avenue SE), a Civil War–era edifice that today is surrounded by yuppified coffee shops, delis, and antiques shops. The market itself is a fully functioning food purveyor offering a good selection of locally grown produce, meat, and poultry.

On weekends, vendors selling everything from used books to organic vegetables and arts and crafts line the streets around the market. It is one of the truly enjoyable areas of the city, creating the small-town feel so many people seek. Nevermind that people from Northern Virginia suburbs flock to Eastern Market to take part in the Saturday morning ritual.

When looking for addresses on Capitol Hill, Washington's quadrant system comes most heavily into play. Remember, the Capitol is the nexus for the four quadrants, and the Northeast and Southeast quadrants merge at East Capital Street, behind the Capitol Building itself. As a result, for example, 2nd Street NE runs into 2nd Street SE at the East Capitol Street intersection, and the house numbers begin anew. When house-hunting on the Hill, make sure of where you're going; ask "Southeast or Northeast?" to avoid any confusion. You can also speak like an old-timer and simply ask "House side?" (Southeast) or "Senate side?" (Northeast).

Finally, a few words about crime on The Hill. While Washington, D.C., has seen a fairly dramatic improvement in crime in the past two years, it still remains a problem in some neighborhoods, including Capitol Hill. Robberies, burglaries, car thefts exceed the national average by more than 50 percent. Murders, as well exceed the national average by 25 percent. These figures, while disturbing should be taken in the context of location. While muggings and shootings do occur within the area we have profiled, they do not occur with as much regularity as other areas of Southeast. Petty crimes, such as purse-snatchings and pickpockets can be common, as are muggings. Capitol Hill streets, especially side streets, can be poorly lit. The one advantage a Hill dweller has is that both the federal Capitol Hill police force and the D.C. police patrol the area we are discussing regularly.

Neighborhood Statistical Profile

Average Housing Costs

2-bedroom house:	$150,000 to $200,000
3-bedroom house:	$400,000 to $600,000

Average Rental Costs

Studio:	*$700 to $800*
1-bedroom:	*$895 to $1,200*
2-bedroom:	*$1,500 to $2,500*
Group home:	*$300 to $500*

Other Statistics

Average annual income:	*$30,000*
Average crime risk:	*Robberies, burglaries, car thefts exceed the national average by more than 100 percent. Murders exceed the national average by 2 to 1.*
Estimated commuting times:	*20 minutes to anywhere in Washington.*

Important Places Nearby

Grocery Stores

Capitol Hill Market
241 Massachusetts Avenue SE
(202) 543-7428

Safeway
4th Street and Rhode Island Avenue NE
(202) 234-6012

415 14th Street SE
(202) 547-4333

Pharmacies

CVS
661 Pennsylvania Avenue SE
(202) 547-9325

Mortons Care Pharmacy
8th and East Capitol Streets NE
(202) 543-1616

Banks

Bank of America
210 Pennsylvania Avenue SE

First Union
400 North Capitol Street NE

Hardware Stores

Ace Hardware
505 8th Street SE
(202) 547-8326

Frager's
1115 Pennsylvania Avenue SE
(202) 543-6157

Washington, D.C., General Hospital
1900 Massachusetts Avenue SE
(202) 675-5000

Hospitals/Emergency Rooms

Medlink Hospital, Capitol Hill
700 Constitution Avenue NE
(202) 675-0500

FOGGY BOTTOM

Foggy Bottom isn't so much a neighborhood as it is a housing center. It's said that the area takes its funny name from the fact that the land runs along the banks of the Potomac, and when it was undeveloped river lowland back in the early 1800s, dense fog rose off the river in the early mornings and evenings.

Today the only things rising off the river in Foggy Bottom are apartment buildings and co-ops, the most famous of which is the Watergate complex. There, influential politicians, journalists, and Washington socialites reside (and not so long ago a certain notorious White House intern). You most likely will want to look at the many other apartment buildings that are in the area.

Foggy Bottom is just south of Georgetown: Its borders include M Street to the north, 26th Street Northwest to the west, 18th Street to the east, and Constitution Avenue to the south. The neighborhood encompasses parts of downtown Washington (almost to the White House's front door), and all of the seemingly ever-expanding George Washington University, which is now one of the largest property owners in the area. Because of the college campus, some areas of Foggy Bottom have an "Animal House" feel to them. (GW is regularly listed as one of the best party schools in the country and the student body works hard to keep its high ranking.) The Kennedy Center and the U.S. State Department are also located here.

This is prime apartment country in terms of variety, availability, and price. There are high-rises and small Victorian brownstones.

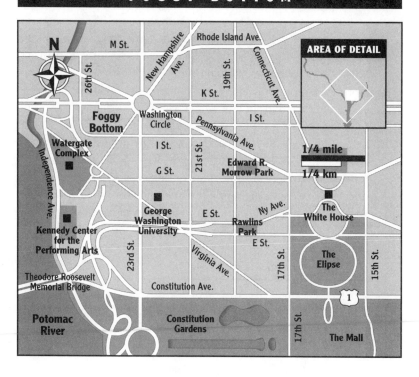

Many cater to the young professionals who work in the area's bureaucratic centers: the State Department, the World Bank, law offices, and the White House's Old Executive Office building (now the Eisenhower Office Building).

Most of the buildings are 1950s and 1960s construction, nothing terribly fancy. Many resemble the standard apartment buildings one might find on the Upper East Side of Manhattan. During and after World War II, Washington saw a boom in housing construction, in part because the government grew so large during the FDR years. The result: Foggy Bottom has many large apartment buildings, almost all of them with vacancies on a regular basis. Most commonly, they are efficiency or one-bedroom apartments. This is not an area intended for families, although there are pockets of single-family homes, especially as you get closer to Georgetown.

The area is serviced by several Metro stops, and like so many areas of Washington, you will probably want to use the Metro instead of trying to find parking for a car. It can be next to impossible, especially when GW classes are in session. In fact, in this neighborhood you won't even miss not having a car. You are within walking distance of just about everything of interest in downtown Washington.

And that's a good thing, because for an area with a large college campus, there is little neighborhood nightlife that might appeal to a nonstudent. This is perhaps the result of Foggy Bottom being only blocks away from Georgetown and the singles bars that run along 18th and M Streets. But a slightly dull neighborhood is a small price to pay to be in the center of town, with a wide variety of housing opportunities and a social whirl only blocks from your doorstep.

Neighborhood Statistical Profile

Average Housing Costs

2-bedroom house:	*$165,000*
3-bedroom house	*$240,000*

2-bedroom $1,250-$2,500

1-bedroom $800-$1,100

Studio $550-$800

Average Rental Costs

Studio:	*$550 to $800*
1-bedroom:	*$800 to $1,100*
2-bedroom:	*$1,250 to $2,500*

Other Statistics

Average annual income:	*$70,000*
Average crime risk:	*Robberies and assaults a little more than twice the national average. Higher incidence of vandalism and disorderly conduct (related to George Washington University campus).*
Estimated commuting times:	*By Metro, five to 10 minutes to anywhere downtown.*

Important Places Nearby

Grocery Stores	Hospitals/Emergency Rooms

Safeway
Watergate Complex
2550 Virginia Avenue NW
(202) 338-3628

George Washington University Medical Center
901 23rd Street NW
(202) 994-1000

Pharmacies

CVS
Watergate Complex
2550 Virginia Avenue NW
(202) 338-3628

WOODLEY PARK/CLEVELAND PARK

I am covering Woodley and Cleveland Parks in one section, because Woodley Park is almost an extension of the larger Cleveland Park. Each can be found along what I will call the "Connecticut Avenue Corridor."

Connecticut Avenue is one of the main arteries of Washington and will serve as one of the central streets to your home-hunting. That's because Connecticut Avenue runs through many of the neighborhoods we're examining.

Woodley Park is the first of what are actually a few of Washington's upper Northwest neighborhoods, just across the Rock Creek Bridge, one of Washington's landmarks. Here Connecticut Avenue intersects with Calvert Street. Several blocks north on Connecticut, near the National Zoo, Cleveland Park begins.

Along Connecticut Avenue and Calvert, Woodley Park features large World War II–era apartment buildings mingling with more modern apartment and co-op buildings. Smaller apartment buildings can be found on the numerous side streets in the area. Woodley Park is also the beginning of the large area of middle-class, single-family homes, and smaller rental properties in Washington.

WOODLEY/CLEVELAND PARKS

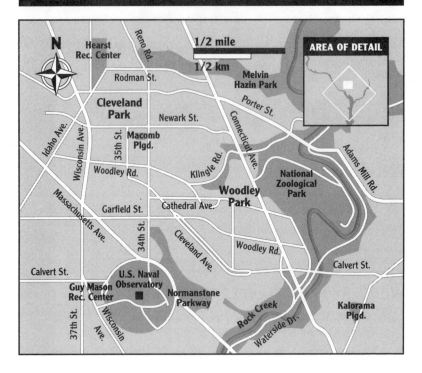

But Woodley Park is probably most known for its high concentration of outstanding restaurants in a two-square-block area. As you walk northward up Connecticut from Rock Creek Bridge, you come across Italian, Thai, Middle Eastern, Chinese, even Irish-American eateries. One of Washington's—indeed, one of the United States'—premier restaurants, New Heights, is also in Woodley Park's restaurant row. The area also features two of Washington's high-end hotels, the Omni Shoreham, once one of the city's top luxury apartment buildings, and the Sheraton Washington.

Although Woodley Park is comparatively small on a map, it has its own Metro stop, making commutes a breeze. Residents have the majestic Rock Creek Park as their backyard playground; it's one of Washington's main recreational resources, with running and bike paths and quick access to other parts of D.C., including Georgetown, Dupont Circle, and Foggy Bottom.

Woodley is considered one of the safest areas in Washington, in part because it is well outside downtown. Other than the restaurants, there is little to attract outsiders to the area except the National Zoo, which people flock to on weekends.

Woodley Park is also considered to be one of the more conservative areas of Washington, not politically, but in terms of lifestyle. Aside from an Irish pub or two, this area is increasingly becoming a bedroom community. If you are a bit older, and you're looking for a nice, calm area to come home to, Woodley Park and Cleveland Park are the places to be.

As you walk up Connecticut Avenue, past the National Zoo, you have entered Cleveland Park. One of the first areas in Washington, D.C., to be developed for residential purposes after Georgetown and Capitol Hill, it was home to the city's business owners and civic leaders as the city grew in the late 19th and early 20th centuries. And for my money, this is Washington's best area to reside in.

First, you have some of the city's nicest large apartment buildings, which usually have a number of vacancies available at any given time. Many of them are beautiful, 40- or 50-year-old buildings, full of history and charm. The crown jewel is the huge Kennedy-Warren next door to the zoo. It features its own convenience store, a dry cleaner—even a ballroom. As you move up Connecticut Avenue, there are a number of such buildings to consider, each with its own advantages.

Second, unlike Georgetown, Cleveland Park is easily accessible for those who choose not to own a car. There are three Metro stops in the Cleveland Park area: Woodley Park, Cleveland Park, and Van Ness. All three are convenient to housing, shopping, and nighttime entertainment. Many apartment buildings offer off-street parking for a monthly fee as well. Taxis are plentiful at almost any hour, particularly along Connecticut Avenue.

Third, Cleveland Park's house prices offer people an opportunity to enjoy the best of D.C. living, without paying Georgetown prices. Prices for homes can reach the high six figures, but there are also houses regularly on the market in the more attainable $200,000 range.

Finally, Cleveland Park offers its residents a real sense of community within the city.

On the downside, Cleveland Park, like Woodley Park and much of D.C. for that matter, does not have plentiful on-street parking. Unmetered street parking is becoming rarer and rarer, and many residents of the area can spend up to a half hour driving about the neighborhood looking for a legal overnight parking space.

Also, while apartment rental prices and home prices remain fairly stable, increasingly there is talk that some of the larger apartment buildings will be going "condo," thus taking those units off the rental market.

Neighborhood Statistical Profile

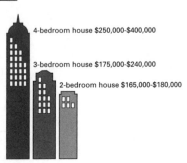

Average Housing Costs

2-bedroom house:	$165,000
	to $180,000
3-bedroom house:	$175,000
	to $240,000
4-bedroom house:	$250,000
	to $400,000

4-bedroom house $250,000-$400,000

3-bedroom house $175,000-$240,000

2-bedroom house $165,000-$180,000

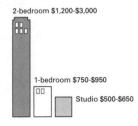

2-bedroom $1,200-$3,000

1-bedroom $750-$950

Studio $500-$650

Average Rental Costs

Studio:	$500 to $650
1-bedroom:	$750 to $950
2-bedroom:	$1,200 to $3,000

Other Statistics

Average annual income:	$45,000
Average crime risk:	Robberies and assaults on par with national average.

Important Places Nearby

Grocery Stores

Brookville Supermarket
3427 Connecticut Avenue NW
(202) 244-9114

Safeway
4310 Connecticut Avenue NW
(202) 244-0180

Pharmacies

Cathedral Pharmacy
3000 Connecticut Avenue NW
(202) 265-1300

CVS
2616 Connecticut Avenue NW
(202) 265-6818

Banks

Bank of America
3401 Connecticut Avenue
(202) 624-4350

SunTrust Bank
3435 Connecticut Avenue NW
(202) 879-7030

Hardware Stores

Adams Morgan Hardware
2200 18th Street NW
(202) 265-3205

Fast Food

Uptown Bakers
3313 Connecticut Avenue NW
(202) 362-6262

Vace Italian Store
3315 Connecticut Avenue NW
(202) 363-1919

Hospitals/Emergency Rooms

Georgetown Hospital
3800 Reservoir Road NW
(202) 687-2000

George Washington University Medical Center
901 23rd Street NW
(202) 994-1000

CATHEDRAL HEIGHTS/TENLEYTOWN

West of the Connecticut Corridor and north of Georgetown is upper Wisconsin Avenue, which intersects with Massachusetts Avenue. A few hundred feet from that intersection lies one of Washington's most majestic sights: the towers and spires of the National Cathedral, the Episcopal Church's contribution to the skyline of the nation's capital.

The cathedral was 40 years in the making, and around it a nice residential community grew as well. None of the housing stock competes with the church, however. There are four- or five-story apartment buildings and an assortment of two-story garden walk-ups and second-story apartments.

Cathedral Heights is no competition for those neighborhoods that surround it: Georgetown and Cleveland Park. But it doesn't have to compete. On its merits, the Heights suits its residents just fine. It offers an affordable alternative to some of the other higher-priced neighborhoods, often times in similar settings. For example, a one-bedroom apartment in Cathedral Heights oftentimes can be had for about $100 to $150 less than a similar one in Cleveland Park. A few modern townhouse developments have been built here, offering young couples an opportunity to buy into the area.

Cathedral Heights doesn't offer some of the amenities that other D.C. locales might, it doesn't have the character, but it does have one of the most attractive monuments in the city to offer as a view from many of the apartments in the area.

On the downside, Cathedral skews older in terms of its population's age and lifestyle, which is fairly staid. It also doesn't have a Metro station as close by as Cleveland Park or Dupont Circle do, although the Tenleytown Metro is certainly within walking distance.

Less than a mile from the staid confines of Cathedral Heights is Tenleytown, located to the north along Wisconsin Avenue. Washington has a number of university campuses within its city limits, and Tenleytown has one of the largest and most vibrant in American University. As a result, you have a neighborhood filled with group homes, several bars, billiard rooms, pizza parlors, and burrito take-out shops.

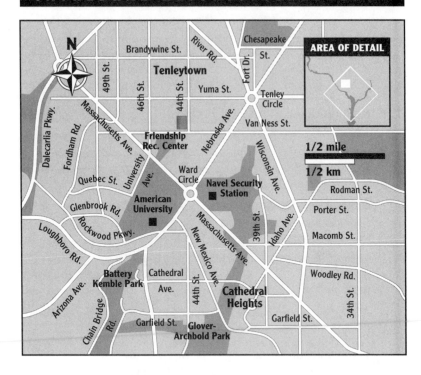

CATHEDRAL HEIGHTS/TENLEYTOWN

Tenleytown is also convenient for commuters to Montgomery County, Maryland, which is less than five miles away up Wisconsin Avenue and is accessible by Metro. If you are looking at employment opportunities in one of the Maryland suburbs, but want to live in the District, then Tenleytown or Cathedral Heights may be a good options for you.

Once again, home prices and rent will be lower here than in Cleveland Park and Georgetown, in part because you're living further out from downtown. But the distance is mitigated by the convenient Metro stop, and if you choose to drive, on-street parking is bit easier to come by than in other neighborhoods.

On the negative side of the ledger, traffic in Tenleytown has become a serious problem in the past couple of years, as more and more commuters driving in from neighboring Montgomery County, Maryland, use Wisconsin Avenue to get downtown. And the college atmosphere can wear thin if it's been a few years since your own graduation.

Neighborhood Statistical Profile

Average Housing Costs

2-bedroom house:	$165,000
3-bedroom house:	$200,000
4-bedroom house:	$275,000
	to $300,000

Average Rental Costs

Studio:	$600
1-bedroom:	$700 to $850
2-bedroom:	$1,025
3-bedroom:	$1,025 to $2,000

Other Statistics

Average annual income:	$35,000 to $40,000
Average crime risk:	Robberies and assaults on par with national average. Higher incidence of vandalism and disorderly conduct related to American University campus.
Estimated commuting times:	By Metro, 15 minutes into D.C., 20 minutes to Maryland, 30 minutes to Virginia. By car, 35 to 40 minutes into D.C., an hour or more into Virginia, and 30 minutes into lower Montgomery County, Maryland.

Important Places Nearby

Grocery Stores

Fresh Fields
2323 Wisconsin Avenue NW
(202) 333-5393

Safeway
1855 Wisconsin Avenue NW
(202) 333-3223

Pharmacies

CVS
Wisconsin Avenue and Newark
Street NW
(202) 966-9268

Banks

Citibank
1901 Wisconsin Avenue NW
(202) 926-1067

First Union
37th Street and Calvert Street
NW
(202) 637-3273

Hardware Stores

G.C. Murphin and Sons
3314 Wisconsin Avenue
(202) 537-1155

Fast Food

Armands Pizza
3636 Wisconsin Avenue NW
(202) 686-9450

McDonald's
3414 Wisconsin Avenue NW
(202) 966-6131

Popeye's Chicken
3701 Wisconsin Avenue NW
(202) 966-6131

Hospitals/Emergency Rooms

Georgetown Hospital
3800 Reservoir Road NW
(202) 687-2000

Sibley Memorial Hospital
5255 Loughboro Road NW
(202) 537-4000

FRIENDSHIP HEIGHTS/CHEVY CHASE

North of Tenleytown along the Connecticut Avenue and Wisconsin Avenue corridors are Friendship Heights and Washington's Chevy Chase (Maryland also has a town named Chevy Chase—it's just across the border from this one).

Both areas feature some small apartment buildings, but it is the high-rise buildings that catch one's eyes. Despite the somewhat upscale urban feel that pervades Wisconsin Avenue, both Friendship Heights and Chevy Chase have become more bedroom communities than social centers.

On the side streets that stretch into Chevy Chase, Maryland, and down toward Connecticut Avenue, the housing is primarily single-family homes. In and around the large malls and Metro station that anchor the Friendship Heights/Chevy Chase shopping center, a number of high-rise apartment and condominium developments can be found.

Apartments in the larger buildings offer all the modern amenities: air-conditioning, swimming pools, gyms, and 24-hour security. These buildings are generally on the higher end of the apartment spectrum, as is the neighborhood. But deals can still be found in these neighborhoods, particularly for smaller homes that are for rent in the surrounding area.

Home rentals in the area have been common in the past, although some homes that only five years ago were rentals have recently been sold due to the hot real estate market in the area. Still, group homes are not difficult to find, particularly in the Connecticut Avenue area; apartments are more plentiful along Connecticut as well.

Both Friendship Heights and Chevy Chase feature self-sustaining shopping and social areas. Coffeehouses, restaurants, gourmet food stores, even clothing boutiques can be found along upper Wisconsin and Connecticut Avenues. So while you are a good 30 minutes from downtown Washington, there is something of an urban feel to the communities. Street parking is a bit easier than in other areas of the city, although, as elsewhere, a parking permit is required. Off-street parking is also more commonly available here.

FRIENDSHIP HEIGHTS/CHEVY CHASE

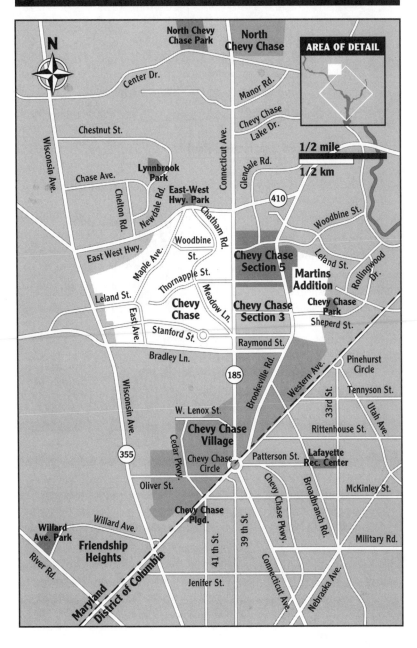

For commuters headed downtown or into Maryland or Virginia, Metro stops are less convenient. The Red Line's stops at Tenleytown and Friendship Heights are the last in the District before crossing over into Maryland. Both those stops can be found along Wisconsin Avenue. So while living along Connecticut Avenue might be more affordable for apartment dwellers, it isn't as convenient if you don't own a car or mind taking a longer walk or paying about $4 for a cab ride to the Metro station.

Neighborhood Statistical Profile

4-bedroom house $400,000

3-bedroom house $220,000

2-bedroom house $157,500

Average Housing Costs

2-bedroom house:	*$157,500*
3-bedroom house:	*$220,000*
4-bedroom house:	*$400,000*

3-bedroom $2,000

2-bedroom $1,200-$1,500

1-bedroom $800-$1,000

Studio $700

Average Rental Costs

Studio:	*$700*
1-bedroom:	*$800 to $1,000*
2-bedroom:	*$1,200 to $1,500*
3-bedroom:	*$2,000*

Other Statistics

Average annual income:	*$45,000 to $50,000*
Average crime risk:	*Burglaries and robberies are slightly higher than the national average; assaults are lower than the national average.*
Estimated commuting times:	*Anywhere in the District or lower Montgomery County, 20 minutes. To Virginia by Metro, 30 minutes; by car, at least one hour.*

Important Places Nearby

Grocery Stores

Giant Food
Chevy Chase Shopping Center
Wisconsin and Western Avenues
(301) 718-6559

Pharmacies

CVS
Chevy Chase Shopping Center
Wisconsin and Western Avenues
(301) 652-4959

Banks

First National Bank of Maryland
2620 Connecticut Avenue NW
(202) 775-4820

Chevy Chase Bank
4455 Connecticut Avenue NW
(202) 966-3672

First Union
4340 Connecticut Avenue NW
(202) 879-7200

Hospitals/Emergency Rooms

Georgetown Hospital
3800 Reservoir Road NW
(202) 687-2000

George Washington University Medical Center
901 23rd Street NW
(202) 994-1000

Sibley Memorial Hospital
5255 Loughboro Road NW
(202) 537-4000

DUPONT CIRCLE

On the other side of Rock Creek Park and Georgetown, the neighborhood known as Dupont Circle is in downtown Washington and is perhaps the most urban neighborhood covered in this book. How urban? How about living in a two-story restored Victorian brownstone next door to a 15-story office building or think tank?

Still, the residents of Dupont Circle have managed to create a neighborhood in this downtown setting. The Dupont Circle area spins out from the eponymous traffic circle on Connecticut Avenue and the streets that branch out from it like so many spokes: P and 19th Streets, Massachusetts, New Hampshire, and Connecticut Avenues. The neighborhood borders are generally accepted to be between 16th and 24th Streets going east to west, P Street to the south, and Florida Avenue to the north.

The neighborhood is today closely identified with a large gay community that has flourished around it, particularly along P Street, where there are several well-known gay bars, such as The Fireplace and Mr. P's. The area's long-standing history as a major center for foreign embassies and a haven for the Washington elite has been eclipsed to a great degree by its newer incarnation as a gay neighborhood.

But single heterosexuals who want to be in the thick of bookstores, coffee houses, trendy restaurants, and boutiques (how all the hip eyewear shops and hair salons in the area stay in business at the same time is one of Washington's unsolved mysteries), should also consider "The Circle." It is the most centrally located neighborhood in the city, convenient to just about everything: Georgetown, the downtown business district, and the major commuting Metro lines. It also offers access to the great outdoors in the form of Rock Creek Park.

Beyond the P Street culture, Dupont Circle is a diverse community. The prestigious Johns Hopkins School for Advanced International Studies is nearby, as are many large professional buildings that house some of D.C.'s most prominent law and lobbying firms. And many of the people who attend the school or work in the buildings also live in the area.

Then there are the embassies. If you are lucky enough to find an apartment near the Brazilian or Argentinean embassies, get ready to party. Both have been known to open their doors to neighbors for huge summer barbecues or cocktail parties.

Particularly along Massachusetts and New Hampshire Avenues, there are quite a few large apartment buildings with studio, one-, and two-bedroom apartments. In addition, in the past 20 years many of the area's old two- or three-story Victorian homes have been converted into small apartment buildings with large, airy flats. On-street parking is next to impossible to find on a consistent basis, although monthly underground parking can be had in many of the large office buildings in the area.

Dupont Circle is not especially conducive to family life because of the urban setting, the expense, and the heavy traffic that clogs the streets almost all day. You also should be aware that in the past year crime in the area, particularly violent robberies and attacks on gay men, has increased dramatically. There are also a large number of homeless people in the neighborhood, mostly around the Dupont Circle park. At night, people sometimes use apartment building entrances as shelter.

Neighborhood Statistical Profile

2-bedroom condo $150,000
2-bedroom house $150,000

1-bedroom condo $80,000

Average Housing Costs

1-bedroom condo:	*$80,000*
2-bedroom condo:	*$150,000*
2-bedroom house:	*$150,000*

2-bedroom $1,500-$2,000

1-bedroom $800-$1,000

Studio $500-$600

Average Rental Costs

Studio:	*$500 to $600*
1-bedroom:	*$800 to $1,000*
2-bedroom:	*$1,500 to $2,000*

Other Statistics

Average annual income:	*$35,000 to $40,000*
Average crime risk:	*Robberies and assaults are three times the national average.*
Estimated commuting times:	*Anywhere in the District, 20 minutes. To Virginia by Metro, 20 to 30 minutes; by car, at least one hour.*

Important Places Nearby

Grocery Stores

Metro Market No. 1
2130 P Street NW
(202) 833-3720

Safeway
1800 20th Street
(202) 483-3908

Pharmacies

CVS
6 Dupont Circle (P Street and New Hampshire Avenue)
(202) 833-5704

Tschifflely Pharmacy
1330 Connecticut Avenue NW
(202) 331-7176

Banks

SunTrust Bank
1369 Connecticut Avenue NW
(202) 879-7070

Riggs Bank
1913 Massachusetts Avenue NW
(202) 835-6000

Hardware Stores

Candey Hardware
1210 18th Street
(202) 659-5650

Hospitals/Emergency Rooms

Georgetown Hospital
3800 Reservoir Road NW
(202) 687-2000

George Washington University Medical Center
901 23rd Street NW
(202) 994-1000

ADAMS MORGAN/KALORAMA

Just a few blocks north up Connecticut Avenue from Dupont Circle is another popular area for the young, the hip, and the artistically/culturally inclined: Adams Morgan. The area's two major streets are Columbia Road, which splits off from Connecticut Avenue, and 18th Street NW, which runs into Columbia Road at the tip of the Adams Morgan neighborhood.

Adams Morgan is one of the liveliest areas of the city any night of the week. The neighborhood is filled with bars, nightclubs, art galleries, and numerous ethnic restaurants—Mexican, Salvadoran, Thai, Chinese, Japanese, Ethiopian, French-Algerian, to name a few. There's even a Ben and Jerry's ice-cream parlor.

The area is quite similar in style and substance to the Haight-Ashbury district in San Francisco and the SoHo district in New York. Adams Morgan is the site of the city's best annual street festival, with live bands, ethnic foods, and arts and crafts sales.

On the side streets between Columbia Road and 18th Street are quite a few apartment buildings. Some are large and regularly have vacancies. As with other popular residential areas in Washington, however, there has been a push here to convert some of the larger buildings into co-ops. Still, if you focus on this area, an apartment shouldn't be too difficult to find.

There are many one- and two-bedroom apartments to be rented, and one- and two-bedroom co-ops to be purchased, in the large apartment buildings that line Columbia Road. Group homes have been a staple of the area for quite some time, particularly among college students who find the area conducive to an active, or overactive, social life.

If you choose to live in the Adams Morgan area expect to pay premium prices for your space. The neighborhood has remained one of the most popular for single young professionals for many years, because of its artsy, bohemian character and great nightlife.

North of Columbia Road, across Connecticut Avenue and west of 18th Street to Calvert Street, is the area known as Kalorama. It is a quieter, more "adult" neighborhood than Adams Morgan—also more

ADAMS MORGAN/KALORAMA

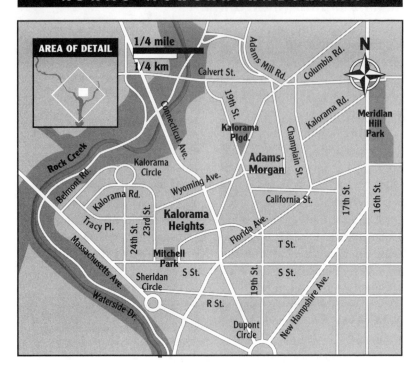

expensive and exclusive. It is filled with large apartments, co-ops, and single-family brownstones. Kalorama is also known for its large embassy community. Homes and apartments are snapped up quickly in the area, but occasionally some apartments or co-ops are available for sub-letting (if you find the right real estate office).

Neither Adams Morgan nor Kalorama is serviced by a Metro station, although the Woodley Park Metro stop is fairly close (a 15-minute walk north), as is the Dupont Circle Metro (about a 10-minute downhill walk south). Parking, therefore, is always at a premium. There is little on-street parking, and because Adams Morgan is so popular at night, the streets are always congested well past midnight with people looking for parking spaces.

The parking and traffic are among the negative aspects of these neighborhoods, as is a heavy homeless and panhandler presence. Because of the late-night social scene along 18th Street and Columbia Road, it is not uncommon to find drunken revelers using apartment building entrances for bathrooms—or even impromptu bedrooms. In the past couple of years, D.C. police have increased their presence in the area. Still, incidents of muggings, robberies, car break-ins, and vandalism remain common, particularly on the side streets between Columbia Road and 18th Street and east of 18th toward 17th Street Northwest.

Neighborhood Statistical Profile

Average Housing Costs

2-bedroom house:	*$220,000*
	to $250,000
3-bedroom house:	*$275,000*

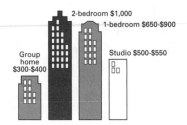

Average Rental Costs

Studio:	*$500 to $500*
1-bedroom:	*$650 to $900*
2-bedroom:	*$1,000*
Group home:	*$300 to $400*

Other Statistics

Average annual income:	*$20,000*
Average crime risk:	*Robberies and assaults are three times the national average. Also the area has seen an increase in aggressive panhandling by the homeless.*
Estimated commuting times:	*In D.C., 20 minutes via Metro.*

Important Places Nearby

Grocery Stores

Safeway
1747 Columbia Road
(202) 667-0774

7-11
1900 Wyoming Avenue
(202) 234-5956

Pharmacies

CVS
1700 Columbia Road
(202) 265-7548

Banks

SunTrust Bank
1800 Columbia Road NW
(202) 879-7090

Hardware Stores

Adams Morgan Hardware
2200 18th Street
(202) 265-3205

Hospitals/Emergency Rooms

Children's Hospital
111 Michigan Avenue NW
(202) 745-5000

Washington Hospital Center
110 Irving Street NW
(202) 877-7000

OTHER NEIGHBORHOODS TO CONSIDER

Catholic University/Brookland

Brookland is located in Northeast D.C., with Michigan and South Dakota Avenues and 12th Streets as its borders. In the past 10 years the area has seen a rebirth, in part due to the presence and growth of Catholic University and Trinity College. Another factor has been the National Catholic Shrine on the CU campus, one of the most impressive churches in Washington.

CATHOLIC UNIVERSITY/BROOKLAND

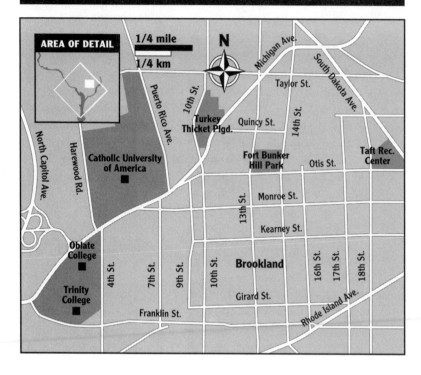

CU is not a commuter school—most of its students live in university housing or in apartments near the campus (many upperclassmen, tired of dorm life, live in off-campus rentals). Students at Trinity College and Gallaudet University, a school for the deaf, also have created markets for housing in the area.

Brookland lies east of Adams Morgan and Mount Pleasant. In the 1940s, it was a central neighborhood for the African-American community. In the 1960s and 1970s Brookland fell on hard times. But by the late 1980s and early 1990s, with house prices remaining low in the area, young families looking to buy moved into the neighborhood and Brookland became gentrified and diversified. In addition, several large real-estate developers bought up many small bungalow-style homes in the area for rental property. Since 1995, many Catholic University students have populated those homes.

Apartment buildings also have sprouted up; they tend to be far more affordable than similar spaces downtown. And because the buildings are newer, they generally offer amenities such as patios or decks and off-street parking. An added plus is that these new buildings are close to Catholic University, in areas often patrolled by the school's security service. There are still some rough spots to this community, but the price may be right for you, especially if you are a recent college graduate or a grad student who can't get on-campus housing.

Brookland is a stop on the Red Line Metro; the station is less than a quarter mile from the CU campus.

Apartments can be had for between $500 to $600 for one-bedrooms; $750 to $1,000 for two-bedroom models. As well, group homes costing about $300 to $400 per person are also plentiful, especially during the school year.

Shaw and U Streets

Shaw remains one of the most diverse neighborhoods within D.C. In the past, it has been one of the most troubled, but as the city begins to get back on its feet, and civic pride takes hold, Shaw is once again on the rise. It was once Duke Ellington's neighborhood and is close to Howard University, one of America's finest African-American universities.

For years, blocks of Shaw were uninhabitable, with rampant violence, prostitution, and drug dealing. But in the last five years gentrification has taken hold in a big way. Apartment buildings are beginning to open up where rundown brownstones once stood. Single family homes and rentals are growing as fast as the weeds once did.

The Shaw neighborhood runs from North Capitol Street to 15th Street NW, north of M Street. While it remains a predominantly black neighborhood, white and Hispanic residents have been moving in as well, in part because rents and property can be had at lower prices than in other areas of the city. The area has a ways to go before it is on par with, say, Adams Morgan or even Mount Pleasant. But if you are looking for a one-bedroom in the $500-to-$600 range, and feel comfortable in an urban setting, then consider Shaw.

SHAW/U STREET

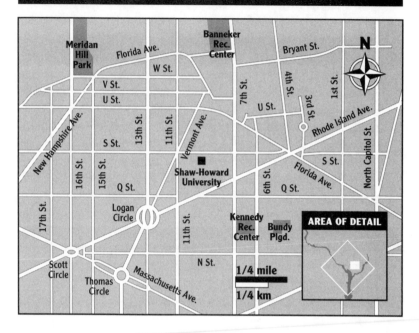

Next to Shaw along U Street NW between 12th and 17th Streets is what is known as the "U Street Corridor." It can be found below Adams Morgan and, like its more well-known neighbor, U Street is home to a diverse crowd. Like Shaw, U Street has a checkered history; thanks to high crime and few desirable properties, it has not been conducive to long-term living until recently.

As rents and property values have increased in Adams Morgan and Dupont Circle, however, some of those neighborhoods' lower-income residents have found U Street to be a fine alternative. The area features used-book stores, ethnic restaurants, and cheaper rents than other parts of the city. Rents are on par with Shaw.

A word to the wise: As you move farther away from 17th, toward 12th, the neighborhood becomes less safe. It would be best to use a real-estate agent or apartment-finders service to help you weed through the selections and make a safe choice for housing.

Both areas are served by the Metro and bus service. Commuting time to anywhere in D.C. is less than 20 minutes by either bus or rail. Cars are not advisable for this area; on-street parking is plentiful, but for all the wrong reasons.

16th Street Corridor

West of Shaw and east of Dupont Circle is what has come to be known as the "16th Street Corridor." The area is sometimes considered part of the Logan Circle neighborhood, which adjoins it. Like Shaw and U Streets, 16th Street has a diverse population, although more white and Hispanic residents can be found in the area than in Shaw or U Street.

The neighborhood has a nice mix of residential styles; there are Victorian homes with porches, brownstones, and small apartment

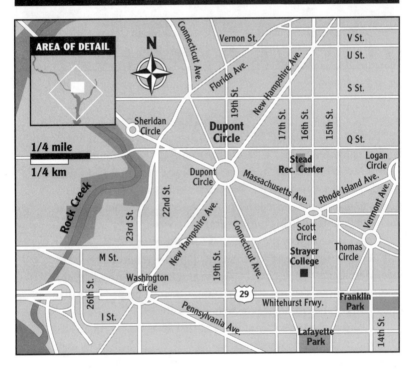

buildings. Because of nearby Howard University, the area also has a young, vibrant feel. Rents are affordable—$500 to $600 for a one-bedroom. Houses with two or three bedrooms can sometimes be had for $100,000.

The 16th Street Corridor does have its problems, especially crime, but it is going through a revitalization, especially in those areas closest to Dupont Circle and Adams Morgan. It is expected that within five years this area will rival Adams Morgan in terms of housing opportunities.

Again, it might be best to use an apartment-finders service if you wish to consider this area. And as with Shaw and U Streets, a car might not be advisable here.

The Palisades

West of Georgetown and below Glover Park lies an almost suburban neighborhood right in the city. Streets lined with large, single-family homes are the norm. The name of the area, Palisades, imparts a sense of stability and calm. And that's just what you get.

MacArthur Boulevard is the main roadway in this area, one of the most established of the city. During the morning and evening commutes, MacArthur is a major commuting artery for people taking a back route from Montgomery County, Maryland, into the city. Hence traffic during the week can be a real pain.

Closer to the Georgetown side of the Palisades, especially along MacArthur, one can find a number of apartment buildings and small townhouse developments, many used as rentals. These tend to appeal to couples and young families, many with the intent of buying into the neighborhood if the opportunity avails itself.

Further west on MacArthur is the neighborhood center, which features a Safeway, CVS, take-out delis, dry cleaners, and a fine wine/liquor shop. Sibley Hospital, one of the better medical facilities in the District, is but a few blocks away. There is a lovely neighborhood park that features year-round recreational programs for both adults and children. After the community's Fourth of July parade, everyone converges here for free hot dogs and soda.

THE PALISADES

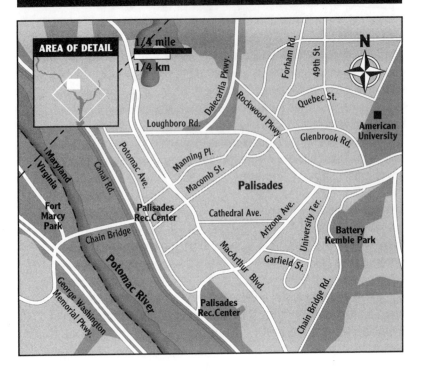

Apartments dot the area (average monthly rent for a one-bedroom apartment is $800; for a two-bedroom townhouse, about $1,500), but there is mostly house-hunting material here. The homes are older (circa 1950s and 1960s) and well-built. Average home prices have skyrocketed in recent years: a large three-bedroom home sells for about $275,000. Recently, some construction of small townhouses and new homes has taken place in the Palisades, allowing younger home buyers to find a slot in the neighborhoods, but it probably isn't enough to lower the overall cost of moving into the area.

Aside from the price of moving in, the other downside here is lack of commuting options. There are several bus lines that run through the area, but no Metro stop (the closest is Tenleytown, about a 10-minute drive from anywhere in Palisades). This doesn't seem to bother the residents of the area, who stay for the quiet, tree-lined streets, good schools, and convenience to Georgetown and downtown by car.

Virginia

West of Washington, D.C., across the Potomac River, is the Commonwealth of Virginia. In what is known as the state's "Washington metropolitan area," there are no major cities, only sprawling communities with a distinctly suburban feel. Some of these communities are areas rich in American history and have been developing and evolving for more than 200 years; others are less then five years old.

The two Virginia communities closest to Washington are Arlington County and the city of Alexandria. Both were actually part of the original plan for the District of Columbia in the late 18th century, but were returned to the commonwealth a few years later in what can only be termed as one of the great real-estate steals of all time. Since then, with the exception of a threat a few years back to tax Virginia commuters working in Washington, the relationship between D.C. and Northern Virginia has been a good one.

The major Virginia suburbs we'll be discussing are Arlington, Alexandria, and Fairfax County. Each has convenient Metro connections to the city as well as major roadway connections for commuters with cars.

ARLINGTON

Drive west down Constitution Avenue, across the Roosevelt Bridge, and you find yourself in Arlington. Your first sights are the high-rise office buildings of Rosslyn, a comparatively new business district that runs along the Potomac River and is a five-minute walk across the Key Bridge from Georgetown. As you turn onto Route 50 (keep this roadway in mind, it will be critical to your home-hunting, as well as shopping), you see the huge Iwo Jima Memorial at Arlington National Cemetery. Each of these sites is representative of an important part of Arlington's indentity: the explosive growth of big business in the area, and its rich military and political history, which dates back to the 17th century.

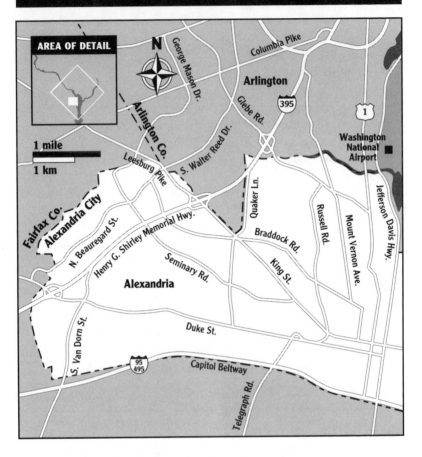

VIRGINIA

AREA OF DETAIL

N

1 mile

1 km

George Mason Dr.

Columbia Pike

Arlington

395

Glebe Rd.

1

Arlington Co.

Washington National Airport

Leesburg Pike

S. Walter Reed Dr.

Jefferson Davis Hwy.

Fairfax Co.

Alexandria City

N. Beauregard St.

Henry G. Shirley Memorial Hwy.

Quaker Ln.

Braddock Rd.

Russell Rd.

Mount Vernon Ave.

Seminary Rd.

King St.

Alexandria

S. Van Dorn St.

Duke St.

95 495

Capitol Beltway

Telegraph Rd.

Arlington is actually a county, with no incorporated cities, towns, or villages within its borders. Rather, it is an amalgam of distinct neighborhoods or business districts that have adapted and grown according to the needs of Washington, D.C., and the surrounding, expanding Virginia business community.

Arlington County is an area that is filled with large apartment buildings, small garden apartment complexes, townhouses, and houses for rent or purchase. There are actually two Arlingtons: North

Arlington and South Arlington. The county is essentially split down the middle by Route 50, which is the dividing line for streets designated "North" and "South." Washington Boulevard, for example, is called North Washington above Route 50 and South Washington below it. Keep this in mind when tracking apartment addresses.

I will focus on North Arlington communities because they're closest to Washington and because the area is serviced extremely well by the Orange Metro line. It passes through practically every North Arlington district of note.

Rosslyn is a community with a number of large apartment buildings and two-story apartment complexes as well as townhouses and homes for rent. Lower Rosslyn, where the Metro station is located, is within easy walking distance of Washington across the Key Bridge to Georgetown. Many of the residential buildings in Rosslyn are within a five- to 10-minute walk of the Metro station.

But once the business day is over, Rosslyn rolls up the sidewalks. With the exception of a couple of casual bars and an old-fashioned prime-rib restaurant, there is not much in Rosslyn in the way of a social life.

You'll find more of one less than a mile away in the Courthouse district—the downtown, if you will, of Arlington. There are two major roadways in this area: Wilson Boulevard and Clarendon Boulevard. Each roadway runs from Rosslyn through the next district of note.

In the Courthouse section of Arlington you will find extensive rental possibilities on Wilson or Clarendon Boulevards as well as the side streets. Fourteenth Street and the neighborhood that runs behind the large Courthouse Shopping Center have numerous large, modern apartment buildings and townhouses.

Courthouse also offers any number of social and entertainment outlets, including a large brew pub, an Irish bar, and several fine restaurants as well as bookstores, coffee houses, and movie theaters. All are within a five-minute walk from the Metro stop.

Further west up Wilson Boulevard is the Clarendon Metro stop. The neighborhood is known as Clarendon, also Lyon Village and Lyon Park. In the past 10 years, Clarendon has become one of the most ethnically diverse areas of Virginia. Within a one-block area of the Metro stop you can find restaurants featuring the following cuisines: French, Italian, Greek, Indian, Korean, Vietnamese, Chinese, Cuban, and

Mexican. Again, apartment rentals, as well as home rentals, are widely available.

It is also the first community in our metro survey that begins to have any kind of suburban feel to it. As you walk streets with names such as Stafford, Irving, Jackson, and Highland, you come across tree-lined, quiet neighborhoods with single-family homes, well-manicured lawns, and small parks. Lyon Park and Lyon Village have become two of the most popular neighborhoods in all of Northern Virginia, with the price of a small, two-bedroom bungalow sometimes reaching as high as $350,000. The seemingly absurd prices are the result of the demand for homes close to Washington, D.C.

Apartment hunters in the area would be best served by keeping close to the Metro stops and walking the neighborhood. You will find a number of apartment and condominium buildings with available space along Route 29 (Lee Highway) between North 20th Street and Spout Run as well.

Finally, there are Virginia Square and Ballston, two areas that have literally grown up around the Metro stops. High-rise apartment buildings and townhouses—many of them less than five years old—surround the Metro stops. Restaurants, bars, and shops can be found within feet of the Metro stations and the apartments that are in these areas. Rental properties are plentiful, and some apartment buildings don't even require a year lease.

The key streets for touring purposes are Fairfax Drive, Wilson Boulevard, and North Glebe Road. On each you will find extensive apartment choices as well as townhouse developments.

Ballston and Virginia Square are also the major stops for George Mason Law School, one of the area's more prestigious institutions, which is associated with George Mason University, a state-funded, four-year college in suburban Fairfax County. The law school is particularly well known for its evening program, which caters to young Washington professionals.

Past Ballston, you'll find neighborhoods that feature primarily single-family homes, although home rentals are not uncommon.

For newcomers to the Washington area, Arlington may be the best option for several reasons. It offers its residents convenient access to the city in an area that has been developed, in part, for the commuter. Rental costs for apartments or townhouses tend to be lower than in Washington. And because so many of the buildings in Arlington are newer, you usually get more space and modern amenities, like air-conditioning (although less charm than found in older properties). Off-street parking for these buildings is generally plentiful, and often provided to residents at no extra cost.

The downsides? Traffic in the area has become increasingly bad. If you choose to drive to work during morning and evening rush hours, it can take as along as 45 minutes to reach Capitol Hill or downtown. And while nightlife in Arlington has improved dramatically, particularly for the under-25 crowd around Courthouse and Clarendon, the area still has a suburb feel.

Being closer to the city, Arlington also has some city problems. Crime tends to be a bit higher in the lower parts of Arlington, but mostly it's of the nonviolent variety—car break-ins, vandalism, purse-snatchings, and the like.

As for transportation, the Metro can usually get you where you want to go in the area, but you might find that a car is useful, particularly if you wish to explore the region further on weekends.

Neighborhood Statistical Profile

Population: 175,334

Population by Ethnicity

64%	Anglo
17%	Hispanic
11%	Black
8%	Asian

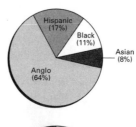

Population by Gender

53%	male
47%	female

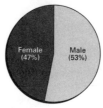

Average Housing Costs

2-bedroom house:	$175,000 to $200,000
3-bedroom house:	$257,000
4-bedroom house:	$325,000 to $500,000

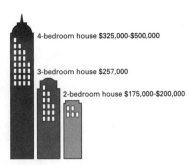

4-bedroom house $325,000-$500,000

3-bedroom house $257,000

2-bedroom house $175,000-$200,000

Average Rental Costs

Studio:	$495 to $600
1-bedroom:	$595 to $1,000
2-bedroom:	$1,500 to $2,500
3-bedroom:	$2,000 to $2,500
2- or 3-bedroom townhouse:	$2,000 to $3,000

2-3-bedroom townhouse $2,000–$3,000

3-bedroom $2,000–$2,500

2-bedroom $1,500–$2,500

1-bedroom $595–$1,000

Studio $495–$600

Other Statistics

Average annual income:	$34,216
Average crime risk:	Three times lower than in Washington, D.C., for violent crime and robbery.
Estimated commuting times:	By Metro, 20 to 30 minutes to anywhere in downtown Washington. By car, 30 minutes into Washington, 30 minutes to Fairfax County.

Important Places Nearby

Grocery Stores

Fresh Fields
2700 Wilson Boulevard
(703) 527-6596

Giant Food
3115 Lee Highway
(703) 527-9453

3450 North Washington
Boulevard
(703) 358-9343

Safeway

5101 Wilson Boulevard
(703) 524-1528

2500 North Harrison
(703) 538-6700

3713 Lee Highway
(703) 841-1155

1525 Wilson Boulevard
(703) 276-9315

Pharmacies

CVS

256 North Glebe Road
(703) 243-4992

2900 North 10th Street
(703) 524-2617

Lyon Village Shopping Center
Spout Run and Lee Highway
(703) 532-2205

Rite Aid

3263 Columbia Pike
(703) 920-4741

Banks

Chevy Chase Bank

3532 Columbia Pike
(703) 553-3750

1100 South Hayes Street
(703) 418-2926

4700 Lee Highway
(703) 812-8550

First Virginia

2200 Wilson Boulevard
(703) 284-0515

3001 Washington Boulevard
(703) 284-0535

1100 South Walter Reed Drive
(703) 553-1166

SunTrust Bank

249 North Glebe Road
(703) 838-3295

3040 North Clarendon Boulevard
(703) 838-3291

900 North Taylor Street
(703) 838-3020

Hardware Stores

Arlington Hardware

2914 Columbia Pike
(703) 920-2449

Cherrydale Hardware Co.

3805 Lee Highway
(703) 527-6177

Virginia Hardware Co.
2915 Wilson Boulevard
(703) 522-3366

Vencor Hospital
601 South Carlin Springs Road
(703) 671-1200

Hospitals/Emergency Rooms

Arlington Hospital
1701 North George Mason Drive
(703) 558-5000

ALEXANDRIA

Much of what has been written here about Arlington can be said about Alexandria. The city of Alexandria, or "Old Town" as it is called, is most readily identified by its cobbled streets and historic Georgian clapboard-and-brick homes. It is one of the most evocative communities in all of the Washington metropolitan area. And as a result, it is one of the most desirable areas to live in.

The main drag is Washington Street, which runs north to south through Alexandria. If you're driving from Washington, the easiest route is across the Memorial, or 14th Street, Bridge, onto the George Washington Parkway, which eventually becomes Washington Boulevard and takes you into downtown Alexandria. North Washington and Duke Street are ground zero for the neighborhood.

Stroll a few blocks to take in the flavor of the area. Walking east down Duke Street, you pass office buildings, small shops, and restaurants, and find yourself standing at the shore of the Potomac River. Along the way, look up and down the side streets to see Alexandria's many homes from the colonial era, which remain exquisitely kept private residences to this day. Walking east up Duke, you will notice a few bars and restaurants, banks, and clothing stores, and a greater feel of modernity. There is still some old-fashioned architecture here, but also new homes, apartment buildings, and townhouses.

Downtown Alexandria's souvenir shops, bookstores, clothing stores, and restaurants mix with small colonial homes and walk-up apartments. Further south along Washington Boulevard, you will find large two- or three-story apartment buildings with mostly one- and two-bedroom units. Beyond the 10- or 12-square-block area of downtown, Alexandria quickly becomes a typical Virginia suburb, complete with single-family homes, strip malls, and shopping centers.

The Blue and Yellow Metro lines serve Alexandria. Both stop at King Street and Braddock, which are the sole stops in the urban center of Alexandria. Apartment buildings and other housing have sprung up around the other Alexandria stops—Eisenhower and Huntington along the Yellow Line and Van Dorn on the Blue Line—but these areas do not offer as many housing options as other parts of suburban Virginia. Much of downtown Alexandria is within easy walking distance of the Metro, however, and some of the larger apartment buildings offer shuttle service to and from the Metro station.

Alexandria has always been a desirable area in which to live, and rents and home prices here have remained steadily higher than in many other parts of suburban Virginia. Most rents are reminiscent of Washington.

In the past five years, with an increased emphasis on economic development, Alexandria has lured many businesses from D.C., among them lobbying organizations, special-interest and advocacy groups, law firms, and several large newspaper and Internet wire services. Unfortunately, most employees of these companies can't afford to live in the community they work in, and at press time there didn't appear to be any major housing initiatives under way in the area.

But "greater" Alexandria is a sprawling area, and rental apartments and townhouses are more common several miles away from the Metro and downtown area. If you own a car, life in Alexandria can be bearable. But while car owners have a wider choice of residential areas, the lifestyle remains the same. Those areas with lots of housing options tend to have little else besides a few shopping centers, large-chain bars and restaurants, and fast-food joints.

Beyond Old Town Alexandria, there are several main streets you will want to traverse in looking for apartments: Duke Street (Route 236), Van Dorn Street, Seminary Road, and Braddock Road. Each is easily accessible from Old Town or via Interstate 395, which cuts across the region from Washington to the western edge of Interstate 495 (The Beltway).

If you don't have a car and choose to use public transportation, your options aren't that limited. Metro bus service is dependable, particularly in the high-traffic areas of upper Alexandria, where so many large apartment complexes have been built. Several of the large apartment developers in the area provide shuttle bus service to the Old Town Metro station during morning and evening commutes.

Prices and sprawl aside, traffic is again a big issue here. In a recent national survey, Washington, D.C., was ranked as one of the three worst areas for traffic congestion. To a great degree this is due to the many people who commute from areas like Alexandria and Arlington into the District. In Alexandria, particularly in Old Town, parking and traffic can be terrible. You are competing against year-round tourism, daytime workers, and night-time revelers. Farther out, traffic is more bearable, but the distances you drive become longer. It can often be a no-win situation.

Neighborhood Statistical Profile

Population: 117,586

Population by Ethnicity

60%	Anglo
12%	Hispanic
23%	Black
5%	Asian

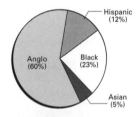

Population by Gender

51%	male
49%	female

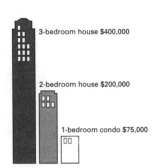

3-bedroom house $400,000

2-bedroom house $200,000

Average Housing Costs

1-bedroom condo:	*$75,000*
2-bedroom house:	*$200,000*
3-bedroom house:	*$400,000*

1-bedroom condo $75,000

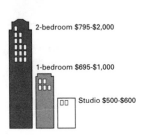

2-bedroom $795-$2,000

1-bedroom $695-$1,000

Average Rental Costs

Studio:	*$500 to $600*
1-bedroom:	*$695 to $1,000*
2-bedroom:	*$795 to $2,000*

Studio $500-$600

Other Statistics

Average annual income: $34,023

Average crime risk: Three times lower than Washington, D.C., for violent crime and robbery.

Estimated commuting times: By Metro, 20 minutes to downtown Washington. By car, 20 minutes to Alexandria, 30 minutes into Washington, 45 minutes to Fairfax.

Important Places Nearby

Grocery Stores

Giant Food
530 1st Street
(703) 845-0851

Safeway
1624 Belle View Boulevard
(703) 765-3434

299 South Van Dorn Street
(703) 313-8800

7900 Fort Hunt Road
(703) 765-0924

Pharmacies

CVS
415 East Monroe Avenue
(703) 836-7058

8628 Richmond Highway
(703) 360-5112

Timberman's
106 North Washington Street
(703) 549-0091

Banks

Chevy Chase Bank
3690 King Street
(703) 998-6502

6800 Richmond Highway
(703) 768-6900

500 South Washington Street
(703) 838-2891

SunTrust Bank
3610 King Street
(703) 838-3280

3101 Duke Street
(703) 838-3110

2809 Mt. Vernon Avenue
(703) 838-3272

First Virginia
6618 Richmond Highway
(703) 718-0090

7716 Telegraph Road
(703) 924-2785

5203 Franconia Road
(703) 924-2790

Hardware

Sears Hardware
7844 Richmond Highway
(703) 360-2125

Village Hardware
7934 Fort Hunt Road
(703) 765-1555

Hospitals/Emergency Rooms

Inova Alexandria Hospital
4320 Seminary Road
(703) 504-3000

Inova Mount Vernon Hospital
2501 Parker Lane
(703) 664-7000

CRYSTAL CITY/PENTAGON CITY

Crystal City is a name that sounds like something out of *The Wizard of Oz*. But with one look at it, you'll know that you aren't in Kansas anymore—and you certainly aren't in some fantasy world, either.

Crystal City is an area nestled between Arlington and Alexandria, behind Ronald Reagan International Airport. It features an extensive underground shopping center accessible from the Metro stop, as well as many above-ground, high-rise office buildings. Every major hotel chain has at least one large facility in the area as well.

Crystal City is in many ways the creation of the Pentagon, which lies less than a mile away from its downtown. Many of the offices that are housed in Crystal City are extensions of the Pentagon or house companies that do business with the Pentagon or with Washington's bureaucracy.

The area began solely as a business center. But with an increasing need for housing for the area's many employees, in the past five years apartment buildings and townhouses that are easily accessible to the Crystal City Metro stop have sprouted up. Most of the city's apartment buildings are less than 10 years old and feature all the modern amenities. There are also a small number of houses that occasionally come on the market for rent. In almost all cases, you will find rental prices to be noticeably less than those in Washington or Alexandria.

Crystal City stops being metropolitan at about 6 P.M. Many of the restaurants that cater to a boisterous lunch crowd close for the evening. If you're looking for compelling nightlife, look elsewhere. But if that's not important to you, consider Crystal City as a place to live. Keep in mind that while Metro service is available, you might find a car to be a necessity, particularly on weekends.

A word about nearby Ronald Reagan National Airport is in order, too. While airport noise never seems to end, in fact, noise restrictions end plane arrivals and takeoffs at 10 P.M., and don't allow takeoffs or arrivals until after 7 A.M. The noise hasn't inhibited the area's growth as a residential community, but it may explain why rents are a bit lower around here.

Pentagon City has many similarities to Crystal City. The U.S. military headquarters for which this area is named is a city of sorts unto itself. What surrounds it doesn't quite pass muster. It is an amalgam of apartment buildings, small houses, and small industrial parks, with a large, splashy shopping mall in the middle of it.

Apartments are more affordable, larger, and more comfortable than others you might find in more desirable neighborhoods. But they are also convenient to public transportation and freeways. If an easy commute is important to you, Pentagon City could be a prime area for you to consider.

Neighborhood Statistical Profile

Average Housing Costs

2-bedroom house:	*$150,000*
3-bedroom house:	*$200,000*
	to $275,000

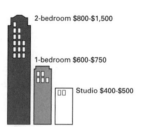

2-bedroom $800-$1,500

1-bedroom $600-$750

Studio $400-$500

Average Rental Costs

Studio:	*$400 to $500*
1-bedroom:	*$600 to $750*
2-bedroom:	*$800 to $1,500*

Other Statistics

Average annual income:	*$34,117*
Estimated commuting times:	*By Metro, 20 minutes to downtown Washington. By car, 30 minutes to downtown Washington, 45 minutes to Fairfax County, 10 minutes to Pentagon, 20 minutes to Alexandria.*

Important Places Nearby

Grocery Stores

Costco
1200 South Fern Street
(703) 413-7240

Safeway
Crystal City Underground
2303 Columbia Pike
(703) 413-2900

Pharmacies

Rite Aid
Crystal City Underground
2303 Columbia Pike
(703) 413-0525

Target
3101 Jefferson Davis Highway
(703) 706-3852

Banks

Chevy Chase Bank
1621-B Crystal Square Arcade
(703) 416-2720

SunTrust Bank
3108 Columbia Pike
(703) 838-3410

First Virginia
2113 Crystal City Arcade
(703) 415-0312

2221 South Eads Street
(703) 553-1166

Hospitals/Emergency Rooms

Pentagon City Hospital
2455 Army Navy Drive
(703) 920-6700

FAIRFAX COUNTY

Surrounding Alexandria and Arlington to the west is Fairfax County, one of the wealthiest and most diverse communities in the United States. Within Fairfax County are the incorporated communities of Falls Church and the city of Fairfax. Other areas of Fairfax County are unincorporated, including McLean, Vienna, Great Falls, Reston, and Herndon.

Ten years ago, this huge area was inhabited by wealthy businessmen, politicians, and patrician families with large tracts of acreage

FAIRFAX COUNTY

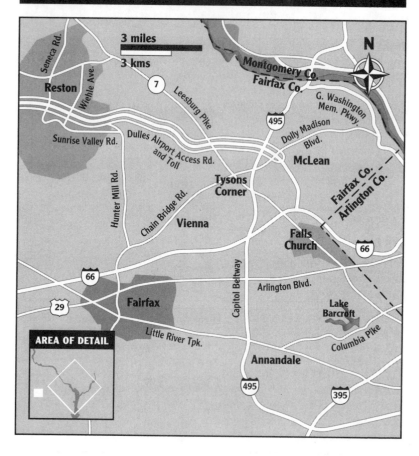

just begging to be bought up and developed. Well, develop it did. Next to Silicon Valley in California, Fairfax County is the single largest producer of high-tech innovation in the world, with America Online's corporate headquarters being the greatest monument to the area's development.

The building and business explosion is due mostly to the two major roadways in the area. The "Beltway," I-495, rings the Washington metro area and runs north to south through much of Fairfax County, and Interstate 66 slices through Northern Virginia from the Potomac River to Vienna and points west. These major commuting arteries, along with the Metro Orange Line and extensive bus routes, meant that prospective employees could live in almost any part of the Washington metropolitan area—D.C., Maryland, Alexandria—and get to work in the Northern Virginia high-tech area. The result after 10 years of development: traffic in the morning and evening rush hour can be a huge headache. The Beltway and I-66 are regularly rated as two of the worst commuting routes in the entire country. Rush hour in the Washington area often starts before 7 A.M. and can run past 7 P.M.. A contributing factor to the traffic problem is that there is no Metro train service to areas such as Tysons Corner, Reston, and Herndon, where much of the new development has occurred. While there is extensive bus service to the area, the closest Metro stations are Dunn Loring and Vienna.

Traffic will probably get worse. The focus of much of the development these days is in the area of Fairfax County known as Tysons Corner. Once farming country, its claim to fame is now being the site of one of the area's premier shopping malls, also called Tysons Corner. Today it is "the downtown"—if that is the correct term—for much of Fairfax County, and it grows by the day as more and more high-tech and business firms make the move to suburbia.

Home to AOL, Fairfax County will soon welcome *USA Today* and Gannett newspapers, too. Sprint Telephone and MCI have offices here, as do several large defense contractors. United Airlines operates its worldwide ticketing from a huge facility near Dulles International Airport. If they haven't already done so, all of the major accounting and law and brokerage firms will be opening offices in the area to cater to the business interests here.

What it all means is that Fairfax is the region of the future. While Washington will remain the employment hub, increasingly people will be finding work beyond the Beltway, particularly in the areas of computers, telecommunication, the Internet, and related industries.

It also means that what were once suburban bedroom communities are now becoming residential centers for young, single professionals and entrepreneurs and newly married couples. That means more apartment buildings, townhouse developments, and social centers filled with bars and restaurants, coffee houses, and gourmet food shops.

What won't change is that Fairfax County, along with its neighbor, Maryland's Montgomery County, remains one of the five most affluent areas of the United States, with one of the most highly rated school systems in the country.

Given the large area that is Fairfax County, we will give a very brief overview of each community.

Neighborhood Statistical Profile

Population: 902,492

Population by Ethnicity

73%	*Anglo*
8%	*Hispanic*
8%	*Black*
11%	*Asian*

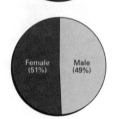

Population by Gender

49%	*male*
51%	*female*

Other Statistics

Average annual income:	*$32,422*
Average crime risk:	*About two to three times less than Washington, D.C., for violent crime. Comparable to the Dristrict for burglaries.*
Estimated commuting times:	*20 minutes to anywhere in Washington.*

Falls Church

There is both an incorporated city of Falls Church and a broader community outside of it bearing the same name. Main thoroughfares for each includes Route 50 (Arlington Boulevard), Route 7 (Leesburg Pike), and Route 29 (Lee Highway). All are major daily commute routes into Washington, D.C.

Falls Church is considered to be mostly a bedroom community, with home prices ranging from $175,000 for a two-bedroom ranch to more than $700,000 for a three- to four-bedroom colonial. Apartment complexes as well as small townhouse developments can be found, particularly along Route 7. But because of their close proximity to Washington and the East and West Falls Church Metro stations, housing is often at a premium. This area will have appeal for people without cars. A number of apartment complexes in the area offer free shuttle service to the Metro stations.

Average Housing Costs

1-bedroom townhouse: *$150,000*

2-bedroom house: *$175,000*
to 200,000

3-bedroom house: *$250,000*
to $400,000

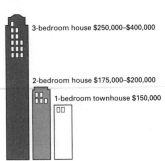

3-bedroom house $250,000–$400,000

2-bedroom house $175,000–$200,000

1-bedroom townhouse $150,000

Average Rental Costs

Studio: *$500 to $800*
1-bedroom: *$795 to $900*
2-bedroom: *$895 to $2,000*

2-bedroom $895-$2,000

1-bedroom $795-$900

Studio $500-$800

Other Statistics

Estimated commuting times: *By Metro, 30 minutes to downtown Washington. By car, 30 to 45 minutes into Washington, 30 to 45 minutes to Fairfax.*

Important Places Nearby

Grocery Stores

Safeway
6118 Arlington Boulevard
(703) 241-4131

7397 Lee Highway
(703) 573-2057

Giant Food
Baileys Cross Roads Shopping Center
(703) 845-0446

Seven Corners Shopping Center
6300 Leesburg Pike
(703) 533-0390

Pharmacies

CVS
134 West Broad Street
(703) 538-5961

6637 Arlington Boulevard
(703) 538-6918

Rite Aid
157 Hillside Avenue
(703) 532-6111

7395 Lee Highway
(703) 698-5356

Banks

Chevy Chase Bank
6367 Seven Corners Center
(703) 534-2540

1100 West Broad Street
(703) 237-1023

3026 Gatehouse Plaza
(703) 560-2170

SunTrust Bank
6300 Leesburg Pike
703-838-3310

603 Broad Street
(703) 838-3264

First Virginia
191 West Broad Street
(703) 241-3505

3010 Annandale Road
(703) 241-3535

7393 Lee Highway
(703) 280-0170

Hospitals/Emergency Rooms

Dominion Hospital
2960 Sleepy Hollow Road
(703) 536-2000

Inova Hospital for Children
3300 Gallows Road
(703) 204-6777

Hardware Stores

Brown's Hardware
100 West Broad Street
(703) 532-1168

Annandale

Like its neighboring communities, Annandale is evolving as of this writing, although compared to areas such as Tysons Corner or Baileys Crossroads, it remains more of a neighborhood-oriented community of single-family homes. Major roadways in the area include Route 236 (Little River Turnpike), Route 244 (Columbia Pike), Gallows Road, and Annandale Road. Apartment complexes and townhouse developments are plentiful, as are large shopping centers, particularly on the Little River Turnpike and Columbia Pike.

With Annandale and other parts of Fairfax County, it's important that you distinguish between neighborhoods "inside the Beltway" and "outside the Beltway." Inside 495, one is closer to D.C., neighborhoods and developments tend to be older, and traffic can be heavier at all hours of the day. Beyond the Beltway, property values tend to be higher and homes are roomier, but apartments and single-living are more rare.

Annandale is serviced by two Metro stations: West Falls Church and Dunn Loring. Neither is particularly convenient to housing, although that has improved in recent years. Each features extensive day parking for commuters and bus service throughout the county. Commuters who live in Annandale have also been known to use East Falls Church Metro because of its proximity to I-66.

Annandale also features one of the most popular recreational areas in Fairfax: Lake Barcroft, which offers swimming, boating, fishing, tennis, and extensive picnicking areas.

4-bedroom house $295,000-$600,000

3-bedroom house $250,000-$400,000

2-bedroom house $200,000

Average Housing Costs

2-bedroom house:	*$200,000*
3-bedroom house:	*$250,000*
	to $400,000
4-bedroom house:	*$295,000*
	to $600,000

2-bedroom $800-$1,500

1-bedroom $595-$900

Studio $450-$600

Average Rental Costs

Studio:	*$450 to $600*
1-bedroom:	*$595 to $900*
2-bedroom:	*$800 to $1,500*

Other Statistics

Estimated commuting times: *By Metro, 30 to 45 minutes to downtown Washington (allowing for bus or car ride to Metro stations). By car, 45 minutes to an hour into Washington, 30 minutes to business centers in Fairfax and Alexandria.*

Important Places Nearby

Grocery Stores

Giant Food
Heritage Mall
6219 Little River Turnpike
(703) 941-6544

Safeway
7414 Little River Turnpike
(703) 941-3874

Shoppers Food Warehouse
6255 Little River Turnpike
(703) 941-1745

Pharmacies

CVS
4707 Lee Highway
(703) 243-4990

5017 Columbia Pike
(703) 671-1031

Banks

Chevy Chase Bank
7030 Little River Turnpike
(703) 941-5770

SunTrust Bank
7617 Little River Turnpike
(703) 813-4100

4250 John Marr Drive
(703) 813-4110

First Virginia
7205 Little River Turnpike
(703) 813-1290

Hardware Stores

Annandale Hardware
4709 Backlick Road
(703) 256-1200

Fischer's
6129 Backlick Road
(703) 451-3700

Hospitals/Emergency Rooms

Dominion Hospital
2960 Sleepy Hollow Road
(703) 536-2000

Inova Fair Oaks Hospital
2600 Joseph Siewick Drive
(703) 391-3600

Inova Hospital for Children
3300 Gallows Road
(703) 204-6777

Fairfax City

This is the county seat, where the county courthouse and government center can be found. It is also the closest community to George Mason University. Fairfax City is perhaps the most established development in the area, and also the oldest. Parts of it have an almost industrial park feel to them.

Major roadways in the area include Route 123 (in this area also known as Chain Bridge Road), Braddock Road, and Route 50. Apartment buildings are most plentiful around the GMU campus, although smaller apartment developments can be found throughout. But for the most part, Fairfax City is a heavily suburban, single-family area.

Average Housing Costs

1-bedroom townhouse:	*$100,000*
2-bedroom house:	*$175,000*
	to 200,000
3-bedroom house:	*$200,000*
	to $400,000
4-bedroom house:	*$375,000 and up*

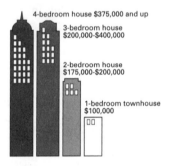

4-bedroom house $375,000 and up
3-bedroom house $200,000-$400,000
2-bedroom house $175,000-$200,000
1-bedroom townhouse $100,000

Average Rental Costs

Studio:	*$500 to $600*
1-bedroom:	*$695 to $800*
2-bedroom:	*$800 to $1,500*

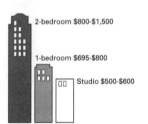

2-bedroom $800-$1,500
1-bedroom $695-$800
Studio $500-$600

Other Statistics

Estimated commuting times: *By Metro, 45 minutes to downtown Washington (allowing for bus or car ride to station). By car, one hour into Washington, 20 to 30 minutes to business centers in Fairfax by car.*

Important Places Nearby

Grocery Stores

Safeway
9525 Braddock Road
(703) 560-6696

6118 Arlington Road
(703) 241-4131

Shoppers Food Warehouse
9622 Main Street
(703) 978-7188

Pharmacies

CVS
10390 Willard Way
(703) 591-0851

Rite Aid
10521 Lee Highway
(703) 273-4515

Banks

Alliance Bank
12735 Shoppes Lane
(703) 631-6411

Chevy Chase Bank
3941 Pickett Road
(703) 425-0687

3095 Nutley Street
(703) 205-2990

13043 Lee/Jackson Highway
(703) 631-7030

SunTrust Bank
9401 Lee Highway
(703) 838-3329

12001 Lee/Jackson Highway
(703) 838-3444

Hardware Stores

Annandale Hardware
4709 Backlick Road
(703) 256-1200

Hospitals/Emergency Rooms

Inova Fair Oaks Hospital
2600 Joseph Siewick Drive
(703) 391-3600

Vienna

One of the farthest communities from Washington that is serviced by the Metro system, Vienna is nonetheless convenient to both D.C. and the burgeoning Tysons Corner area. It is an incorporated community, with its own Metro station.

Surrounding the Vienna Metro station is an extensive development of apartment buildings, condominiums, and townhouses. This residential area is also in close proximity to I-66, making it a highly appealing area for commuters into the District. Other major roadways include Maple Avenue (Route 123), which leads directly into Tysons Corner, Courthouse, and Nutley. Rental property is widely available in these areas.

Despite the growing availability of rental property, Vienna remains a family-oriented bedroom community with a definite suburban feel. For those single people looking for group home opportunities, Vienna offers some rental properties with three or four bedrooms at prices sometimes under $2,000. These homes can be large enough to house five, or even six, people comfortably.

In nearby Fairfax City is the main campus for George Mason University, one of the larger state-run schools in the region. Because of its location, Vienna has become home to many GMU students looking for off-campus housing.

Vienna offers its residents a quiet community convenient to work and shopping. What it does not offer is an extensive nightlife, beyond the occasional TGI Friday's or late-night diner.

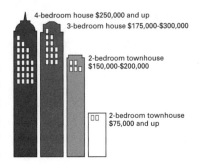

4-bedroom house $250,000 and up
3-bedroom house $175,000-$300,000
2-bedroom townhouse $150,000-$200,000
2-bedroom townhouse $75,000 and up

Average Housing Costs

2-bedroom townhouse: $75,000 and up

2-bedroom house:	*$150,000*
	to 200,000
3-bedroom house:	*$175,000*
	to $300,000
4-bedroom house:	*$250,000 and up*

Average Rental Costs

1-bedroom: *$600 to $800*
2-bedroom: *$795 to $1,500*

Other Statistics

Estimated commuting times: *By Metro, 45 minutes to downtown Washington. By car, one hour into Washington, 30 minutes to Fairfax business centers.*

Important Places Nearby

Grocery Stores

Magruder's
180 West Maple Street
(703) 938-4700

Safeway
225 East Maple Street
(703) 281-4071

Pharmacies

Safeway Pharmacy
225 East Maple Street
(703) 281-0501

Vienna Drug Center
150 West Maple Street
(703) 938-7111

Banks

Chevy Chase bank
234 West Maple Avenue
(703) 255-9544

SunTrust Bank
8219 Leesburg Pike
(703) 838-3512

First Union
212 East Maple Street
(703) 255-7091

Hardware Stores

Annandale Hardware
4709 Backlick Road
(703) 256-1200

Sheets Wholesale
430 Mill Street
(703) 938-9110

Hospitals/Emergency Rooms

Inova Fair Oaks Hospital
2600 Joseph Siewick Drive
(703) 391-3600

Tysons Corner

It doesn't have a Metro station, its roadways are constantly congested, yet it is the hottest location in the region. Why? Business, business, and more business. Tysons Corner offers miles of strip malls, super-stores, and the twin shopping heavens of Tysons Shopping Center and Tysons Galleria, which feature every high-end department store and national chain store imaginable.

The shopping meccas have been around for more than a decade. What has driven the recent explosive growth in Tysons Corner are the high-tech firms that have sprouted up all across the area. As a result of the business growth, in the past five years there has been similar growth in residential development. With old-line residential communities Vienna and McLean on either side of Tysons, single-family homes have always been plentiful. Only recently has apart-ment and townhouse development caught up. Today, plentiful and always-available rental properties can be found along large portions of Route 7, off Route 123. These areas feature both high-rise apart-ments and townhouse communities.

Major roadways in the area include Route 7 and Route 123, as well as the Dulles Toll Road, which deserves special mention. The toll road, which is accessible from I-495, I-66, Route 7, and Route 123 has become a major commuting artery into D.C. for residents residing in parts of Fairfax, Reston, and Herndon. It costs 50 cents to enter and exit the toll road and an additional quarter to enter and exit each of seven off-ramps on the toll road. These on- and off-ramps lead to major residential areas and commercial office parks. Running parallel to the toll road is the Dulles International Airport Access Road; there is no toll for this road, which is intended solely for airport traffic.

Average Housing Costs

1-bedroom condo:	*$75,000*
	to $120,000
2-bedroom townhouse:	*$175,000*
	to 200,000

Average Rental Costs

1-bedroom: *$695 to $1,000*
2-bedroom: *$795 to $2,000*

Other Statistics

Estimated commuting times: *By Metro, 45 minutes to an hour to downtown Washington (allowing for car or bus ride to station). By car, one hour into Washington, 20 minutes to Fairfax business centers, 30 minutes to Reston.*

Important Places Nearby

Grocery Stores

Fresh Fields
7511 Leesburg Pike
(703) 448-1600

Giant Food
1445 Chain Bridge Road
(703) 845-1446

Safeway
9881 Georgetown Pike
(703) 759-3802

Pharmacies

Dart Drugs
8369 Leesburg Pike
(703) 893-7165

McLean's
6823 Chain Bridge Road
(703) 827-0990

Banks

Chevy Chase Bank
7935-L Tyson's Corner Center
(703) 883-3915

Riggs National
8002 Tysons Corner Shopping Center
(703) 887-6000

Hardware Stores

Falls Hardware Limited
9912 Georgetown Pike
(703) 438-1700

Sheets Wholesale
430 Mill Street
(703) 938-9110

Hospitals/Emergency Rooms

Dominion Hospital
2960 Sleepy Hollow Road
(703) 536-2000

Inova Hospital for Children
3300 Gallows Road
(703) 204-6777

McLean

It's the home of the Central Intelligence Agency, members of the Kennedy family, any number of U.S. Senate and House members, bureaucrats, businessmen, and high-profile journalists. It can be your home, too.

Despite McLean's image of wealth and power, as you drive along Route 123 it looks like any number of subdivisions you might find in the Washington area. So why the rep of exclusivity? Well, before the large acres of farmland were sold off for development in the 1950s, McLean was a community of estates and large private homes. It has always been home to the wealthy and powerful.

But today much of the old money is gone, and many of those estates have long been sold off for planned developments in which numerous expensive, cookie-cutter mansions and large brick colonials have been built. If you buy into McLean, you're paying as much for the zip code as you are for the actual property.

And *buying* is the operative word here. While there is rental property available in both townhouse and house form, there are few apartment developments in the area. It should be noted, however, that several large undeveloped tracts of land were sold in late 1999 and early 2000, with the buyers announcing that townhouse and apartment complexes were to be built. So if you want to rent, the area may still be worth a look.

Much of the housing exists in either old-line neighborhoods or new subdivisions, almost all of which are accessed through the major roadways in the area: Route 123, Route 738 (Old Dominion Drive), and Route 194 (Georgetown Pike). McLean is also accessible by way of the Beltway and the George Washington Parkway. All of these roads serve as morning and evening commuting byways.

Keep in mind that McLean remains an extremely quiet community, with a small shopping area that features several fine restaurants, a gourmet pizza shop, and a couple of take-out shops. There is no nightlife to speak of beyond the restaurants. And because there is no Metro station in the area, a car is needed to get to and from Washington or the nightlife that exists in nearby Arlington.

4-bedroom house $325,000 and up

3-bedroom house $275,000–$400,000

Average Housing Costs

2-bedroom townhouse: $175,000

                                           to $200,000

3-bedroom house: $275,000

                                           to 400,000

2-bedroom townhouse
$175,000–$200,000

4-bedroom house: $325,000 and up

Average Rental Costs

1-bedroom: *$800 to $1,200*

2-bedroom: *$1,275 to $2,000*

Other Statistics

Estimated commuting times: *By Metro, 45 minutes to an hour to downtown Washington (allowing for car or bus ride to station). By car, 45 minutes to an hour into Washington, 30 minutes to Fairfax.*

Important Places Nearby

Grocery Stores

Giant Food

1445 Chain Bridge Road
(703) 448-0800

McClean Shopping Center
(703) 893-8593

Safeway

7401 Colshire Drive
(703) 356-1354

6244 Old Dominion Road
(703) 538-6539

Pharmacies

McLean Medical Center Pharmacy
1515 Chain Bridge Road
(703) 356-0356

McLean's
6823 Chain Bridge Road
(703) 827-0990

Banks

Riggs National
6805 Old Dominion Drive
(301) 887-6000

8002 Tysons Corner Center
(301) 887-6000

First Virginia
6220 Old Dominion Drive
(703) 241-3366

1455 Chain Bridge Road
(703) 847-4345

Hardware Stores

McLean Hardware
6811 Old Dominion Drive
(703) 356-5496

Stalcup Hardware
6254 Old Dominion Drive
(703) 241-7477

Hospitals/Emergency Rooms

Dominion Hospital
2960 Sleepy Hollow Road
(703) 536-2000

Inova Hospital for Children
3300 Gallows Road
(703) 204-6777

Reston/Herndon

At some point, these two communities may deserve separate sections, but not now. They are virtually identical in character and design.

Reston is one of the largest planned communities in the Washington area, a mixed-use development that features single-family homes, apartments, condominiums, and office parks all in a highly controlled environment. There are restrictions on colors and sizes of homes, on parking, even on the size and color of fences. With the exception of several large commuter arteries, most roads are two lane.

Reston is accessible via the Dulles Toll Road, which has four on- and off-ramps into the community. Residents also use Route 673 (Lawyers Road), Hunter Mill Road, and the Reston Parkway. Large apartment, condominium, and townhouse complexes dot the entire community and mix seamlessly with the single-family housing subdivisions.

Nightlife for the area can be found almost exclusively in the Reston Town Center, an open-air mall that features a multiscreen movie theater, specialty shops, and several bar/restaurants. Around the Reston Town Center, other large strip mall developments have been built, featuring some chain restaurants and take-out shops.

But people expect that as more and more large companies set down roots in the area, more diverse social and entertainment options will become available as well. That is already happening to some extent in Reston's neighbor, Herndon.

Herndon is an incorporated community across the Dulles Toll Road from Reston. It is increasingly becoming the hub of the region's high-tech development. Single-family home subdivisions and townhouse and apartment complexes compete for the ever-shrinking undeveloped land in the area.

Even as recently as five years ago, most of what was being built here was single-family homes. But as more and more Internet startups opened shop in the comparatively inexpensive office parks in the area, Herndon found itself having to cater to a younger and single clientele. The community remains a work in progress.

Be aware that, depending on traffic, both Reston and Herndon can be a good hour's drive from Washington, D.C. There is no Metro train service to either area, although Metro bus service is extensive, particularly in Reston. To attract young computer-savvy talent, some employers are offering shuttle service to the Vienna Metro station. But increasingly those same employers are encouraging their workers to take advantage of the comparatively inexpensive housing prices in the area—and, with the money they save, to buy a car to drive to the city on weekends.

Average Housing Costs

2-bedroom townhouse: $95,000
                        to $175,000
3-bedroom house: $200,000
                        to 275,000
4-bedroom house: $290,000
                        to $400,000

4-bedroom house $290,000-$400,000

3-bedroom house $200,000-$275,000

2-bedroom house $95,000-$175,000

Average Rental Costs

1-bedroom: $550 to $700
2-bedroom: $800 to $1,300

Other Statistics

Estimated commuting times: By Metro, one hour to downtown Washington (allowing for car or bus ride to Metro station). By car, one hour into downtown Washington, 30 minutes to Fairfax business centers, 15 to 20 minutes to Reston business centers.

Important Places Nearby

Grocery Stores

Safeway
11120 South Lake Drive
(703) 620-3400

2304 Hunter Woods Plaza
(703) 716-4193

Pharmacies

CVS
11122 South Lake Drive
(703) 938-9490

Rite Aid
2260A Hunter Woods
(703) 860-0300

Banks

Bank of America
11303 Sunset Hills Road
(703) 834-6520

Chevy Chase Bank
11874 Spectrum Center
(703) 435-1578

First Virginia

11100 South Lakes Drive
(703) 476-5275

1490 North Point Village Center
(703) 481-2316

2513 Fox Mill Road
(703) 476-5270

Hardware Stores

Sears Hardware
13348 Franklin Farm Road
Herndon
(703) 481-5270

The Home Specialty Store

1821 Fountain Drive
Reston
(703) 709-5757

Hospitals/Emergency Rooms

Reston Hospital Center
1850 Town Center Parkway
(703) 689-9000

Maryland

MONTGOMERY COUNTY

Across the Potomac River from Fairfax County is another affluent and highly developed region: Montgomery County. In many ways, the two are mirror images of each other.

Close to Washington are more deeply developed, more deeply rooted communities weighted heavily to single-family homes. Further out are newer communities, with more developments that cater to the younger, single workers who are increasingly looking for housing closer to the high-tech firms they work for.

Montgomery County also has a strong high-tech and biotechnology industry. But for whatever reason, housing and communities seem to have more closely developed along the Metro lines than in some parts of Virginia. As a result, newcomers to the area tend to find more convenient living situations in Maryland, especially in what could be called lower Montgomery County.

Parts of Montgomery County are serviced by three different Metro lines, the Red, Orange, and Blue lines. For commuters in cars, the Beltway is the major connector, as is I-270, which connects many of the upper county communities to the Beltway.

Closer to Washington, some of the major streets in the District also service the lower county. This is especially true of Wisconsin Avenue, which becomes what is known as the "Rockville Pike," Connecticut Avenue, and Georgia Avenue.

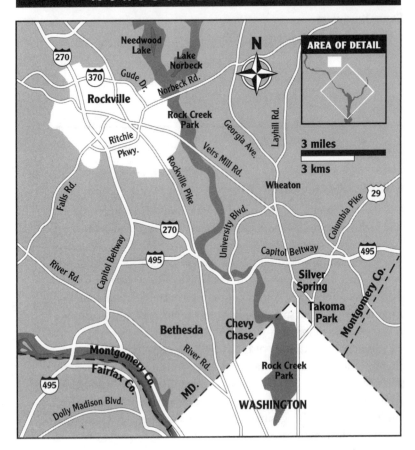

Traffic is an ongoing problem in Montgomery County, in part because of the bottlenecking that occurs as cars head into Washington. In Virginia, the traffic slows at the bridge crossings into the District. In Maryland, the traffic congestion occurs on the Beltway and on the streets leading into D.C.-River Road, Wisconsin, Connecticut, and Georgia Avenues.

Like Fairfax County, Montgomery County is extremely large and spread out. We will look at three of the most popular and most heavily developed areas in lower Montgomery County and two communities a bit farther out.

Demographically, the county breaks down as follows:

Neighborhood Statistical Profile

Population: 816,999

Population by Ethnicity

67%	Anglo
9%	Hispanic
14%	Black
10%	Asian

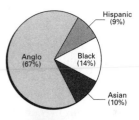

Population by Gender

| 47% | male |
| 53% | female |

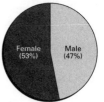

Other Statistics

Average annual income: $34,299

Average crime risk: *Violent crime rate is three to four times lower than Washington, D.C. Home burglaries are on par with other suburban areas in the Washington area.*

Bethesda/Chevy Chase

Just over the D.C. line at Friendship Heights is Chevy Chase; Bethesda is farther north. Both are among the region's most popular residential areas, and combined they make for one of the most affluent areas in America. As a result, both have top-flight school systems and infrastructure, and residents pay for both, either in higher rents or higher mortgage and property tax payments. The two communities, while distinct, are often listed together because of their close proximity to each other and the seamlessness between the two.

The exclusive community of Chevy Chase, Maryland, is one of several Chevy Chases in the area: there is a neighborhood in D.C. that is known as Chevy Chase, and there is a village of Chevy Chase and an unincorporated neighborhood of Chevy Chase, both of which are in Montgomery County, along the D.C. line.

Rental property is hard to come by in Chevy Chase. Apartment rentals or co-ops can mostly be found in and around the Friendship Heights/Chevy Chase area, and smaller and older apartment buildings are located along River Road and Connecticut Avenue. The lack of apartments is due, mostly, to the fact that Chevy Chase is an old, established community with little undeveloped land.

Responsibility for newer housing, then, fell to Bethesda. And boy, has it shouldered the responsibility well. Due to a sensible development plan rolled out over the past 15 years, Bethesda is a gem of a community, filled with "downtown" apartment buildings of all sizes and prices. Houses, mostly of the expensive variety, can be found in longstanding, traditional neighborhoods that ring the downtown. And the social scene and nightlife rivals (surpasses, some say) Washington, D.C. The so-called "Woodmont Triangle," the streets within the border of Old Georgetown Road, Woodmont Avenue, and Battery Lane, offers the highest concentration of bars and restaurants in all of the D.C. metro area. The place is hopping every night of the week. The National Institute of Health, located on the Rockville Pike outside of Bethesda proper, is one of the area's largest employers.

Major rental residential areas include East-West Highway, Bradley Boulevard, Old Georgetown Road, Woodmont Avenue, Wisconsin Avenue, Bethesda Avenue, and Hampden Lane.

Can't find an apartment in downtown Bethesda? Two Metro stops up from Bethesda on the Red Line is the White Flint stop, also known as "North Bethesda." Here are large tracts of apartment and townhouse developments, again of varying prices, styles, and sizes. In fact, there is a seemingly endless selection of apartments and townhouses all the way up what is known as the Rockville Pike.

For that reason, lower Montgomery County has become the most popular location for single people or young married couples. Most residential developments are fairly new, with modern amenities, including off-street parking. Metro stops are easily accessible either by foot or by shuttle service. And at night, the area is alive with blocks upon blocks of bars and restaurants that cater to almost any taste.

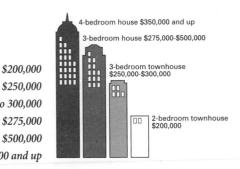

Average Housing Costs

2-bedroom townhouse:	$200,000
3-bedroom townhouse:	$250,000 to 300,000
3-bedroom house:	$275,000 to $500,000
4-bedroom house:	$350,000 and up

4-bedroom house $350,000 and up

3-bedroom house $275,000-$500,000

3-bedroom townhouse $250,000-$300,000

2-bedroom townhouse $200,000

Average Rental Costs

Studio:	$600 to $650
1-bedroom:	$700to $850
2-bedroom:	$950 to $1,500

2-bedroom $950-$1,500

1-bedroom $700-$850

Studio $600-$650

Other Statistics

Estimated commuting times: By car, 30 to 45 minutes into Washington, 45 minutes to an hour to Northern Virginia, 25 minutes to business centers in Montgomery County.

Important Places Nearby

Grocery Stores

Giant Food
Arlington Road
(301) 718-2470

Safeway
7625 Old Georgetown Road
(301) 907-0700

Pharmacies

The Apothecary
5415 West Cedar Lane
(301) 530-0800

CVS
Bradley Boulevard and Arlington Road
(301) 656-2522

Banks

Chevy Chase Bank
8401 Connecticut Avenue
(301) 986-6600

5424 Western Avenue
(301) 320-3800

First Union
7500 Old Georgetown Road, #3
(301) 656-2633

7901 Wisconsin Avenue
(301) 907-2034

Hardware Stores

Glen Echo Hardware
7303 Macarthur Boulevard
(301) 229-3700

Strosniders Hardware Store
Arlington Road and Bradley Boulevard
(301) 654-5688

Hospitals/Emergency Rooms

Suburban Hospital
8600 Old Georgetown Road
(301) 896-3100

Silver Spring

East across Montgomery County from Bethesda is Silver Spring. Like Bethesda, Silver Spring is serviced by the Metro Red Line. But, for now, the similarities end there. For any number of reasons too complex to get into here, Silver Spring was not the jewel in the developers' eyes that Bethesda was 20 years ago. As a result, the area is just beginning to see the growth other areas of the county saw some time ago.

That said, the situation affords newcomers to the area some interesting opportunities, especially for housing. Silver Spring does have a downtown similar in layout to Bethesda. There are large apartment and townhouse developments to be found near the Metro stations. Colesville Road, East-West Highway, Georgia Avenue, Piney Branch Road, and Sligo Avenue are major points to check out rental property.

In addition, single-family home prices, while higher because they are "inside the Beltway," remain considerably lower than most home prices in the Bethesda area. There are also more houses for rent in the Silver Spring area.

Silver Spring's close proximity to Washington makes the area convenient for city workers or even commuters to the Pentagon or Rosslyn. Georgia Avenue is a major commuter auto route into the city. What's missing from Silver Spring right now is the social scene and the breadth of housing options that is now in place in the Bethesda corridor. Thanks to newly approved development plans, that may change for the better in time.

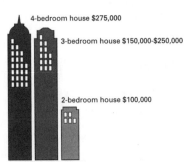

Average Housing Costs

2-bedroom house:	*$100,000*
3-bedroom house:	*$150,000*
	to $250,000
4-bedroom house:	*$275,000*

4-bedroom house $275,000

3-bedroom house $150,000-$250,000

2-bedroom house $100,000

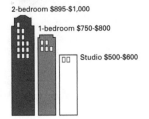

2-bedroom $895-$1,000

1-bedroom $750-$800

Studio $500-$600

Average Rental Costs

Studio:	*$500 to $600*
1-bedroom:	*$750 to $800*
2-bedroom:	*$895 to $1,000*

Other Statistics

Estimated commuting times: By Metro, 30 minutes to downtown Washington.
By car, 30 to 45 minutes into downtown
Washington.

Important Places Nearby

Grocery Stores

Giant Food
13490 New Hampshire Avenue
(301) 384-1572

8750 Arliss Street
(301) 587-3450

Safeway
1101 West University Boulevard
(301) 434-2777

909 Thayer Avenue
(301) 565-0686

Pharmacies

Best-Care Pharmacy
9801 Georgia Avenue
(301) 593-3022

Fairway Pharmacy
531 Dale Drive
(301) 588-9300

Banks

Chevy Chase Bank
11261 New Hampshire Avenue
(301) 681-5500

115 West University Boulevard
(301) 754-1662

Citizens Savings Bank
8485 Fenton Street
(301) 589-9610

First Union
13601 Connecticut Avenue
(301) 460-4420

3852 International Drive
(301) 598-4902

8701 Georgia Avenue
(301) 650-1003

Hardware Stores

A & A Hardware
9441 Georgia Avenue
(301) 589-5330

Hardware City Home Center
11105 New Hampshire Avenue
(301) 593-2990

Washington Adventist Hospital
7600 Carroll Avenue
Takoma Park
(301) 891-7600

Hospitals/Emergency Rooms

Holy Cross Hospital
1500 Forest Glen Road
(301) 587-878

Takoma Park

Next door to Silver Spring, but seemingly a world away, is Takoma Park, one of the most unique and interesting communities in the area. And that may be putting it mildly.

We're talking about a community that is one of only three in America that has designated itself a "nuclear-free" zone and campaigns against the use of gas-powered lawnmowers and leaf-blowers. Because of its generally accepted leftist political leanings, it is often called "The People's Republic of Takoma Park." Takoma Park has its own city government, although it lies between both Montgomery County and Prince Georges County.

That said, Takoma Park is one of the most livable areas around. The tree-lined streets and small-town feel of this planned community are inviting to newcomers and present an appealing alternative to fast-growing communities that surround it. The result is a racially diverse city that is both family-friendly and accessible to the single professional.

For all of its small-town feel, more than half of Takoma Park's housing stock is rental property. Larger apartment buildings can be found along Maple Avenue and dotting the rest of the area. Unfortunately, much of the rental properties are not in close proximity to the Metro station that bears the community's name, which is technically within the Washington, D.C., city limits.

Average Housing Costs

3-bedroom house:	*$150,000*
4-bedroom house:	*$200,000*
	to $375,000

Average Rental Costs

1-bedroom:	*$495 to $600*
2-bedroom:	*$550 to $800*

Other Statistics

Estimated commuting times: *By Metro, 20 minutes to downtown Washington.*
By car, 30 to 45 minutes into Washington.

Important Places Nearby

Grocery Stores

G & H Food Market
8000 Flower Avenue
(301) 587-5595

Shoppers Food Warehouse
6875 North H Avenue
(301) 270-5324

Pharmacies

Takoma Park Family Pharmacy
7610 Carroll Avenue
(301) 891-6077

University Boulevard Professional Pharmacy
831 University Boulevard East
(301) 439-1657

Banks

Bank of America
6950 Carroll Avenue
(301) 270-7095

Hardware Stores

A & A Hardware
9441 Georgia Avenue
(301) 589-5330

Hardware City Home Center
11105 New Hampshire Avenue
(301) 593-2990

Hospitals/Emergency Rooms

Holy Cross Hospital
1500 Forest Glen Road
(301) 754-7740

Washington Adventist Hospital

7600 Carroll Avenue
(301) 891-7600

Rockville

Farther north up the Rockville Pike lies that roadway's namesake. Rockville is the seat of Montgomery County, and the courthouse and government center are based here. But if one ventures out onto the Pike, beginning in Bethesda and heading north, the trip is seamless: just miles and miles of strip malls, apartment buildings, shopping centers, gas stations, and more of the same. It's difficult to tell where Rockville ends and Bethesda or North Bethesda begins.

With that in mind, there isn't much to distinguish Rockville from other parts of the county. It is mostly a bedroom community, easily accessible from I-270 or the Pike. Apartment buildings and townhouse developments are common and plentiful. Most come at slightly lower rates than those closer to the city. And because many of these properties have been built near a Metro station, commuting from Rockville is a bit easier for those without a car.

Closer to "downtown" Rockville are neighborhoods with older single-family homes that for some reason tend to carry higher price tags than in other areas of the county. This may be due to the larger lots that the homes sit on, or their location away from the major highways and roadways that have cut through the area in the past 15 years. Farther out from downtown are numerous new subdivisions of single-family homes. Many are no more than 15 years old; many more are less than five years old.

The advantage some may see in Rockville comes with employment opportunities. Because high-tech and bio-tech firms have opened up in the area, many people find it convenient to live here and cut down their commuting time.

Average Housing Costs

2-bedroom house:	*$130,000*
3-bedroom house:	*$175,000*
	to 250,000
4-bedroom house:	*$225,000*
	to $500,000

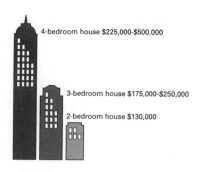

4-bedroom house $225,000-$500,000

3-bedroom house $175,000-$250,000

2-bedroom house $130,000

Average Rental Costs

1-bedroom:	*$550 to $700*
2-bedroom:	*$750 to $1,000*

Other Statistics

Estimated commuting times: *By Metro, 45 minutes to downtown Washington.*
   By car, 45 minutes to an hour into Washington.

Important Places Nearby

Grocery Stores

Giant Food
12051 Rockville Pike
(301) 881-4541

2401 Wootton Parkway
(301) 340-9378

275 North Washington Street
(301) 340-9037

Safeway
13069 Wisteria Drive
(301) 428-9256

Pharmacies

Fairway Pharmacy
13617 Russett Terrace
(301) 588-9300

Lotte Pharmacy
11716 Parklawn Drive
(301) 770-2654

Banks

Chevy Chase Bank
215 North Washington Street
(301) 251-1434

2409 Wootton Parkway
(301) 251-9272

Citibank
1400 Research Boulevard
(301) 762-8000

14405 Laurel Place
(301) 217-0236

First Union
502 Hungerford Drive
(301) 294-6860

1110 Congressional Lane
(301) 650-1045

Hardware Stores

Macks Hardware
8 West Middle Lane
(301) 424-5656

Strosniders Hardware
Falls and River Roads
(301) 299-6333

Hospitals/Emergency Rooms

Childrens National Medical Center at Shady Grove
14804 Physicians Lane
(301) 424-1755

Columbia Hospital for Women Medical Center at Shady Grove
9707 Medical Center Drive
(301) 309-9114

Germantown/Gaithersburg
Even farther up Rockville Pike and on either side of I-270 are Germantown and Gaithersburg. Both communities were almost rural in nature, until developers began moving in 25 years ago to construct single-family homes on the large lots that were available along I-270.

Because of their close proximity to this major commuting artery, Germantown and Gaithersburg have seen an amazing amount of growth in just the past five years. In fact, a new apartment, condo, townhouse, or single-family housing subdivision seems to open in the area every week.

Gaithersburg is probably the older of the two communities. It features an Olde Town historic district, and a more interesting and diverse selection of real estate in the town center. From there, it's almost all newer development. Residents tend to work for the corporations and agencies that have built up the area. Defense contractor Hughes has a large presence here, as do several federal government agencies, including the Bureau of Weights and Measures and the Department of Energy.

Germantown lies about five miles northwest of Gaithersburg and is the fastest growing community in the region. It features extensive and moderately priced apartment and townhouse complexes, many of which offer shuttle service during commuting hours to the Shady Grove Metro station.

Lying between Germantown and Gaithersburg is the 30-year-old planned community known as Montgomery Village. It features the full range of housing choices: single-family homes, townhouses, apartments, and a retirement community. The community also offers a number of open spaces, parks, swimming pools, and recreation centers, some with tennis courts and playing fields. Montgomery Village is easily accessible from I-270 and the major commuting arteries in the area.

Housing development may be explosive in Gaithersburg and Germantown, but the same cannot be said about the social scene. It is essentially nonexistent. While there are a few restaurants and movie multiplexes, residents seeking nightlife must look along the Rockville Pike or go down into Bethesda or into D.C. to find it.

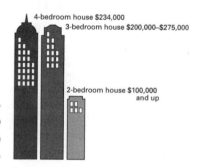

4-bedroom house $234,000
3-bedroom house $200,000–$275,000
2-bedroom house $100,000 and up

Average Housing Costs

2-bedroom house:	$100,000 and up
3-bedroom house:	$200,000 to 275,000
4-bedroom house:	$234,000

Average Rental Costs

1-bedroom: $500 to $750

2-bedroom: $700 to $900

Other Statistics

Estimated commuting times: By Metro, 45 minutes to downtown Washington.
By car, an hour into Washington.

Important Places Nearby

Grocery Stores

Giant Food
842 Muddy Branch Road
(301) 948-8148

19721 Frederick Road
(301) 428-9314

Pharmacies

CVS
Goshen Plaza
18080 Mateny Road
(301) 916-9305

7230 Muncaster Mill Road
(301) 330-9333

Banks

First Virginia Bank Maryland
19801 Frederick Road
(301) 540-4407

Lincoln National Bank
14106 Seneca Road
(301) 948-4650

Potomac Valley Bank
12801 Wisteria Drive
(301) 916-0200

Hardware Stores

Christopher's Hardware
25 Sandy Spring Road
(301) 977-9393

N & S Rentals Inc.
19600 Frederick Road
(301) 428-3200

Hospitals/Emergency Rooms

Childrens National Medical Center at Shady Grove
14804 Physicians Lane
(301) 424-1755

PRINCE GEORGES COUNTY

Next to Montgomery County and abutting Washington, D.C., farther to the southeast is Prince Georges County. It is less well known than Montgomery County, perhaps because its communities tend to be smaller and more racially diverse. Next to Washington, D.C., it is the most predominantly African-American region in the metro area.

Because much of the county is connected to the poorer areas of the District, there is the unfair perception that Prince Georges County is riddled with crime itself. This isn't necessarily so. Crime is a problem along the borders of D.C. and Prince Georges County, but beyond that, crime rates are about 25 to 30 percent lower in the county than its District neighbor.

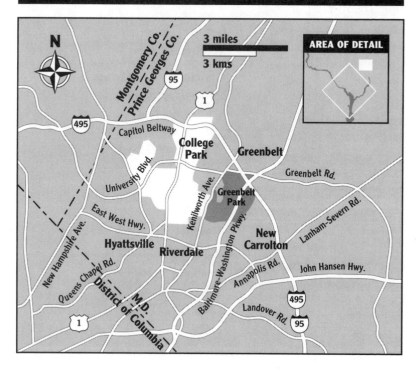

That said, Prince Georges isn't without its problems. Its school system lags badly behind Montgomery, Arlington, and Fairfax County schools. Development in the area is lagging a bit as well. Most communities in Prince Georges County are accessible by Metro rail, Interstate-495 (the Beltway), and I-395. Major thoroughfares inside the county include Rhode Island Avenue (coming out from the District of Columbia), New York Avenue, and Kenilworth Avenue. University Avenue serves as a cross-county connector.

While development and nightlife may not measure up to other parts of the region, Prince Georges County does afford newcomers some options. Communities here tend to be a bit more rural and wide open. To follow are snapshots of four of the better-known Prince Georges communities to consider. Two are closer to the District, two are farther out. Demographically, the county shapes up this way:

Neighborhood Statistical Profile

Population:　　　　　　　773,810

Population by Ethnicity

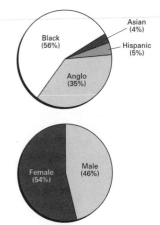

35%	Anglo
5%	Hispanic
56%	Black
4%	Asian

Asian (4%)
Black (56%)
Hispanic (5%)
Anglo (35%)

Population by Gender

46%	male
54%	female

Female (54%)　Male (46%)

Other Statistics

Average annual income:　$32,422
Estimated commuting times:　20 minutes to anywhere in Washington.

College Park

This community has grown up around the large main campus of the University of Maryland. As a result, the residents of this area tend to be younger and more transient than in other areas. This can be a good thing, however. Apartments and other rental properties are plentiful, and leasing terms tend to be a bit more flexible to accommodate the college students.

The area has been compared to Berkeley, California (home to the University of California), in atmosphere and lifestyle, although it is not as politically active or urban. Residents tend to be federal government employees or university staff.

College Park's "downtown" is along Baltimore Avenue. Here you'll find much of your shopping opportunities and some social settings, mostly bars and moderately priced restaurants inside the strip malls.

Along with the numerous apartment buildings there are single-family houses here, particularly in neighboring University Park. This community has few apartments, but many houses both for rent and for sale. Some have compared University Park to Takoma Park in favorable terms.

College Park offers extensive public transit options, including a Metrorail station, and the District is easily accessible by car.

4-bedroom house $200,000 and up
3-bedroom house $125,000-$200,000
2-bedroom house $100,000 and up

Average Housing Costs

2-bedroom house:	*$100,000 and up*
3-bedroom house:	*$125,000 to 200,000*
4-bedroom house:	*$200,000 and up*

Group home $1,750-$2,000
2-bedroom $875-$1,500
1-bedroom $600-$800
Studio $500

Average Rental Costs

Studio:	*$500*
1-bedroom:	*$600 to $800*
2-bedroom:	*$875 to $1,500*
2- to 3-bedroom group home:	*$1,750 to $2,000*

Other Statistics

Estimated commuting times: *By Metro, 30 to 45 minutes to downtown*
Washington. By car, 45 minutes to an hour into
downtown Washington.

Important Places Nearby

Grocery Stores

Safeway
7595 Greenbelt Road
(301) 345-0150

Pharmacies

Dumfries Pharmacy
10001 Rhode Island Avenue
(301) 345-4700

Rite Aid
Chestnut Hill Shopping Center
10456 Baltimore Avenue
(301) 937-4020

Banks

Chevy Chase Bank
6107 Greenbelt Road
(301) 345-2424

10800 Baltimore Avenue
(301) 595-1860

First National Bank of Maryland
6303 Ivy Lane
(301) 397-5501

Suburban Bank of Maryland
7505 Greenway Center Drive
(301) 220-0733

Hospitals/Emergency Rooms

Holy Cross Hospital
1500 Forest Glen Road
Silver Spring
(301) 587-878

Washington Adventist Hospital
7600 Carroll Avenue
Takoma Park
(301) 891-7600

Hyattsville/Riverdale

Less than five miles from Washington, along the Anacostia River, lie these two small, quiet communities. Both feature large parklands, which add to the suburban, sometimes rural, feel. Neither has seen heavy development in some time, perhaps because the Metro line bypasses the more heavily populated, more residential areas.

Hyattsville does have Metro service at its West Hyattsville and Prince Georges Plaza stations. Riverdale has no Metro rail station. Rhode Island Avenue, Queens Chapel Road, and Route 1 serve as the main roadways for commuters. Rental property can be found in those areas as well.

Riverdale can be reached by Route 1 or through Route 410 (East-West Highway). It is an extension of College and University Park, although less developed than both. Northwest Branch Park runs along it, affording residents fine recreational opportunities.

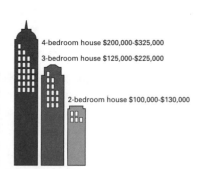

4-bedroom house $200,000-$325,000

3-bedroom house $125,000-$225,000

2-bedroom house $100,000-$130,000

Average Housing Costs

2-bedroom house:	*$100,000*
	to $130,000
3-bedroom house:	*$125,000*
	to 225,000
4-bedroom house:	*$200,000*
	to $325,000

Average Rental Costs

1-bedroom:	*$500 to $7,500*
2-bedroom:	*$620 to $1,000*

Other Statistics

Estimated commuting times:	*By Metro, 30 minutes to downtown Washington.*
	By car, 30 to 45 minutes into downtown Washington.

Important Places Nearby

Grocery Stores

Giant Food
6300 Sheriff Road
(301) 248-1333

6524 Landover Road
(301) 322-7441

Safeway
8484 Annapolis Road
(301) 577-6277

3511 Hamilton Street
(301) 864-6026

Pharmacies

Chandlers Drugs & Medical Supplies
7037 Annapolis Road
(301) 577-9000

Drug Emporium
5416 Annapolis Road
(301) 985-3070

Banks

Citizens Bank
12301 Annapolis Road
(301) 206-6000

Commerce Bank
3004 52nd Avenue
(301) 985-3740

SunTrust Bank
4805 Annapolis Road
(301) 864-2745

Maryland Federal
3505 Hamilton Street
(301) 779-1200

Hardware Stores

Bill's Hardware
7431 Annapolis Road
(301) 577-7100

East-West Hardware
6571 Ager Road
(301) 422-7474

Hospitals/Emergency Rooms

Laurel Regional Hospital
3001 Hospital Drive
(301) 618-3100

Greenbelt

This large suburban community lies about halfway between Washington and Baltimore and is perhaps one of the most convenient locales in the region. It is accessible from the Beltway, Kenilworth Avenue, Route 1, and the Baltimore-Washington Parkway.

Greenbelt was a planned community constructed by the federal government in 1934. More than 1,500 simple row houses were built, forming what was then one of the largest co-ops in the area. Despite development around them, the co-op buildings remain as such today.

Like other areas outside of Washington, Greenbelt has a large federal-government presence, although it's a particularly interesting branch of the federal government. The NASA Goddard Space Flight Center is based here, and many Greenbelt residents work there.

Surrounding what could be termed "Old Greenbelt" is newer development along and around Greenbelt Road. Here one can find a wide variety of rental properties, both apartments and townhouses. In addition to the historic co-op, Greenbelt boasts what at one time was the largest apartment complex outside of New York—Springhill Lake Apartments, with more than 2,500 units. Due to frequent turnover, the property often has apartments available. It also offers shuttle service to the Metro station and to the University of Maryland campus at College Park.

The surrounding area is full of single-family homes, many of which are far more affordable than anything one might find in Montgomery or Fairfax County. This is in part due to Greenbelt's distance from Washington, although the many roadways that travel directly into the city make for a fairly easy commute. In addition, Greenbelt recently opened its own Metrorail station on the relatively new Green Line.

Average Housing Costs

2-bedroom house:	*$90,000 to $115,000*
3-bedroom house:	*$125,000 to 175,000*
4-bedroom house:	*$200,000 to $265,000*

4-bedroom house $200,000-$265,000

3-bedroom house $125,000-$175,000

2-bedroom house $90,000-$115,000

Average Rental Costs

1-bedroom: *$500 to $650*
2-bedroom: *$700 to $1,000*

Other Statistics

Estimated commuting times: *By Metro, 45 minutes to downtown Washington.*
                               By car, 45 minutes to an hour into downtown
                               Washington.

Important Places Nearby

Grocery Stores

Giant Food
13490 New Hampshire Avenue
(301) 384-1572

Safeway
1101 West University Boulevard
(301) 434-2777

909 Thayer Avenue
(301) 565-0686

Pharmacies

Greenbelt Consumers Pharmacy
121 Centerway
(301) 474-4400

Banks

First National Bank of Maryland
6303 Ivy Lane
(301) 397-5500

Suburban Bank of Maryland
7505 Greenway Center Drive
(301) 474-6694

Hardware Stores

Beltway Plaza Hardware
6210 Greenbelt Road
(301) 345-2662

Hospitals/Emergency Rooms

Childrens National Medical Center at Shady Grove
14804 Physicians Lane
(301) 424-1755

Landover/New Carrollton

Landover was once best known for its sports arena, home to the then Washington Bullets basketball team, Washington Capitols hockey team, and Georgetown University basketball team. Today, what was once a sports center is being converted into a large shopping and housing development, but Landover is probably still one of the more well-known communities in the area. It has a Metro station and is easily accessible from the Beltway, Route 50, and the Baltimore Washington Parkway.

Landover Road is the major roadway, running east to west, and it is lined with numerous apartment buildings. But recognition and convenience aside, it doesn't have much more to offer. The area has large apartment buildings, convenient to the District and Montgomery County, and rental prices tend to be lower than in other areas. Nightlife tends to be limited to the restaurants or bars in the strip malls. Most residents make their way to the District for fun.

New Carrollton, the last Metrorail stop on the Orange Line, is a similarly quiet community. It offers commuters the convenience of apartment buildings and townhouses around the station. In addition to Metrorail service it offers Maryland Area Rapid Transit train service to Baltimore and Amtrak train service up and down the East Coast. So for the person with wanderlust, New Carrollton is the place to live.

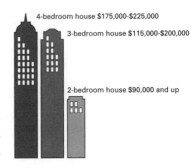

Average Housing Costs

2-bedroom house:	*$90,000 and up*
3-bedroom house:	*$115,000*
	to 200,000
4-bedroom house:	*$175,000*
	to $225,000

Average Rental Costs

1-bedroom:	*$500 to $650*
2-bedroom:	*$650 to $950*

Other Statistics

Estimated commuting times: *By Metro, 45 minutes to downtown Washington. By car, 45 minutes to an hour into downtown Washington.*

Important Places Nearby

Grocery Stores

Giant Food
6300 Sheriff Road
(301) 248-1333

6524 Landover Road
(301) 322-7441

Safeway
8484 Annapolis Road
(301) 577-6277

3511 Hamilton Street
(301) 864-6026

Pharmacies

Landover Hills Drug Store
7037 Annapolis Road
(301) 577-9000

Rite Aid
8048 New Hampshire Avenue
(301) 439-6188

Banks

Chevy Chase Bank
6200 Annapolis Road
(301) 773-7177

Provident Bank of Maryland
4552 Edmondson Avenue
(410) 281-7383

Suburban Federal Savings Bank
7467 Annapolis Road
(301) 577-7000

Susquehanna Bank
6669 Security Boulevard
(410) 265-1140.

Hospitals/Emergency Rooms

Prince Georges Hospital Center
3001 Hospital Drive
(301) 618-2000

Outside the Area

In recent years, areas outside of what is considered to be the metropolitan area of Washington are seeing increased development designed to attract families of Washington workers. Why? Simply put, it's the only land left to develop and there is a huge demand for single-family housing in this region.

Families looking for larger houses at lower prices—and willing to put up with longer commutes to get them—are moving to these areas. And the communities are welcoming them with open arms, allowing more commercial development to support the growing populations: more shopping centers, more grocery stores, and wider roads with better access to freeways. Prince William County, Virginia, for example, constructed two light-rail systems to carry commuters into Alexandria and Washington, D.C.

VIRGINIA

In Virginia, two counties outside of the traditional Washington metro area are developing the kinds of communities that families would find appealing: Loudon County, to the northwest beyond Fairfax County, and Prince William County, to the south of Fairfax County.

Neither of these areas is really of interest to young, single people, in part because the communities are more than 30 miles from Washington. This kind of distance makes for a difficult social life, which for most singles would outweigh whatever minor savings on housing costs one might gain.

Some young professional couples, willing to make the more than one-hour commute into Washington, are buying homes in Loudon and Prince William counties because they expect the value of the homes will increase in the coming years as even these counties become saturated with residents and development.

There are virtually no large-scale apartment buildings or other rental properties going up in the areas. Instead, single-family homes and townhouses are making up the majority of new construction. Here is a quick overview of the two counties, along with some details about each:

Prince William is a county of about 250,000 residents in towns with mostly suburban, semi-rural, and rural settings. The farther south one goes, the more rural the communities tend to be. Average income in the county is $20,921. Demographics are as follows:

77%   white
13%   black
4%   Asian
6%   Hispanic

The most populated and popular communities on the map today are Manassas, Fredericksburg, Woodbridge, Dumfries, Dale City, and Haymarket.

Manassas, the site of one of the bloodiest Civil War battles and now home to a major national park, may be the best known. It is one of the closer communities to Washington, about 20 miles outside of town. It offers a fairly convenient commute for workers in Fairfax County, and quite a few government employees in the District make the drive every day.

In 1995, Prince William County launched a light-rail system in conjunction with Washington Metro and Amtrak. Today, the Manassas and Fredericksburg lines of the Virginia commuter rail system carry about 30,000 workers a week into the metropolitan area. Tickets are between $2 and $7 a day, round-trip, depending on which station you travel from. Weekly and monthly passes are available. Trains make stops in Fairfax, Alexandria, Crystal City, and Washington D.C.

Despite the trains, cars remain the most popular commuting mode for the area and, given extensive road construction projects, traffic has become a terrible problem. Unfortunately, it's one that transportation experts say will continue well into 2005. Commutes of more than an hour into Washington are not uncommon.

But the hassles may seem worth it when you compare the average home prices in Prince William County to those of areas closer in to the city. On average a new three-bedroom house on a one-acre lot costs $171,000. Older homes in more established areas may cost even less.

Just north of Prince William County is Loudon County, considered to be one of the fastest growing counties in the region. Its current population is about 125,000 people. Average income is $26,430, and the ethnic breakdown is as follows:

85%	*white*
8%	*black*
3%	*Asian*
4%	*Hispanic*

Loudon County is suburban to semi-rural. The area has developed as the region surrounding Dulles International Airport has seen an explosion of growth. Today, housing subdivisions full of new brick colonials dot the landscape like so many haystacks.

The most popular areas of the county currently are the towns of Leesburg, Sterling, and Ashburn. Commuters to the high-tech firms located in parts of Fairfax County don't mind the 30-minute drive to work, and there continues to be an exodus of Washington, D.C., dwellers way out to these suburbs, in part because of the reasonable home prices.

The town of Ashburn is northwest of Dulles Airport and east of Leesburg. It remains in many ways much as it was when it was founded in the early 20th century. Some farmers remain, as does the W & OD Railway. But at that time only about 200 people resided in the area; today, about 11,000 residents are based here. Schools and infrastructure are just beginning to catch up with development.

The Greenway Toll Road, an extension of the Dulles Toll Road, opened in 1997 and makes commuting easier than following the back roads into Fairfax County. Ashburn's growth is due, in part, to business development. America Online has opened a large facility here, and the NFL Washington Redskins have announced plans to expand their facility to be a year-round recreational center and tourist attraction. Home prices range from $175,000 to $300,000; townhouses are priced $120,000 to $165,000.

Located about 40 miles from Washington, Leesburg is the largest town in Louden County, with a population of about 20,000. It is considered to be one of the most architecturally noteworthy communities in the area, with beautiful old Victorian-era homes in the downtown area. Such homes sell for upwards of $300,000. More modern homes sell for about $165,500.

MARYLAND

The demand for new housing and development isn't as great outside of Montgomery County as it is in the outlying counties of Virginia, because parts of the county still have room for growth. This is especially true in Germantown and Gaithersburg, where new housing start-ups continue at a rapid pace that should carry on until 2005. At that point, area residents will be hearing about housing development in Frederick County, north of Germantown. Upper Montgomery County is still a bargain for housing, and remains convenient to Washington because of the Metro rail system. That said, some people are turning to communities between Washington and Baltimore because of the lower home prices and the close proximity to two urban centers.

Some people just prefer Baltimore to Washington. The inner harbor, world-class aquarium and museum, the Baltimore Orioles, and the more urban setting of Charm City are attractive lures to people who consider Washington somewhat bland and characterless.

Unlike those Virginia areas that are attracting almost exclusively families, one Maryland community that would be considered "way out," Columbia, is popular with both single professionals and families alike. This is probably due to the fact that commuting into Washington is made easier by an older and more established mass transit system and a number of freeways. Maryland runs a commuter train service between Baltimore and Washington, and I-95 feeds into the Washington Beltway. There is also the Baltimore-Washington Parkway. Still, commutes from Columbia and Bowie into Washington can take more than an hour.

Columbia is a planned community in Howard County that lies just off of I-95 about halfway between Washington and Baltimore. Construction of the community began in 1963 by the Rouse Company, one of the largest builders in the country. Today the 14,000-

acre development features single-family homes, townhouses, and apartments. Columbia has over 32,000 residential units ranging from government-subsidized apartments to single-family homes ranging in price from $160,000 to over $1 million. There are more than 500 stores and restaurants in the area and approximately 2,800 businesses employing over 60,000 people. Businesses from both Washington and Baltimore continue to seek the so-called "middle ground" in this part of Maryland.

Columbia has been compared favorably to Reston, Virginia, although many people who know both places say that Columbia has more of a "community" feel than Reston. That may be because Columbia is a bit less suburban and because of its easy access to area freeways.

Those people who commute into Washington from Columbia often hit the road before 6:30 A.M. and leave the office before 4 P.M. to avoid heavy traffic tie-ups on the Beltway. But those hours aren't considered terribly out of the ordinary. In fact, most government offices in Washington now encourage flex-time to reduce rush-hour traffic.

So if you're looking for a bit more space and perhaps a better price on a home or townhouse, consider Columbia.

CHAPTER 2

Advice on Finding an Apartment

Now we will deal with the basic issues of finding and renting the apartment or house that will meet your needs, your expectations, and your bank account.

Preliminary Considerations

Before you begin an in-depth, intensive search, there are a couple of broader issues you should take into account. The most important are:

What kind of life do you have?

What kind of life do you want to have?

Will you be a single stranger in a strange town? Perhaps you'll need a jump-start for your social life. The area you live in may mean the difference between a hopping weekend and a slow boat to boredom. Maybe, on the other hand, you enjoy the quiet neighborhood you already reside in, and you want the same thing in Washington. In either situation, you have a choice to make. And thanks to one-year leases, it's a decision that you will have to live with for a while.

When considering where to live, also take into account your daily habits and routines:

Do you enjoy an evening walk?

Do you prefer lots of take-out food options to home cooking?

Do you like using self-serve Laundromats as opposed to an apartment building's laundry room? (Some people like to give laundry day a social dimension.)

Some of these points may seem trivial, but consider how many small or trivial points help to make your lifestyle what it is. In the end, some of these things—or others like them—may be more important than you think. You've just taken them for granted.

Also think about your job:

Do you already have one, and if so, do want to live near your place of employment?

Do you require close proximity to public transportation?

How far of a commute are you willing to make?

Most neighborhoods inside Washington are no more than 20 to 30 minutes away from the major employment centers of the District. So if you want to live in the city, this gives you some flexibility.

After considering the various lifestyle questions, come up with a realistic monthly housing budget. When calculating what you can spend on an apartment, keep in mind that almost all apartment buildings in Washington require first and last month's rent and a nonrefundable fee of between $25 to $50 for a credit and reference check up front. That means you may be spending between $2,000 and $3,000 before you move in. If you can't afford this, you might want to consider living in a group home, where such fees are not usually required.

As you try to figure out what you can afford to spend on rent, don't forget your other monthly expenses: car or other transportation, food, clothing, entertainment, home furnishings, etc., etc., etc. Washington can be an expensive place to live. For an overview of prices in the region, go online to *www.washingtonpost.com*. What you see may be eye-opening—and should be helpful as you search for the right area to live in.

Selecting a Neighborhood

You've addressed some of the big and little issues of your life. Now you need to focus on Washington, the city, and what it has to offer in terms of shelter.

One thing you should know about the area is that there are a lot of renters and rental properties out there. Unlike many other cities and suburbs, where homeownership and rentals tend to run neck and neck, many D.C. neighborhoods boast a 3-to-1 rental-versus-owner-ship ratio. This is especially true in many of the downtown neighborhoods we've highlighted.

That said, you should also be aware that, as of this writing, the Washington rental market is considered "tight." This doesn't mean that apartments aren't plentiful, it's just that those that are available get snapped up quickly. If an apartment sounds good to you, it probably sounds good to a few other prospective tenants, as well. So be aggressive, move quickly, and be prepared to make a commitment and full application immediately.

The business of real estate is all about location, location, location. Finding real estate is all about research, research, and more research. Hopefully, you've already bought this book instead reading it in an easy chair at the bookstore, so your research has begun.

MOVING TIP

Compare the cost of making your move on a do-it-yourself basis or hiring a professional mover. If you go the pro route, get multiple estimates and lock in the price before you begin the process—get it in writing. Remember, a one-way move can be costly if you are not using a full relocation service.

When looking at Washington neighborhoods, perhaps the first question you should consider is: "How hot is it?" We're talking about popularity here, not the temperature. The thumbnail sketches following will help answer that question, but a look at the rental ads and a quick discussion with real estate agents in Washington will help round out your knowledge. Keep in mind that in Washington it's possible to live near a popular neighborhood, take advantage of all it has to offer, and not pay the rent others pay for the same privilege.

Another question to consider: Do you want older, more classic architecture or modern amenities? Where you live in Washington will determine the types of apartments or houses available to you. In general, the city has three kinds of housing for rent: apartments in older, large buildings and townhouses; modern buildings with modern amenities; and older, single-family homes that have been retrofitted for multiple residents. You must also decide whether you prefer a mature community with convenient grocery stores, playgrounds for the kids, and family-oriented activities, or a cutting-edge neighborhood with a pulsing nightclub beat, coffee bars, and gourmet-food shops.

Detailed descriptions of the neighborhoods of Washington, D.C., and the surrounding suburbs of Virginia and Maryland can be found in chapter 1. The following is an overview of Washington neighborhoods from the point of view of the renter, including an outline of the prevalent housing choices and a quick look at the pros and cons of renting in each area.

GEORGETOWN

West of downtown D.C. in the Northwest quadrant, Georgetown borders Rock Creek Park, Georgetown University, and the Potomac River. Its northern border is Massachusetts Avenue. The area is filled with restaurants, bars, nightclubs, and specialty stores along the main streets of Wisconsin Avenue and M Street.

Housing is varied, but there are few modern, large apartment buildings in the neighborhood. Those few that do fit that category are generally condominiums. The most common types of rental properties are townhouses converted for multiple residents in a group home setting, small efficiency or one-bedroom apartments, and garden apartments. On the outer edges of upper Georgtown, near N and P Streets, some larger apartment buildings may be found.

Availability: Rentals are common year-round, but expect a broader selection after May 1, when Georgetown University students leave at the end of the school year, and before August 15, when they arrive back in town.

Pros: Most desirable neighborhood in Washington. Great social whirl, with bars and restaurants galore. Convenient to downtown D.C.

Cons: Little to no off-street parking in many areas of Georgetown. Traffic, especially on Friday and Saturday nights, is nightmarish. No Metro station. Apartments and houses tend to be smaller and more expensive per square foot than elsewhere.

Rating: Hot

CAPITOL HILL

This is one of the oldest neighborhoods in the District. The prime rental area is limited to the section behind the Capitol Building—about 20 to 25 square blocks. Boundaries for Capitol Hill run along Massachusetts Avenue to the north, 11th Street to the east, Virginia Avenue SE to the south, and the Capitol itself to the west.

There are a few large apartment buildings, particularly along Independence Avenue on the House side of the Hill, and Massachusetts Avenue on the Senate side. But more common are smaller, single-family dwellings that have been remodeled to serve as rental properties or converted into two or three small apartments. Smaller brick and brownstone homes often serve as group homes for younger congressional staffers.

Availability: Always good for a wide range of rental property in all price ranges, from $350 a month for a slice of a group home to more than $2,000 per month for a three-story single-family house.

Pros: Convenient to Capitol Hill and downtown via Metro.

Cons: Some of the neighborhoods bordering the Hill are high-crime areas, and the crime problem spills over. Lack of on-street parking day and night is an ongoing problem.

Rating: Warm

FOGGY BOTTOM

An apartment-seeker's nirvana, Foggy Bottom is just south of Georgetown. Its borders include M Street to the north, 26th Street NW to the west, 18th Street to the east, and Constitution Avenue to the south.

The neighborhood encompasses parts of downtown Washington (almost to the White House's front door), and all of George Washington University's urban campus. Because of the college campus, some parts of the neighborhood have a very young feel to them. There aren't many stores or restaurants—the college-y ambience mostly comes from the attitude of the residents and the late-night partying that can go on here. (This is one neighborhood where inquiring about the ages of other tenants and any noise or party restrictions is a good idea.)

Most of the large apartment buildings come equipped with many modern amenities, including central air. This is not the case in the smaller, older, brownstone apartment buildings that can be found down numerous side streets.

Availability: Fair. Because of the heavy concentration of students, apartments can be snapped up quickly. The larger buildings are appealing to professionals who work in the area and who tend to stay for two to three years at a time.

Pros: Within walking distance to all of downtown, Georgtown, the Mall, and government buildings. Good Metro service. Many modern buildings with updated amenities.

Cons: George Washington University lends overly college feel to some areas. Little "character" to neighborhood when compared to areas such as Georgetown, Capitol Hill, and Cleveland Heights.

Rating: Warm

WOODLEY PARK/CLEVELAND PARK

As you head north up Connecticut Avenue and across the Rock Creek Bridge, you'll reach Woodley Park and then Cleveland Park.

Connecticut Avenue and Calvert Street in Woodley Park are lined with large World War II–era apartment buildings as well as more modern apartment and co-op facilities. Smaller apartment buildings can be found on the side streets in the area. Woodley Park is also the beginning of a large area of middle-class, single-family homes and smaller rental properties.

Cleveland Park is similar in style and housing options, with many large apartment buildings and private homes.

Availability: Always good, with a wide selection of efficiency, one-, and two-bedroom apartments.

Pros: Large neighborhoods full of rental property of all kinds. Stylish buildings with character. Many restaurants, bars, movie theaters, and shopping options. Good Metro access.

Cons: On-street parking at night is a problem on side streets. Traffic along Connecticut Avenue during rush hours.

Rating: Hot

CATHEDRAL HEIGHTS/TENLEYTOWN

West of the Connecticut Corridor and north of Georgetown is upper Wisconsin Avenue, which intersects with Massachusetts Avenue. This is where Cathedral Heights begins. Housing in the area can be a bit less expensive than in the areas of Georgetown or Cleveland Park, while offering just as many amenities.

Availability: Good selection always.

Pros: Less expensive area than neighboring communities, but not by much. Convenient to downtown and Georgetown via Massachusetts and Wisconsin Avenues. Area has many apartment buildings and some townhouses.

Cons: No nearby Metro station (Tenleytown Metro is closest). Traffic on main thoroughfares can be heavy at rush hour. Not as broad a selection of restaurants and bars as in other areas.

Rating: Warm

FRIENDSHIP HEIGHTS/CHEVY CHASE

North of Tenleytown, along the Connecticut Avenue and Wisconsin Avenue corridors, are Friendship Heights and D.C.'s Chevy Chase neighborhood. Both areas feature some small apartment buildings, but the high-rise buildings are what catch one's eyes. Despite the somewhat upscale, urban feel that pervades Wisconsin Avenue, both Friendship Heights and Chevy Chase have become more bedroom communities than social centers.

Availability: Less than in other areas of D.C. Still, apartments regularly become available.

Pros: Close to Metro stop. Easy commute to Maryland suburbs. Extensive, high-end shopping. Plenty of on-street parking. Some apartment buildings feature such amenities as tennis courts and swimming pools.

Cons: Apartment prices tend to be high because of the amenities. Heavy Friday and Saturday night traffic along Wisconsin Avenue. Longer commutes to downtown and Capitol Hill.

Rating: Warm

DUPONT CIRCLE

It's one of the most urban neighborhoods in Washington, D.C.—which is not surprising since it's smack dab in the middle of downtown. Dupont Circle has shaped a unique and diverse identity for itself, in part as the social and residential center for Washington's gay community.

CITY FACT

Never say you live in "Washington, D.C." You live in "D.C." or "the District."

On the other side of lower Rock Creek Park and Georgetown, the Dupont Circle neighborhood spins out from the traffic circle on Connecticut Avenue that gave it its name. Streets that intersect with the circle like so many spokes are P and 19th Streets and Massachusetts, New Hampshire, and Connecticut Avenues. The neighborhood borders are 16th Street to the east, 24th Street to the west, P Street to the south, and Florida Avenue to the north.

Besides the gay community, much of the area's character is drawn from its long-standing history as a major center for foreign embassies. Today the embassies remain, along with museums and large private residences.

Availability: Good, but better apartments in some of the smaller, more exclusive buildings are snapped up quickly. Prices for apartments tend to be high, regardless of size or amenities.

Pros: Area is convenient to downtown and Georgetown by foot, Capitol Hill by Metro. A thriving urban center with lots of social and cultural activities. A diverse community with many bookstores, fashionable boutiques, and art galleries.

Cons: Heavy traffic. More crime than in other areas of the city. On-street parking a constant problem. Limited amount of affordable housing.

Rating: Hot

ADAMS MORGAN/KALORAMA

Just a few blocks north of Dupont Circle is another popular area for the young, the hip, and the artistically/culturally inclined: Adams Morgan. The area's two major streets are Columbia Road, which splits off from Connecticut Avenue, and 18th Street NW, which runs into Columbia Road at the neighborhood's tip.

Adams Morgan is filled with bars, nightclubs, art galleries, and numerous ethnic restaurants. The area is often compared in style and substance to the Haight-Ashbury district in San Francisco or the SoHo district in New York.

Northwest of Adams Morgan, along part of upper Columbia Road and Connecticut Avenue and west of 18th Street to Calvert Street, is the area known as Kalorama. It is a quieter, more "adult" neighborhood than Adams Morgan—also more expensive and exclusive. Filled with large apartments, co-ops, and single-family brownstones, Kalorama is also known for its large embassy community.

Availability: In both Adams Morgan and Kalorama, rentals are in great demand. Move quickly on opportunities, as many won't last more than a day or two. This applies to the group homes in the area as well.

Pros: Great social scene, stylish and diverse neighborhood. Within walking distance of Woodley and Cleveland Park.

Cons: Tight rental market, leading to higher rents for smaller spaces. Metro stations in other neighborhoods—at least a 10-minute walk away. Weekend traffic a nightmare in an area where parking is bad almost all of the time. Large, aggressive panhandler presence.

Rating: Hot

MOUNT PLEASANT

Located east of Adams Morgan along Columbia Road, Mount Pleasant offers renters daily contact with Adams Morgan—without Adams Morgan rents.

The area is full of large buildings with efficiency, one-, and two-bedroom apartments. Mount Pleasant is a racially diverse community with a heavy Latin-American accent.

Availability: Good, although in the past three years the area has seen increased runoff from Adams Morgan.

Pros: Cheaper and with a greater selection of housing than Adams Morgan, with the attractions of Adams Morgan close by.

Cons: Bad parking situation. Some parts of the neighborhood are high-crime areas. No Metro station nearby.

Rating: Warm

CATHOLIC UNIVERSITY/BROOKLAND

Brookland is based in Northeast D.C., east of Adams Morgan and Mount Pleasant, with Michigan and South Dakota Avenues and 12th Streets as its borders. In the past 10 years the area has seen a rebirth, in part due to the presence and growth of Catholic University and Trinity College.

Modern apartment buildings and small townhouse complexes stand along Michigan Avenue. Residents are a mix of professionals and students from the area colleges. Farther east on Michigan is the broader neighborhood of Brookland. It's almost entirely made up of single-family homes, many of which are available for rent. Rents for such homes are considerably lower than in other home-rental centers such as Capitol Hill and upper Connecticut Avenue.

The entire area is short on social amenities, bars, and restaurants, however. Most students and professionals make their way down North Capitol Street to the Hill or across town to Adams Morgan for entertainment and nightlife.

Availability: Compared to other areas of the city, a bit tight, in part because there are fewer apartments and other rentals. Still, rentals are available year-round.

Pros: For college students and recent college grads, a good neighborhood to transition into the real world. Metro station within walking distance of most residential areas. Both on-street and off-street parking are plentiful. Less expensive than many other parts of the city.

Cons: Some parts of the neighborhood are marginal when it comes to safety and crime. More limited choice of rentals compared to other areas.

Rating: Cold

SHAW AND U STREETS

The Shaw neighborhood runs from North Capitol Street to 15th Street NW, north of M Street. For years, blocks of Shaw were uninhabitable, with criminal violence, prostitution, and drugs running rampant. But in the last five years, gentrification has taken hold in a big way. Apartment buildings are beginning to open up where old rundown brownstones once stood.

Single-family homes and rentals are also popping up. While it remains a predominantly black neighborhood, white and Hispanic residents have been moving in, in part because apartments and property can be had at lower prices than in other areas of the city.

Availability: It seems as though more apartments are opening up in the area each month. Good bargains are to be found if one is willing to live in a transitional area.

Pros: Close proximity to downtown business district, Adams
Morgan, Dupont Circle, and Capitol Hill. Good Metro access.
Apartments of good size at lower prices.

Cons: Crime remains a problem, although the situation is much
improved in the past few years. On-street parking remains a
risky proposition.

Rating: Warm

16TH STREET CORRIDOR

West of Shaw and east of Dupont Circle is an area that has come to be
known as the 16th Street Corridor. It is sometimes thrown in with the
Logan Circle neighborhood, which adjoins it. Like Shaw and U Streets,
16th Street is diverse, although today more white and Hispanic residents can be found in the area than in Shaw or U Street.

Victorian homes with porches mix with brownstones and small
apartment buildings to provide a nice urban mix. Because of nearby
Howard University, the area also has a young, vibrant feel.

Availability: Good. Gentrification continues at a fast pace.
Efficiencies and one-bedrooms are most common.

Pros: Good location, with access to Metro, downtown, Capitol Hill,
and Adams Morgan. Diverse neighborhood that offers good-
size living space at lower cost.

Cons: Neighborhood remains in transition, although it has made
advances thanks to the presence of Howard University and a
growing business district.

Rating: Warm

Apartment Hunting Resources

Now that you have a good handle on the neighborhoods, you should
take a gander at some classified ads to get a sense of the marketplace.
In Washington, there are a number of resources you can use that won't
require you to pay a service fee or a real estate agent finder's fee.

NEWSPAPER CLASSIFIED ADS

Most newspaper classified ads will clearly identify the neighborhoods in which the rentals are available, using the same neighborhood designations as this book.

The Washington Post

www.washingtonpost.com

This is the region's biggest newspaper, with the most comprehensive rental and real estate listings. Some people insist the *Post's* online listings aren't as comprehensive, but the paper claims what you see is what you get both on paper and on the Net.

The best days for real estate rental and sales listings in the *Post* are Saturday and Sunday.

MOVING TIP

If you're dealing with a professional mover, make sure you set a schedule that both you and the moving company can stick to.

On Saturday, the paper features a special apartment pullout section, with features and advertisements for apartments in Washington, Virginia, and Maryland. (If you buy a paper in Washington, you'll get the Washington apartment section. If you want the Virginia section, with regional content, you need to get it in Virginia).

The Sunday *Post* features a complete real estate section. If you reside on the East Coast, it may be possible to get that section with the *Post* that is sold at major newsstands in your area. Elsewhere in the country, your best bet may be looking at the online listings.

The Blade

www.washingtonblade.com

The city's free weekly newspaper for the gay community.

The City Paper

www.dccitypaper.com

D.C.'s free weekly alternative newspaper carries extensive rental information and is also a great resource for roommate hunting.

You'll also find ads for inexpensive furniture, used cars, and events. It's a great resource for finding out what's going on around town.

A tip: The *City Paper*'s classified ads are available online on Tuesdays, but the paper itself doesn't usually hits the streets until late Wednesday or Thursday. So if you can check online, you might get a leg up on your competition.

The Hill

www.thehill.com

This Capitol Hill weekly is similar to *Roll Call* (next).

Roll Call

www.rollcall.com

A weekly paper on Capitol Hill, it covers politics in the House and Senate and also has a small, but helpful, classified section listing employment opportunities, house and apartment rentals, and roommate searches.

The Washington Times

www.washingtontimes.com

The *Times* puts out a real estate section on Fridays. The rental and sales listings are not as comprehensive as those in the *Washington Post*.

INTERNET SERVICES

All of the following Internet services are free to the prospective tenant. Some are accessible over the phone as well as over the Internet.

Apartments.com

www.apartments.com

An online service operated in joint partnership with the online company and the *Washington Post*. One of the most popular and comprehensive services in the area.

The Apartment Connection
(202) 237-8000; (800) 916-APTS

www.theapartmentconnection.com

A full-service apartment-location service offered at no cost to prospective tenants. Call and use their referral service or use their Internet site to match yourself up with an apartment. It's one of the better search engines around.

The Apartment Locators
(800) 999-RENTS

www.apartmentlocators.com

Another popular service, it specializes in apartments in the Maryland and Virginia suburbs.

Apartment Search
(202) 483-8160 for D.C.; (301) 656-3733 for Maryland; (703) 379-3733 for Virginia

www.apartmentsearch.com

An online service for Washington, Virginia, and Maryland that features extensive apartment listings. This free service also provides information and resources to help relocaters.

CITY FACT

The first tourist to arrive in Washington, D.C., after it became the nation's capital is said to have been Captain John Smith of Jamestown and Pocahontas fame.

HomeHunter.com

www.homehunter.com

Another free online service.

Move.com

www.move.com

A full-service Web site that includes apartment and home searches, furniture rental and purchase—even moving company contacts. One of the better online sites, it is operated in conjunction with the Yellow Pages.

The Registry

www.theregistry.com

An online service for Washington, Virginia, and Maryland that features extensive apartment listings. It can be difficult to wade through, but is a good resource.

Rent.com

www.rent.com

Another free, full-service apartment and house search engine for Washington and the suburbs.

Living on Your Own Versus with a Roommate

Given the cost of living in Washington and the large number of young people who move to the D.C. area to begin careers in government or to work on Capitol Hill while pursuing law or graduate degrees, roommates and group homes are extremely common.

In some towns, landlords might look down on prospective tenants seeking to rent a house for a group home, or three young women looking to take a two-bedroom apartment on Capitol Hill. But in Washington, landlords have to be pretty flexible about such things.

Of course, so too do the roommates or housemates. The advantages to a group home or an apartment shared with one or more roommates are twofold: financial and social.

If you are a newcomer to Washington, don't know anyone here, and/or are uncertain about how long you might stay, a roommate or a group home are perfect options. First of all, they allow you to save money on rent. On average, sharing an apartment saves a roommate about $400 a month on rent; a housemate pays about $600 less than he might if he rented a small house on his own. Socially, if you hit it off with your new roomy or roomies, you have built-in friends to hit the town with.

All of the newspaper and online classifieds listed previously are good resources for finding a roommate or a group home, especially the *City Paper*. Remember that group homes generally are established in the late summer (when colleges in the area are opening their doors) and the spring (when college graduates are making the move out of the dorms and into their own digs).

COLLEGE AND UNIVERSITY ROOMMATE FINDER SERVICES

Because so many college students in the area look for off-campus housing, some of the area colleges offer roommate and housemate matching at low cost to non-students. Among them are:

American University

www.ngen.com/housing/ameri-can

For a $25 fee, the university's Office of Student Housing will match up prospective roommates and housemates.

Georgetown University

data.georgtown.edu/student-affairs/och

Offers off-campus housing postings on the Web site.

George Washington University

www.och.gwu.edu

The Office of Student Housing offers a free roommate service.

ONLINE ROOMMATE FINDER SERVICES

If you'd prefer not to go the student housing route, there are several good online services that will match you with prospective roommates.

The Roommate Assistant

www.roommate-assistant.com

A free service worth giving a shot.

The Roommate Locator

www.roommatelocator.com

This free service lists prospective roommates as well as apartments for rent. Keep in mind that many of the listings are posted by those seeking roommates and have not been screened.

Roommates Preferred

3000 Connecticut Avenue NW
North Entrance Suite 136
Washington, DC 20008
(202) 965-4004

www.roommatespreferred.com

Perhaps the best resource for people seeking roommates, the firm provides both a Web site and a great in-person screening process. For a $75 fee the staff will interview you and match you up with the kind of housing and roommate(s) most compatible to your interests, work location, etc. While some of the preliminary screening can be done over the phone, the company usually requires an in-office interview, particularly when you review the potential roommates they've found for you.

Urban Apartments

www.UrbanApartments.com

Another site that matches up roommates and housemates. It's not as comprehensive as the others.

Things to Ask/Consider While Looking for an Apartment

You've pulled together a list of apartments and you're ready to take a look. Here's a list of things to look at and ask when apartment hunting.

- Before you even look at the interior of the apartment unit you're to be shown, eyeball the building's exterior. Note whether or not it is well-maintained. Inquire whether the building has a full-time maintenance crew or just a once-a-week handyman.
- Take a look at the foyer and the stairwells. Are they clean, with a good coat of paint? Is the building handicapped accessible?
- Ask about security. Is access to the lobby and elevators controlled? Many of the larger buildings in Washington have a full-time desk staff.
- Are emergency exit doors visible but also securely closed?

- If there is a garage, is it well-lit and secure?
- Is there a well-lit and secure laundry room?
- Ask to speak to a couple of current tenants. It's especially helpful to meet any prospective neighbors before you sign on the dotted line. If the noise coming from 6B are going to affect you in 6C, it's better to find out sooner rather than later.
- Ask tenants about the building's management. How much of a rent increase did they make last year? Are the tenants happy with the building, the service, the amenities? Do they feel safe? Best question: Would they encourage their friends or family to move into the building?
- If the building offers special facilities, check them all out. Don't wait until after you move in to find that the "exercise room" is a closet with an old rowing machine on the floor. Inspect the swimming pool, the fitness center, and/or the rec room.
- Ask about controlled access to building facilities. Are there additional charges for their use above and beyond rent?
- What about guests? Are there any kind of visitation limits or entertaining restrictions on weeknights or weekends? Any cohabitation restrictions?
- Inquire about utilities. Most D.C. apartments include all utilities (heat, water, electricity) except cable service in the rent. In some smaller buildings, especially on Capitol Hill and in the suburbs, utilities are billed individually.
- Can you control heat or air-conditioning from your apartment or is the thermostat centralized?
- Check out cable access. Most D.C. apartments are now cable ready, but some landlords or long-term tenants may not have had cable installed.
- Look for the phone jacks. Is there at least one in each room? Most apartment buildings will charge extra for such additions after you move in. A manager might not hit you with the charge if you ask about it beforehand.
- Many older buildings feature hardwood floors. Inspect them for any serious damage. Most buildings in Washington will re-wax and treat the floors before a new tenant moves in.

- As you conduct your walk-through, write down what you are seeing—and not seeing. You'll then know what things need to be repaired before you move in: a toilet that needs a new handle, a leaky shower head or faucet, gauges in the wall, cracked window panes, loose door hinges, etc. Have the manager or rental agent sign or initial this document so that if the repairs aren't completed to your satisfaction (or at all), you have legal recourse (should it go that far). Also, if you should move out, you have documentation about damages that existed before you moved in. These notes also give you a handy guide when you sit down to sign a lease.

Now, about that lease. Remember that it is a legally binding document. It says a landlord is bound to give a tenant living space and that the tenant is bound to pay rent for a specified length of time. Leases vary from rental company to rental company, even landlord to landlord. But there are important points that are outlined in each. Make note of the following terms:

- How much notice must you give before moving at the end of the lease?
- Can the rent be increased, and by how much? (Some buildings have apartments opening up that were formerly rent controlled; this is an important point to inquire about.)
- Are pets allowed? (Most buildings allow cats, but dogs may be a dicey subject.)
- Must you pay your last month's rent or can your security deposit count as such?
- Is there a mandated cleaning charge when you move out or is it optional?

Just to see how it would work, I used these guidelines at several apartment buildings in Washington. Running through the list and checking off most of the points took about 75 minutes each time. A small price to pay in time, considering how many headaches you sidestep by asking the right questions.

Now you've run through your list, you've read over the lease, and you're ready to sign your life—well, at least a year of it—away. Your prospective landlord will need references from previous landlords or contact information for each. If you are a first-time renter, letters of reference from an employer may also suffice. In the case of an employer, make sure your salary or some reference to income is included—this is a piece of information the landlord will be interested in knowing.

Most large Washington apartment buildings charge between $25 and $50 for a credit and reference check. The fee is nonrefundable. But in the case of smaller apartments, it's best to have a copy of your credit report in hand, just in case. In the time it might take you to get a copy, you might lose the apartment to someone who came more prepared than you were.

Finally, once you've signed your lease and you're ready to move in, purchase renter's insurance. It's an underused consumer protection tool that covers damage to or loss of your property in the apartment. D.C. landlords aren't required to carry insurance to cover your losses, even any possessions you might place in a storage room in the building. Renter's insurance typically costs between $300 to $500 a year for a $35,000 to $50,000 policy that covers loss due to theft, damage caused by other people, or natural causes.

Now you're signed, sealed, and secured for the big move.

CITY FACT

Want to meet other people from your neck of the woods? Many congressional state delegations have formed associations for state residents living and working in Washington. For example, the Oklahoma Society regularly holds social events in Washington for transplanted Sooners. Southern states, especially, have active groups in the Washignton area. Call your congressman's office for further information, or check in with their district office before you make the move.

RENTING A HOUSE

With the exception of amenities and some of the security points, the renter's checklist is applicable for those people seeking to rent a house in Washington, D.C.

MOVING TIP

Make sure someone other than the movers themselves are watching the loading and unloading process. Make sure to notify the movers quickly about any damage and have it documented.

Additional points you might want to raise are the tenant's responsibilities for upkeep of the yard and exterior of the house during the leasing period. Is there yard and lawncare equipment on site? If not, the landlord should provide them at no cost to the tenant.

Be especially careful to clarify any visitation or cohabitation rules the landlord might have. Many rental homes in areas around D.C. college campuses have some restrictions on entertaining, noise, and cohabitation. Whether or not you are a college student, make sure the points are clearly spelled out.

Also, make sure the lease specifies how and when a landlord is allowed to make repairs or improvements to the house. These should be done in a timely fashion. If not, the tenant should be given some recourse in rent relief.

There is the issue of privacy as well. Make sure the lease spells out who has access to the home and when. Most leases require that a landlord seek permission from the tenant to enter a house, unless there is an emergency.

CHAPTER 3

Advice on Finding a House

The American Dream can be many things to many people. But most commonly, it's the purchase of a home or condominium. In Washington, renters outnumber home owners almost three to one. Clearly, in a city full of transient professionals, renting has more appeal. It provides people with flexibility to move and select housing that they need at the time they need it, without further commitments. And for the short term, it makes sense financially—a renter hasn't locked himself or herself into a long-term financial deal like a mortgage, or a piece of property that requires extensive maintenance and care.

On the other hand, owning a home provides a degree of economic security and a feeling of permanence that rental property does not. Ownership also confers a significant tax break because you can deduct the interest paid on a mortgage. And homeowners know from month to month what their monthly housing costs will be, especially if they are locked into a fixed-rate mortgage.

Without the proper mind-set and resources, however, the dream of home ownership can be a nightmare. This is particularly true in Washington, D.C., with its ever-shifting gentrification plans and development proposals, and the increasing demand for housing in the city.

Finding a house in Washington wasn't a problem five years ago. Crime and poor city services were such problems that residents were fleeing the District for the suburbs at an incredible rate. To stem the exodus, the District of Columbia began offering prospective homebuyers a financial incentive: if they bought a house in the city in certain areas and within a particular price range, they stood to receive a $5,000 tax credit (the credit does not include condo sales).

MOVING TIP

If the apartment building or house you are moving to does not have a loading dock or off-street parking, arranging for street parking in advance will make for a much easier move. This is especially true in Washington, where parking is always at a premium on the street. You will want to make arrangements with neighbors to keep the street in front of your new building clear on the morning of your move.

Washington remains a city heavily weighted toward the renter, but the number of home sales in the area has risen since the late 1990s, following the national trend. With the conversion of some medium-to-large buildings to condominiums, condo sales in the city have increased as well.

In fact, Washington, D.C., has never been a hotter place in terms of residential real estate. The new perception is that D.C. is the place to be; that it's a city making a comeback from its days of heavy crime and poor services. There is even talk of tax cuts for city residents.

Selecting a Neighborhood

There are areas of Washington, D.C., that remain sellers' markets and those where buyers may get a break. Detailed descriptions of the neighborhoods of the District and the surrounding suburbs of Virginia and Maryland can be found in chapter 1. The following is an overview of Washington neighborhoods from the point of view of the prospective homebuyer, including the pros and cons of purchasing a home in each area.

GEORGETOWN

West of downtown D.C. in the Northwest quadrant, Georgetown borders Rock Creek Park, Georgetown University, and the Potomac River. Its northern border is Massachusetts Avenue.

The most common types of properties sold in the neighborhood are connected and unconnected townhouses with two to three bedrooms and one or $1^1/2$ baths; some older homes with modern amenities; and many smaller houses with antiquated electrical systems and small, unremodeled spaces.

Availability: Low turnover, but homes are always on the market.

Pros: Most desirable neighborhood in Washington to buy in. Great resale values. Property here is viewed as a stable, long-term investment.

Cons: Many homes have small rooms and small yards. Most homes are street-front.

Rating: Seller's market.

CAPITOL HILL

Capitol Hill is one of the oldest neighborhood in the District. The prime real estate is limited to the area behind the Capitol building—about 20 to 25 square blocks. Boundaries for Capitol Hill run along Massachusetts Avenue to the north, 11th Street to the east, Virginia Avenue SE to the south, and the Capitol itself to the west.

The area offers good housing prospects. The most common homes on the market are connected and unconnected townhouses with two to three bedrooms and one or $1^1/2$ baths. Many older homes have been remodeled and refurbished. Still, many "fixer-uppers" on the Hill have been on and off the market for a number of years.

Availability: Considered good, especially on the outer edges of the prime real estate area. Homes in need of repair and remodeling are quite common and more affordable.

Pros: Convenient to Capitol Hill and downtown via Metro. Less expensive home prices than Georgetown or Cathedral Heights, but with similar amenities.

Cons: Neighborhoods bordering the Hill can be high-crime areas, which depreciates home values unless you make major improvements. Little on- or off-street parking.

Rating: Close to the Capitol, seller's market. Farther out, buyer's market.

FOGGY BOTTOM

Foggy Bottom is just south of Georgetown: Its borders include M Street to the north, 26th Street NW to the west, 18th Street to the west, and Constitution Avenue to the south. The neighborhood encompasses parts of downtown Washington and all of the George Washington University's urban campus. Because of the college, some parts of the neighborhood have a very young feel to them. There aren't many stores or restaurants—the collegiate feel mostly comes from the attitude of the residents and the late-night partying that can go on here.

The housing stock is a broad mix of older and new townhouses. Newer homes are found around the Watergate complex; older homes tend to be of the same design as those in Georgetown and Capitol Hill. Condominiums are also common in the area, almost all of them of modern design.

Availability: Single-family homes are not as plentiful in Foggy Bottom as in other parts of the city. Condominiums may be a better buy.

Pros: Within walking distance to all of downtown, Georgetown, the Mall, and government buildings. Good Metro service. Stable property values.

Cons: Limited housing market. Not a family-oriented area.

Rating: Due to the proximity to downtown, a seller's market.

WOODLEY PARK/CLEVELAND PARK

As you head north up Connecticut Avenue across the Rock Creek Bridge you'll reach Woodley Park and then Cleveland Park. Woodley

Park is the first of Washington's upper Northwest neighborhoods. Several blocks north on Connecticut, near the National Zoo, Cleveland Park begins.

Large apartment buildings line the main drags of Connecticut Avenue and Calvert, but single-family homes are most common along the side streets. Woodley Park is the beginning of a large area of middle-class, single-family homes. Cleveland Park is similar in style and housing options, with many large apartment buildings and private homes.

Numerous two- to three-bedroom houses with either 1½ or two full baths and small backyards can be found off Connecticut Avenue. Larger homes can be found deeper into Woodley and Cleveland Park, especially as one moves west toward Massachusetts Avenue and Wisconsin Boulevard.

Availability: Always good, with a wide selection of small, medium, and large homes. Because these are two of the most desirable neighborhoods in the city, demand is great.

Pros: Large neighborhoods full of single-family homes lend a real community feel to the areas. Good Metro access. Family-oriented amenities and activities are plentiful. Property values are stable; the area is considered a good investment.

Cons: On-street parking at night is a problem on side streets. Heavy traffic along Connecticut Avenue during rush hours. Toward Connecticut Avenue, homes have small front and backyards. Space is at a premium and expensive.

Rating: Seller's market.

CATHEDRAL HEIGHTS/TENLEYTOWN

West of the Connecticut Corridor and north of Georgetown is upper Wisconsin Avenue, which intersects with Massachusetts Avenue. This is where Cathedral Heights begins. While apartments can be less expensive in this area compared to other D.C. neighborhoods, single-family houses here can be just as expensive as in other areas, with the exception of Georgetown. This is because Cathedral Heights connects to Glover Park and the Palisades, two neighborhoods of single-family homes on the outer edges of Washington along the Maryland border.

Glover Park, just above Georgetown, is an area filled with small, bungalow-style homes, popular as rental property for area students and young professionals. Most houses in the area have two bedrooms, 1½ baths, small front and backyards, and off-street parking (usually by way of a rear alley).

West beyond Wisconsin Avenue in the Palisades are comparatively large single-family homes with three or four bedrooms, off-street parking, and front and backyards. This is one of the more expensive neighborhoods in the District, with home prices in excess of $500,000.

Several townhouse developments and many smaller homes similar to those in Woodley Park can be found along Wisconsin Avenue and its side streets.

Availability: Good selection always.

Pros: Larger homes in an area that is well-suited to families. Stable property values in neighborhoods that are highly desirable. Convenient to downtown and Georgetown via Massachusetts Avenue and Wisconsin.

Cons: Home prices limit the market for young families in some areas. No Metro within walking distance. Traffic on main thoroughfares can be heavy during rush hours.

Rating: Strong seller's market.

FRIENDSHIP HEIGHTS/CHEVY CHASE

North of Tenleytown along the Connecticut Avenue and Wisconsin Avenue corridors are Friendship Heights and D.C.'s Chevy Chase neighborhood. Both areas are considered prime neighborhoods for single-family homes. As with other neighborhoods farther out from downtown, these areas have larger homes, more yard space, and better parking. Friendship Heights and Chevy Chase also have especially strong, family-oriented communities, with parks, playgrounds, and recreational activities. The neighborhoods are "mature," with many homes built prior to 1960.

As is the case with other desirable locations, home prices in Friendship Heights and Chevy Chase have skyrocketed in recent years, with larger houses sometimes selling for $500,000 to $750,000.

Availability: Good, but prices are high.

Pros: Property values are strong, making for a solid investment. Good infrastructure for families. Close to Metro stop, with easy access to both downtown Washington and the Maryland suburbs. Extensive high-end shopping.

Cons: Home prices are high, and properties tend to sell quickly thanks to high demand. Traffic on main thoroughfares remains a serious community issue.

Rating: Extremely strong seller's market.

DUPONT CIRCLE

One of the most urban neighborhoods in Washington, D.C., Dupont Circle is also one of the most diverse, in part because it is the social and residential center for Washington's gay community. The area's character also is drawn from its long-standing history as a major center for foreign embassies.

On the other side of lower Rock Creek Park and Georgetown, Dupont Circle spins out from the traffic circle on Connecticut Avenue that gave the neighborhood its name. Intersecting it like so many spokes are P and 19th Streets, and Massachusetts, New Hampshire, and Connecticut Avenues. The neighborhood borders are 16th Street to the east, 24th Street to the west, P Street to the south, and Florida Avenue to the north.

There is limited property available to homebuyers, and what is on the market tends to be expensive. Walk-up brownstones and small colonials are part of the mix, along with condominums. Dupont Circle is a popular area for real estate investors, particularly those looking to buy "mixed use" buildings with storefronts on the street level and apartments above.

Availability: Poor due to high demand. Condominiums may be more readily available.

Pros: Stable real estate market, but limited appeal. Area is convenient to downtown and Georgetown by foot, Capitol Hill by Metro. Thriving urban center with lots of social and cultural activities.

Cons: Strong urban feel, with lots of businesses in some residential areas. Limited housing market beyond extensive apartment rental and condo sales.

Rating: Seller's market.

ADAMS MORGAN/KALORAMA

Just a few blocks north of Dupont Circle is another popular area for the young, the hip, and the artistically/culturally inclined: Adams Morgan. The area's two major streets are Columbia Road, which splits off from Connecticut Avenue, and 18th Street NW, which runs into Columbia Road at the tip of the Adams Morgan neighborhood.

As in Dupont Circle, there is a limited number of single-family residences here, although there are numerous condominium buildings in the area, particularly along Columbia Road and some parts of Connecticut Avenue.

Availability: In both Adams Morgan and Kalorama, demand for condos is great. While there is the occasional fixer-upper house available, the market for the classic brownstone walk-ups that are common in the area is tight.

Pros: Great social scene, stylish and diverse neighborhood, with popular brownstones.

Cons: Tight market with prices on the higher end of the scale for both condos and houses. Strong urban feel, although some family-oriented activities are available in the Kalorama area.

Rating: Seller's market.

MOUNT PLEASANT

This neighborhood is located east of Adams Morgan along Columbia Road. As you head up 16th Street, more and more private homes and some condos can be found. In the past 10 years, in fact, condominiums have become popular in the area because of its close proximity to Adams Morgan.

Mount Pleasant is a racially diverse community, with a heavy Latin-American accent.

Availability: Good, especially condominiums.

Pros: Less expensive than Adams Morgan, with more properties on the market.

Cons: Neighborhood is still evolving and in the midst of gentrification. Some parts of the neighborhood remain high-crime areas. No Metro station nearby.

Rating: Buyer's market.

CATHOLIC UNIVERSITY/BROOKLAND

Brookland is in Northeast D.C., east of Adams Morgan and Mount Pleasant, bordered by Michigan and South Dakota Avenues and 12th Street. In the past 10 years the area has seen a rebirth due to the presence and growth of Catholic University and Trinity College.

Farther east on Michigan is a neighborhood made up almost entirely of single-family homes. Prices for such homes are considerably less than in Capitol Hill and upper Connecticut Avenue.

The area is short of social amenities, but for first-time home buyers or others looking for a more affordable house in the city, this area may have some appeal.

Availability: Good. But many homes require repair or remodeling.

Pros: Affordable single-family houses with reasonably easy access to downtown and Capitol Hill. Home prices are significantly lower here than in other areas of the city.

Cons: Area is still in the midst of gentrification. Limited—but growing—number of amenities for families. Some areas still have high crime rates.

Rating: Buyer's market.

SHAW AND U STREETS

The Shaw neighborhood runs from North Capitol Street to 15th Street NW, north of M Street. For years, blocks of Shaw were uninhabitable, with criminal violence, prostitution, and drugs running rampant. But in the last five years, gentrification has taken hold in a big way. Apartment buildings are beginning to open up where old rundown brownstones once stood.

Single-family home sales are on the rise, in part because the property prices are so low compared to those in Dupont Circle, Adams Morgan, or Woodley Park. Much of the property is being bought up by investors who are looking to refurbish the houses or convert them to apartments or condos.

Availability: Good.

Pros: Highly affordable housing that may appreciate in value as this neighborhood continues to make its comeback. Close proximity to downtown business district, Adams Morgan, Dupont Circle, and Capitol Hill. Good Metro access.

Cons: Purchasing property here is a gamble. If the city falls back on hard times, the neighborhood could slide once again. Crime remains a problem, although the situation has improved in the past few years. Urban setting may be unappealing for families.

Rating: Strong buyer's market.

16TH STREET CORRIDOR

West of Shaw and east of Dupont Circle is what has come to be known as the 16th Street Corridor. The area is sometimes thrown in with the Logan Circle neighborhood, which adjoins it.

Like Shaw and U Streets, 16th Street is diverse, although today more white and Hispanic residents can be found in the area than in Shaw or U Street. Victorian homes with porches and brownstones create a nice urban mix. Because of nearby Howard University, the area also has a young, vibrant feel.

Availability: Good. Gentrification continues at a fast pace, and home sales have been increasing in the past five years. The perception is that this area is well along on the comeback trail.

Pros: Affordable housing in a neighborhood that has good days ahead of it. Good investment potential, particularly for some of the larger homes that go on the market. Location is good, with access to Metro, downtown, Capitol Hill, and Adams Morgan.

Cons: The neighborhood is still in transition, although it is making progess thanks to a growing business district and the presence of Howard University. Crime remains a problem in the area.

Rating: Buyer's market.

House-Hunting Resources

Once you've identified where you'd like to live, it's time to track down some houses for sale in the neighborhoods that interest you. As with just about any purchase one makes today, the research you perform is an important part of finding the right home. Unless you take out a full-page ad in the *Washington Post* announcing: "I Want to Buy. Call Me!" sellers aren't going to come knocking on your door. As you begin your hunt, there are a number of print and online resources that you can turn to.

NEWSPAPER CLASSIFIED ADS

The Washington Post

www.washingtonpost.com

This is the region's biggest newspaper, with the most comprehensive real estate listings. Some people insist the *Post*'s online listings aren't as complete, but the paper claims what you see is what you get both on paper and on the Net.

The best days for real estate sales listings in the *Post* are Saturday and Sunday. On Saturday, the paper publishes a special pullout section, with features and advertisements for homes on the market in Washington, Virginia, and Maryland. (If you buy a paper in Washington, you'll get the Washington real estate section. If you want the Virginia section, with regional content, you need to get it in Virginia).

The Sunday *Post* features a complete real estate section. If you reside on the East Coast, it may be possible to get that section with the *Post* that is sold at major newsstands in your area. Elsewhere in the country, your best bet may be looking at the online listings.

CITY FACT

To get a sense of the best of Washington in novels, read the mystery series by Margaret Truman set in glamorous Georgetown and the halls of power. For a look at the grittier side of the city, read the mystery novels of George Pelecanos. Both series make the city come alive.

The Blade

www.washingtonblade.com

The city's free weekly newspaper for the gay community. Some private homes and condos for sale are listed, but not many.

The City Paper

www.dccitypaper.com

D.C.'s free weekly alternative newspaper lists some homes for sale, but the listings are not as comprehensive as those in the *Post* or even the *Times*.

A tip: The *City Paper*'s classified ads are available online on Tuesdays, but the paper itself doesn't usually hits the streets until late Wednesday or Thursday. So if you can check online, you might get a leg up on your competition.

The Washington Times

www.washingtontimes.com

The *Times* puts out a real estate section on Fridays. The listings are not as comprehensive as those in the *Washington Post*.

INTERNET SERVICES AND RESOURCES

There's a world of useful information available to prospective home-buyers through their computer modems. Not only does the Internet offer extensive listings of homes for sale, but a number of Web sites can help you get a handle on some of the other issues involved in buying a home.

For a fuller understanding of the financial implications of buying real estate, check out some of the Web sites that offer financial news. Three sites that might be helpful are *www.msnbc.com*, *www.nandonews.com*, and *www.newspage.com*. All feature news articles on banking, finance, real estate, interest rates, bank and loan policies, and other topics of interest to prospective home buyers.

A number of Web sites have "mortgage calculator" features that can help you determine how much of a mortgage you can afford and what your monthly mortgage payments would be. One of the best such sites is *www.homeadvisor.msn.com*. It features links to a number of home loan sites and even shows you the advantages or disadvantages of renting versus buying. Other calculators can be found at the National InterAd site, *www.nia.com,* and at the Dream Home Network, *www.islands.com.*

The Mortgage Market Information Services, Inc. Web site, *www.interest.com/rates.html,* lets you track most of the interest rates available across the nation at various banking and loan institutions, including banks based in Washington, D.C.

Another useful Internet resource is the International Real Estate Digest, *www.ired.com,* which features helpful articles on home buying. It also helps you search for a licensed realtor in the area you are interested in moving to and even lets you put your current house on the market.

You can also use the Internet to access real estate listings in the area you want to move to. Doing a search for a home is just a click away. There are numerous Web sites that provide access to listings of houses for sale. A number of national real estate companies have Web sites; the Century 21 (*www.century21.com*) and Remax (*www.remax.com*) sites are two of the largest and easiest to utilize. At these sites you can narrow your search to neighborhoods, types or models of homes, number of rooms, etc. In some cases you can even take virtual tours of the properties and receive information about the realtors selling them, including e-mail addresses.

Many independent real estate agents or realtors affiliated with firms are also setting up their own Web sites. The easiest way to find such sites in a specific area is to use one of the Internet search engines such as *www.yahoo.com, www.infoseek.com, www.lycos.com,* or *www.askjeeves.com.*

In addition, there are numerous national online real estate sites— new ones seem to crop up almost daily. Following is a list of some of the largest and the best on the Web.

www.ByOwnerSales.com

It's just what it says: properties put up for sale on the Web by their owners. This is a national Web site that allows you to localize your search. Unless you are an experienced homebuyer, the best approach would be to search this site and if you find a home you are interested in, bring in an experienced realtor or real estate attorney to help you make the purchase.

www.FSBO.com

"FSBO" is an acronym for "For Sale By Owner." This is another national Web site that features privately sold homes.

www.HomeBuilder.com

Those looking to buy—or build—a home in the suburbs might want to check out this site. It offers info on private contractors and regional contacts for new homes that are hitting the market.

www.homehunter.com

A Web site operated in conjunction with the *Washington Post,* this may be one of the best real estate sites for the region. The site includes extensive listings for Washington and the Virginia and Maryland suburbs. It also provides links to other useful Web sites such as *www.move.com,* which is a comprehensive site operated in partnership with the Yellow Pages. Together, these sites provide one-stop shopping for home sales and relocation, with information on moving companies, truck rentals, real estate agents, mortgage companies, furniture rentals and sales, and more.

www.Homes.com

Homes, homes, and more homes—this is one of the largest sites around for home sales. It also includes resources for relocation, temporary housing, pre-approval of mortgage loans, and contact information for local real estate agents and attorneys.

www.ired.com

The comprehensive International Real Estate Digest site features links to real estate agencies, mortgage brokers, movers, consumer sites, and independent real estate salespeople.

www.msn.HomeAdviser.com

One of the most comprehensive sites on the Web. It offers local for-sale listings, information on realtors and mortgage lenders, and general advice on how to buy a home, with or without an agent.

www.realtor.com

The Web site operated by the National Realtors Association features good consumer information and links to a number of real estate sites.

The following are some additional sites worth taking a look at, although they are not as comprehensive nor as easy to use as the ones listed previously:

www.Homespace.com

A comprehensive Web site for property sales.

www.iOwn.com and www.homescout.com

These are linked sites that provide comprehensive real estate searches on a regional basis.

www.owners.com

Another homeowner property sale site.

MOVING TIP

While packing, number all of your boxes and list them on a master sheet. This will allow you to track them during the move.

REAL ESTATE AGENTS

Unless you feel comfortable hunting for and then buying a home on your own, you will want the assistance of a real estate professional.

There are three types of agents: the buyer's agent, the seller's agent, and the dual agent. The names are pretty self-explanatory: Given the subject of this book, you will probably be interested in either a buyer's agent or a dual agent. Almost all licensed real estate professionals can handle these tasks.

In almost all cases, unless you have hired an agent on your own and signed a contract with him or her, the seller of the home pays the agent's commission at the closing. It is generally 6 percent of the sale price if the realtor represents both the buyer and seller; if both a seller's agent and a buyer's agent are involved in the sale, each earns a 3 percent commission.

Benefits of Using a Real Estate Agent.

- The realtor helps you find the types of home you are in the market for. One advantage a realtor has, that most people don't, is access to the local computerized real estate listings. If you choose not to use a realtor, it means you will be house hunting on your own time, doing your own research, scanning the papers, and checking out leads.

- The agent arranges house viewings and walks through the property with you, pointing out flaws and attractive features you might have overlooked, and evaluating the home compared to others you have seen. Without an agent, you must make your own arrangements with the seller's agent or the home owner. In some cases, the sellers may not want to deal with you unless you are affiliated with a real estate professional, which may mean having to work with the seller's agent.

- The real estate agent oversees almost all facets of the purchase: the offer, the negotiations, the home inspection, and the closing. Without a realtor, all the financial dealings and arrangements— mortgage applications, home inspection, final closing, etc.—are all in your ball court. Most likely, you will have to turn to an attorney specializing in real estate law to assist you. That's money out of your pocket unless you can get the sellers to pick up the legal bill—and the chances of that are nill.

Questions to Ask a Real Estate Agent

It's important to select the right real estate agent to help you in your quest for a home. Here are some questions you might ask an agent before making a decision.

- How long have you been a licensed real estate agent?
- Do you work full time in that capacity or is this a second job or a hobby?
- Do you live or work in the neighborhood I am interested in? If not, is your agency based in the neighborhood so that others in the office might serve as a resource?
- How many homes did you sell in the last 12 months? How many buyers did you assist in buying a home during that same time? (Perhaps the agent is better at selling homes than at helping buyers to acquire one. If the sale and assistance numbers are similar, ask the agent if he or she prefers to do one or the other. An agent's enthusiasm for you, the buyer, is critical to finding what you want.)
- If the agent specializes in buyers, how many is he or she working with during the period you will be looking for a home?
- Finally, ask for at least three to five references.

Washington, D.C., Real Estate Firms

Following is a list of the major real estate firms in Washington, D.C. Those firms licensed in Washington are allowed to operate offices in Maryland and Virginia, but under different licenses. Some agents may not hold licenses in all three areas. It's something to inquire about, especially since some larger firms make sure their agents can help a home-hunter who wants to look in D.C., Virginia, and Maryland.

Doritha E. Campbell Realtor Co.

1800 11th Street NW
Washington, DC 20001
(202) 387-7037

Century 21 Ashby & Associates

1533 Pennsylvania Avenue SE
Washington, DC 20003
(202) 543-8060

JAshby9980@aol.com

Century 21 Dodson Realty
Washington, DC 20012
(202) 882-2121

c21dodson@aol.com

Peter Ferris & Levin Realtors
5034 Wisconsin Avenue NW
Washington, DC 20016
(202) 686-9830

CITY FACT

The city of Washington does not have true representation in Congress. While there are shadow senators and District of Columbia representatives in the House, they do not have a formal say in the management of the city.

H. A. Gill & Son Inc. Realtors
1722 Wisconsin Avenue NW
Washington, DC 20007
(202) 338-5000

Graham Shanks Realtors
1233 Potomac Street NW
Washington, DC 20007
(202) 333-5252

Long & Foster Realtors
20 Chevy Chase Circle NW
Washington, DC 20015
(202) 686-765

2601 Connecticut Avenue NW
Washington, DC 20008
(202) 483-6300

2121 Wisconsin Avenue NW #100
Washington, DC 20007
(202) 944-8400

3201 New Mexico Avenue NW
Washington, DC 20016
(202) 363-1800

MGMB Inc. Realtors
3301 New Mexico Avenue NW
#105
Washington, DC 20016
(202) 362-4480

W. C. & A. N. Miller Realtors
5518 Connecticut Avenue NW
Washington, DC 20015
(202) 966-1400

4910 Massachusetts Avenue NW
#119
Washington, DC 20016
(202) 362-1300

Al Mirman Realtors Inc.
1529 Pennsylvania Avenue SE
Washington, DC 20003
(202) 543-7000

Murrell Realtors
4201 Georgia Avenue NW
Washington, DC 20011
(202) 726-1100

National Association of Realtors
700 11th Street NW, 2nd Floor
Washington, DC 20001
(202) 383-1000

Pardoe and Graham Real Estate/ERA
Georgetown
(202) 333-6100

georgetown@earthlink.net

Capitol Hill
(202) 547-3525

capitolhill@earthlink.net

Chevy Chase
(202) 362-5800

chevychase@earthlink.net

Bethesda
(301) 718-0010

bethesda@earthlink.net

Prudential Carruthers Realtors
216 7th Street SE
Washington, DC 20003
(202) 393-1111

5025 Wisconsin Avenue NW
Washington, DC 20016
(202) 362-3400

Stevens Realtors
4200 Wisconsin Avenue NW #117
Washington, DC 20016
(202) 686-5000

Washington, D.C., Association of Realtors
1400 I Street NW
Washington, DC 20005
(202) 789-8880

Weichert Realtors
1930 18th Street NW #1
Washington, DC 20009
(202) 326-1010

5034 Wisconsin Avenue NW
Washington, DC 20016
(202) 326-1300

3400 Idaho Avenue NW #100
Washington, DC 20016
(202) 326-1100

Finding and Buying the Right House

Whether or not you have a real estate agent to guide you through the home-purchase maze, the following tips may help you prepare for one of the biggest purchases of your life.

- Create a "Top 10" list of "must have" amenities: fireplace in the master bedroom, swimming pool, play area for the kids, proximity to shopping or public transportation, special kitchen features, etc. Settling on what features you want will help your real estate agent to narrow the search field and show you only homes that meet your criteria. If you have set a criteria and the homes don't meet your expectations, perhaps you need to reconsider the agent or the neighborhood you are searching in.

- Prequalify for a mortgage. Most real estate agents love it when their clients come with a "prequal" letter. If done properly and professionally, the letter eases the negotiations for a home and lets both you and your agent know what you can and cannot afford. A lender, whether it be a bank or a private mortgage company, typically uses the 28 percent formula (your monthly mortgage can't exceed 28 percent of your monthly income). Another rule of thumb is that a home purchase price shouldn't exceed the combined total of three years' salary or joint income. Your prequal letter also may help establish a relationship with a mortgage provider that will hold you in good stead when it comes time to make your deal.

- Shop around for your mortgage. Just because you have been pre-approved by one mortgage lender doesn't mean you have to stick with them. According to the Mortgage Bankers Association of America, there are more than 10,000 banks and mortgage companies ready to take you on as a client. Your real estate agent can recommend a good local bank or mortgage company. But more likely you will find a lender you may have previously used in your hometown, or you will use one of the many mortgage Web sites that can take your application over the Internet. There are great deals to be had, and thanks to the Internet, you're not limited to a few local banks and mortgage companies.

- When you've found a house you want to buy and it's time to have it inspected, your realtor probably will recommend an inspector he or she has used before. Don't arrange the inspection without doing some research first. The home inspection may be the most important tool you have to save money in the short term (what you pay for the house) and in the long-term (on repairs and upkeep). Remember: When a home inspector is recommended by the agent, it's in both their interests to make sure that the house gets a passing grade. Before you just sign off on a home inspector, check around, seek outside recommendations, and choose wisely.

MOVING TIP

If you're using professional movers, make sure that you have enough cash to give them a tip. Of course, if they break half your stuff, don't tip them, unless the movers are really big and never smile.

Packing Up and Moving Out

By Monstermoving.com

CHAPTER 4

Getting Organized and Planning Your Move

Written for both the beginner and the veteran, this chapter contains information and resources that will help you get ready for your move. If money is foremost on your mind, you'll find a section on budgeting for the move and tips on how to save money throughout the move—as well as a move budget-planning guide. If time is also precious, you'll find time-saving tips and even suggestions for how to get out of town in a hurry. You'll find help with preliminary decisions, the planning process, and packing, as well as tips and advice on uprooting and resettling your family (and your animal companions). A budget worksheet, a set of helpful checklists, and a moving task time line complete the chapter.

Paying for Your Move

Moving can certainly tap your bank account. How much depends on a number of factors: whether your employer is helping with the cost, how much stuff you have, and how far you are moving.

To get an idea of how much your move will cost, start calling service providers for estimates and begin listing these expenses on the move budget-planning guide provided at the end of this chapter.

If you don't have the money saved, start saving as soon as you can. You should also check out other potential sources of money:

- Income from the sale of your spare car, furniture, or other belongings (hold a garage or yard sale).

- The cleaning and damage deposit on your current rental and any utility deposits. You probably won't be reimbursed until *after* your move, though, so you'll need to pay moving expenses up front in some other way.

- Your employer, who may owe you a payout for vacation time not taken.

Taxes and Your Move

Did you know that your move may affect your taxes? As you prepare to move, here are some things to consider:

- Next year's taxes. Some of your moving expenses may be tax-deductible. Save your receipts and contact your accountant and the IRS for more information. Visit *www.irs.gov* or call the IRS at (800) 829-3676 for information and to obtain the publication and forms you need.

- State income tax. If your new state collects income tax, you'll want to figure that into your salary and overall cost of living calculations. Of course, if your old state collects income tax and your new one doesn't, that's a factor, too, but a happier one—but remember to find out how much if any of the current year's income will be taxable in the old state.

- Other income sources. You'll want to consider any other sources of income and whether your new state will tax you on this income. For example, if you are paying federal income tax on an IRA that you rolled over into a Roth IRA, if you move into a state that collects income tax, you may also have to pay state income tax on your rollover IRA.

- After you move or when filing time draws near, consider collecting your receipts and visiting an accountant.

The Budget Move (Money-Saving Tips)

Here you'll find some suggestions for saving money on your move.

Saving on Moving Supplies

- Obtain boxes in the cheapest way possible.

    Ask a friend or colleague who has recently moved to give or sell you their boxes.

    Check the classified ads; people sometimes sell all their moving boxes for a flat rate.

    Ask your local grocery or department store for their empty boxes.

- Borrow a tape dispenser instead of buying one.

- Instead of buying bubble wrap, crumple newspaper, plain unused newsprint, or tissue paper to pad breakables.

- Shop around for the cheapest deal on packing tape and other supplies.

- Instead of renting padding blankets from the truck rental company, use your own blankets, linens, and area rugs for padding. (But bear in mind that you may have to launder them when you arrive, which is an expense in itself.)

Saving on Labor

- If you use professional movers, consider a "you pack, we drive" arrangement, in which you pack boxes, and the moving company loads, moves, and unloads your belongings.

- Call around and compare estimates.

- If you move yourself, round up volunteers to help you load and clean on moving day. It's still customary to reward them with moving-day food and beverages (and maybe a small cash gift). You may also have to volunteer to help them move some day. But you may still save some money compared to hiring professionals.

- Save on child and pet care. Ask family or friends to watch your young children and pets on moving day.

Saving on Trip Expenses

Overnight the Night Before You Depart

- Where will you stay the night before you depart? A hotel or motel might be most comfortable and convenient, but you could save a little money if you stay the night with a friend or relative.

- If you have the gear, maybe you'd enjoy unrolling your sleeping bag and "roughing it" on your own floor the night before you leave town. If you do this, try to get hold of a camping sleeping pad or air mattress, which will help you get a good night's sleep and start your move rested and refreshed.

Overnight on the Road

- Look into hotel and motel discounts along your route. Your automobile club membership may qualify you for a better rate. Check out other possibilities, too—associations such as AARP often line up discounts for their members, as do some credit cards.

- When you call about rates, ask if the hotel or motel includes a light breakfast with your stay.

- If your move travel involves an overnight stay and you're game for camping, check into campgrounds and RV parks along your route. Be sure to ask whether a moving truck is allowed. Some parks have size restrictions; some RV parks may not welcome moving trucks; and some limit the number of vehicles allowed in a campsite.

Food While Traveling

Food is one of those comfort factors that can help make the upsetting aspects of moving and traveling more acceptable. Eating also gives you a reason to stop and rest, which may be exactly what you or your family needs if you're rushing to get there. Here are a few pointers to consider:

- Try to balance your need to save money with your (and your family's) health and comfort needs.

- Try to have at least one solid, nutritious sit-down meal each day.

- Breakfast can be a budget- and schedule-friendly meal purchased at a grocery or convenience store and eaten on the road: fruit, muffins, and juice, for example.
- Lunch prices at sit-down restaurants are typically cheaper than dinner prices. Consider having a hot lunch and then picnicking in your hotel or motel on supplies from a grocery store.

Scheduling Your Move

Try to allow yourself at least three months to plan and prepare. This long lead time is especially important if you plan to sell or buy a home or if you are moving during peak moving season (May through September). If you plan to move during peak season, it's vital to reserve two to three months in advance with a professional moving company or truck rental company. The earlier you reserve, the more likely you are to get the dates you want. This is especially important if you're timing your move with a job start date or a house closing date, or are moving yourself and want to load and move on a weekend when your volunteers are off work.

MOVING TIP

Before buying anything for your new apartment or home, stop and consider what you'll need immediately and what you might be able to do without for a while. You'll spend a lot less if you can afford to wait and look for it on sale or secondhand.

WHEN IS THE RIGHT TIME TO MOVE?

If your circumstances allow you to decide your move date, you'll want to make it as easy as possible on everyone who is moving:

- Children adjust better if they move between school terms (entering an established class in the middle of a school year can be very difficult).

- Elders have special needs you'll want to consider.
- Pets fare best when temperatures aren't too extreme, hot *or* cold.

THE "GET-OUT-OF-TOWN-IN-A-HURRY" PLAN

First the bad news: Very little about the move process can be shortened. Now the good news: The choices you make might make it possible to move in less time. The three primary resources in a successful move are time, money, and planning. If you're short on time, be prepared to spend more money or become more organized.

Immediately check into the availability of a rental truck or professional moving service. Next, give your landlord notice or arrange for an agent to sell your home. (If you own your home, you may find it harder to leave town in a hurry.) If your employer is paying for your move, ask if it offers corporate-sponsored financing options that will let you buy a new home before you sell your old one. Then consider the following potentially timesaving choices:

- Move less stuff. Of all the moving tasks, packing and unpacking consume the most time. The less you have to deal with, the quicker your move will go. Consider drastically lightening the load by selling or giving away most of your belongings and starting over in your new location. Although buying replacement stuff may drain your pocketbook, you can save some money by picking up some items secondhand at thrift stores and garage sales. (And after all, everything you have *now* is used, isn't it?)

- Make a quick-move plan. Quickly scan through chapters 4 and 5, highlighting helpful information. Use the checklists and the task time line at the end of this chapter to help you.

- Get someone else to do the cleaning. Before you vacate, you'll need to clean. You can be out the door sooner if you hire a professional cleaning company to come and clean everything, top to bottom, including the carpets. Again, the time you save will cost you money—but it may well be worth trading money for time.

Planning and Organizing

Start a move notebook. This could be as simple as a spiral-bound notepad or as elaborate as a categorized, tabbed binder. Keep track of this notebook. You'll find it invaluable later when the chaos hits. In your notebook, write notes and tape receipts. Of course, keep *this* book with your notebook! You may find the checklists and moving task time lines at the end of this chapter helpful. You may also find it helpful to assign a "do-by" date to each task on the checklist. To help you gauge what you face in the coming weeks, perhaps you will find it useful at this point to scan through the task time lines before reading further.

The section of the Moving Task Time Line that will help you the most at this point is "Decision Making: Weeks 12 to 9," which you'll find at the end of this chapter.

MOVING TIP

Start packing as soon as you get boxes. Some things you can pack long before the move. For example, off-season holiday decorations and off-season clothes can be boxed right away. The more you do early on, the less there is to do closer to move day, when things are hectic anyway.

Preliminary Decisions

Before you even begin to plan your move, there are a number of decisions you'll need to make regarding your current residence, how you will move (do it yourself or hire a professional), and your new area.

LEAVING YOUR CURRENT HOME
(RENTED PROPERTY)

Leaving a rental unit involves notifying your landlord and fulfilling your contractual obligations. This won't be a problem unless you have a lease agreement that lasts beyond your desired move date.

Your rights and options are dictated by state and local landlord/tenant laws and by your lease agreement. Exit fees can be expensive, depending on the terms of your lease. Here are some tips that may help you get out of a lease gracefully and save a few bucks at the same time.

- Know your rights. Laws governing landlord/tenant agreements and rights vary by state and municipality. Consult state and local law and call and obtain a pamphlet on renter's rights for your state and municipality.

- Review your lease agreement. There's no point in worrying until you know whether you have anything to worry about—and no use finding out too late that there were things you could have done.

- Look for a way out. Ask your landlord to consider letting you find a replacement tenant to fulfill your lease term (in some areas, this is a right dictated by law). If your move is due to a corporate relocation, your landlord or the property management company *may* be more willing to be flexible with exit fees—especially if you provide a letter from your employer. (And you may be able to get your employer to pick up the cost if you can't get the fees waived.)

- Adjust the timing. If you need to stay a month or two longer than your current lease allows and you don't want to sign for another six months or longer, ask your landlord for a month-to-month agreement lasting until your move date.

LEAVING YOUR CURRENT HOME (OWNED PROPERTY)

If you own your home, you'll either sell it or rent it out. If you sell, you'll either hire a real estate agent or sell it yourself. If you rent it out, you'll either serve as your own landlord or hire a property management agency to manage the property for you. Here are a few quick pros and cons to help you with the decisions you face.

Hiring a Selling Agent: Pros

- Your home gets exposure to a wide market audience, especially if the agent you choose participates in a multiple listing service.

- Homes listed with a real estate agent typically sell more quickly.

- Your agent will market your home (prepare and place ads and so on), and will also schedule and manage open houses and showings.

- Your agent will advise you and represent your interest in the business deal of selling including offers, negotiation, and closing, guiding you through the stacks of paperwork.

Hiring a Selling Agent: Cons

- Hiring an agent requires signing a contract. If, for whatever reason, you want out, you may find it difficult to break the contract (it's wise to read carefully and sign only a short-term contract. Typical real estate agent contracts are 90 to 120 days in length).
- You pay your agent a fee for the service, typically a percentage of the selling price.

Selling Your Home Yourself: Pros

- You don't pay an agent's fee.
- You retain more control over showings, open houses, walk-throughs, and so on.

Selling Your Home Yourself: Cons

- Selling a home takes time. You must arrange your own showings and schedule and conduct your own open houses. Combined with everything else that happens during move preparation (working, interviewing for jobs, finding a new home, planning your move, packing, and so on), you will probably be swamped already. Add home showings (which are based around the buyer's schedule, not yours), and you may find yourself looking for an agent to help you after all.
- You pay for marketing costs, which can add up. Consider the cost of flyers, newspaper ads, or listing your home on a "homes for sale by owner" Web site.
- Since you don't have a real estate agent to represent you in the sale, you may need to hire an attorney at that point, which could take up some of the savings.

RENTING OUT YOUR PROPERTY

If you prefer to rent out your home, you can turn it over to a property management agency or be your own landlord. The services an agency will perform depend on the agency and your agreement with them.

The following table details some of the rental issues you'll need to consider. As you review these, ask yourself how far away you're moving and whether or not you can handle these issues from your new home. Remember that every piece of work you must hire out cuts into the money in your pocket at the end of the month.

Rental Issue	You As Landlord	Hired Property Manager
Vacancy	You interview candidates, show the property, and choose tenants	The agency finds and selects tenants
Cleaning	You clean or arrange for cleaning services between tenants	The agency arranges for cleaning services between tenants
Late Rent	You collect rent and pursue late rent	The agency collects rent and pursues late rent
Rental Income	The rent you collect is all yours	The agency charges a fee, usually a percentage of the monthly rent
Repairs	You handle repairs and emergencies or find and hire a contractor to do the work	The agency handles repairs and emergencies

Strategic Financial Issues
Related to Renting Out Your Old Home

If your property is located in a desirable neighborhood that is appreciating in value 3 percent or more annually, keeping it may in the long run defray or overcome the cost of management fees. If you rent out your property, it ceases being your primary residence. Find out from your accountant if this will affect your federal or state income taxes or local property taxes (some counties/municipalities give owner-occu-pied credits that reduce the tax burden). If there is an impact, you'll want to figure the difference into your decision of whether or not to sell and into the total you charge for rent.

Deciding How to Move: Hiring Professionals or Moving Yourself

At first, you may be inclined to handle your own move to save money. But there are other factors to consider, and, depending on your situa-tion, you may actually *save* money if you use professional services. Consider the range of service options some professional companies offer. The right combination could save you some of the headache but still compete with the cost of a do-it-yourself move. For example, some professional moving companies offer a "you pack, we drive" arrangement, in which you pack boxes, and the moving company loads, moves, and unloads your belongings. Call around and inquire about rates. Also consider the following list of pros and cons to help you decide what's best for you.

The section of the Moving Task Time Line that will help you the most at this point is "Decision Making: Weeks 12 to 9," which you'll find at the end of this chapter.

The Pros of Using Pros

- *Time.* You may not have the hours it will take to pack, move, and unpack, but professional movers do—that's their day job.
- *Materials.* The moving company provides boxes and packing materials.*
- *Packing.* The movers pack all boxes (unless your contract states that you will pack).*
- *Loading and Unloading.* The movers load your belongings onto the moving van and unload your belongings at your destina-tion.*
- *Unpacking.* The movers remove packed items from boxes and place items on flat surfaces.*
- *Debris.* The movers dispose of packing debris such as boxes, used tape, and padding.*

- *Experience.* The movers will know just what to do to transport your precious belongings in good condition.
- *Safety.* The movers do the lifting, which could save you a real injury.

Professional moving contracts typically include the services marked with an asterisk (*). Don't count on something unless you know for sure that the contract covers it, though—it's a good idea to ask your mover a lot of questions and read the contract carefully.

The Cons of Using Pros

- *Administrative chores.* Using professionals requires you to do some up-front work: obtaining estimates, comparing and negotiating prices and move dates, reviewing contracts, and comparing insurance options.
- *Loss of control.* The movers typically take charge of much of the packing and loading process, and you need to adapt to their schedule and procedures.

The Pros of a Self-Move

- *Control.* You pack, so you decide what items get packed together, how they get packed, and in which box they reside.
- *Cost-cutting.* You may save some money. But as you compare costs, be sure to factor in *all* self-move-related moving and travel costs. These include fuel, tolls, mileage charge on the rented truck, food, and lodging. All these costs increase the longer your trip is.

The Cons of a Self-Move

- *Risk to your belongings.* Because of inexperience with packing, loading, and padding heavy and unwieldy boxes and furniture, you or your volunteers may inadvertently damage your property.
- *Risk to yourself and your friends.* You or your volunteers may injure yourselves or someone else.
- *Responsibility.* Loading and moving day are especially hectic, and you're in charge.
- *Reciprocal obligations.* If you use volunteers, you may be in debt to return the favor.

OTHER THINGS TO KNOW
ABOUT PROFESSIONAL MOVING SERVICES

Your moving company may or may not provide the following services, or may charge extra for performing them. Be sure to ask.

- Disassembling beds or other furniture
- Removing window covering hardware (drapery rods, mini-blinds) or other items from the walls or ceiling
- Disconnecting and installing appliances (dryer, washer, automatic ice maker)
- Disconnecting and installing outside fixtures such as a satellite dish, a hose reel, and so on
- Moving furniture or boxes from one room to another

MOVING INSURANCE IN A PROFESSIONAL MOVE

By U.S. law, the mover must cover your possessions at $0.60 per pound. This coverage is free. Consider taking out additional coverage, though, because under this minimal coverage, your three-pound antique Tiffany lamp worth hundreds of dollars at auction fetches exactly $1.80 if the moving company breaks it.

Your homeowner's or renter's insurance provider may be willing to advise you on moving insurance options, and the moving company will offer you a number of insurance options. Be sure you understand each option—what

MOVING TIP

If you are renting a truck, you'll need to know what size to rent. Here is a general guideline. Because equipment varies, though, ask for advice from the company renting the truck to you.

10-foot truck:

    1 to 2 furnished rooms

14- to 15-foot truck:

    2 to 3 furnished rooms

18- to 20-foot truck:

    4 to 5 furnished rooms

22- to 24-foot truck:

    6 to 8 furnished rooms

it covers and what it costs you. Ask a lot of questions and read everything carefully. No one wishes for mishaps, but it's best to be prepared and well informed should something break or show up missing.

STORAGE

If you want your moving company to store some or all of your possessions temporarily, inquire about cost and the quality of their facilities:

- Are the facilities heated (or air-conditioned, depending on the time of year that applies to you)?
- Does the moving company own the storage facility or subcontract storage to someone else? If they subcontract, does your contract with the moving company extend to the storage facility company?

Moving and Storage Companies in D.C.

Following is a list of some of Washington's recommended moving and/or storage companies. Many will take in storage without moving it if you chose to do it yourself. In the past few years, national and local TV news shows have highlighted the various pitfalls and scams some moving and storage companies will use to hike up the costs of a move or temporary storage.

As with any major move or financial investment, make sure any moving or storage agreement is presented to you in writing, with understandable terms. Get at least two to three estimates for moving companies and feel free to negotiate.

For storage, make sure that you see the space or locker you are going to rent before you pay any money, and make sure that the space you approved and requested is available *before* you arrive with your belongings. It is a common practice of some storage firms to promise you a smaller-size, lower-cost space to rope you in, then once you arrive, tell you they have only larger spaces available.

Anytime Apartment Movers
1806 11th Street NW
Washington, DC 20001
(202) 483-9109

Concord Movers
1933 Montana Avenue NW
Washington, DC 20002
(202) 842-5440

Hughes Moving & Storage
710 Kennedy Street NW
Washington, DC 20011
(202) 726-3517

Lloyd Moving & Storage CO Inc.
5774 2nd Street NE
Washington, DC 20011
(202) 635-8030

Mullens Transfer & Storage
412 V Street NE
Washington, DC 20002
(202) 829-6676

Prime Movers
5646 3rd Street NE
Washington, DC 20011
(202) 882-1414
(301) 588-2336 (fax)

Public Storage
(number of locations in
Washignton Area)
(800) 447-8673

Storage Place
175 R Street NE
Washington, DC 20002
(202) 269-4499

Shurgard Storage Centers
(number of locations in
Washington area)
(800) 748-7427

United Van Lines
1701 Florida Avenue NW
Washington, DC 20009
(202) 234-5600

MOVING TIP

Save the TV, VCR, kids' videos, and a box of toys to be loaded on the truck last. Upon arriving at your destination, if you can't find someone to baby-sit, set aside a room in your home where your young children can safely play. Set up the TV and VCR and unpack the kids' videos along with some toys and snacks.

University Storage & Moving
700 13th Street NW, Suite 950
Washington, DC 20005
(202) 434-4512
(301) 772-9216 (24 hours)
(202) 434-4599 (fax)
(800) 489-9969 (toll-free)

CHOOSING A MOVER

- Start by asking around. Chances are your friends, family, or colleagues will have a personal recommendation.

- Take their recommendations and list them in a notebook, each on a separate sheet. Call these companies to request a no-obligation, free written estimate—and take notes on your conversation.

- Find out if the company you're talking to offers the services you need. For example, if you want to ship your car, boat, or powered recreational craft in the van along with your household goods, ask if this service is available.

- Do a little investigating. Ask the company to show you its operating license, and call the Better Business Bureau to ask about complaints and outstanding claims.

GETTING AN ESTIMATE

You need to know what kind of estimate the moving company is giving you. The two most common are "non-binding" and "binding." A *non-binding estimate* (usually free, but potentially less accurate) is one in which the moving company charges you by the hour per worker per truck and quotes you an approximate figure to use in your planning. Depending on circumstances, your final cost could be significantly greater than what shows up in the estimate.

The second type is a *binding estimate,* which you typically pay for. In this type, the professional mover performs a detailed on-site inspection of your belongings and quotes a flat price based on the following:

- The amount of stuff you're moving, whether it is fragile or bulky, and how complicated it is to pack
- Final weight
- Services provided
- Total length of travel

Once you choose a mover, it's a good idea to have a representative visit your home, look at your belongings, and give you a written (binding) estimate. Getting a written estimate may cost you money, but it helps prevent surprises when it comes time to pay the final bill.

You play a big role in making sure that the estimate you receive is accurate. Be sure you show the moving company representative everything you plan to move.

- Remember to take the representative through every closet, out to the garage, into the shed, down to the basement, up into the attic, and to your rented storage facility if you have one.
- Tell the representative about any item you *don't* plan to move (because you plan to get rid of it before you move). Then be sure to follow through and get rid of it so there are no surprises on moving day.
- Point out any vehicles you want to ship in the van along with your household goods, and ask your representative to include the cost in your estimate.

WHAT MIGHT INCREASE YOUR FINAL BILL

It is reasonable to expect that certain circumstances will unexpectedly increase your final bill, including:

- You do the packing and it's incomplete or done improperly.
- Circumstances unexpectedly increase the time and labor involved in your move. For example:

    You're moving out of or into a high-rise and movers don't have access to an elevator (perhaps it's broken).

    Access at either location is restricted (for example, there is no truck parking close by or the movers have to wait for someone to unlock).

- You change your move destination after you receive your written estimate.
- You require delivery of your belongings to more than one destination.

Researching Your New Area

The section of the Moving Task Time Line that will help you the most at this point is "Decision Making: Weeks 12 to 9," which you'll find at the end of this chapter. Other chapters of this book discuss the details of your destination city. Here are some additional move-related tips and resources.

GENERAL CITY INFORMATION

- Visit your local library and read up on your new area.
- Go online and look for the local newspaper.
- Have a friend or family member mail you a week's worth of newspapers or have a subscription delivered via postal mail.
- Visit *www.monstermoving.com* for easy-to-find city information and links to local services, information, and Web sites.

JOBS, HOUSING, AND COST OF LIVING

Visit *www.monster.com* for career assistance, and visit *www.monster moving.com* for links to apartments for rent, and real estate and other services, as well as free cost-of-living information.

CHOOSING SCHOOLS

Selecting schools is of supreme importance for family members who will attend public or private schools.

Do Your Homework

- Ask your real estate agent to help you find school information and statistics or a list of contacts for home school associations.
- Search the Web.

    Visit *www.2001beyond.com*. There you can compare up to four districts at once. Information on both public and private schools is provided. The extensive twelve-page report provides information on class size, curriculum, interscholastic sports, extracurricular activities, awards, merits, and SAT scores. It also provides the principal's name and phone number for each school in the district. You may need to pay a nominal fee for the twelve-page report (or the cost may be covered by a sponsoring real estate professional, if you don't mind receiving a phone call from an agent).

    Visit *www.monstermoving.com*, which provides links to school information.

Visit Schools

Arrange to visit schools your children might attend, and bring them along. Your children will pick up on subtleties that you will miss. As you talk with your children about changing schools, try to help them differentiate between their feelings about moving to a new school and area and their feelings about that particular school by asking direct but open-ended questions. (An *open-ended* question is one that invites dialogue because it can't be answered with a simple "yes" or "no"—"What was the best or worst thing you saw there?" for example, or "Which electives looked the most interesting?")

MOVING TIP

A few weeks before you move, start eating the food in your freezer. Also use up canned food, which is bulky and heavy to move.

PLANNING AND TAKING A HOUSE- OR APARTMENT-HUNTING TRIP

Preparing and planning in advance will help you make the most of your trip. Ideally, by this point, you will have narrowed your search to two or three neighborhoods or areas.

- Gather documents and information required for completing a rental application:

    Rental history: Landlord name, contact information, dates occupied

    Personal references: Name and contact information for one or two personal references

    Employment information: Current or anticipated employer name and contact info

    Bank account number

- Consider compiling all this information onto a "Rental Résumé." Even though most landlords won't accept a rental résumé in lieu of a completed application, spending the time up front could be helpful in a market where rentals are scarce.

Handing the landlord a rental résumé lets them know you're serious about finding the right place and are professional and organized in how you conduct your affairs.

- Go prepared to pay an application fee and deposits. Deposit the funds in your account and bring your checkbook. Typically, landlords require first and last month's rent and a flat damage and cleaning deposit.
- Take your Move Planning Notebook. List properties you want to visit, one per notebook page. Clip the classified ad and tape it onto the page. Write notes about the property, rent rate, deposit amount, and terms you discuss with the landlord or property manager.

Planning

Now that you've made pre-move decisions, it's time to plan for the physical move. First, you'll need to organize your moving day. Next, you'll need to prepare to pack.

These are the sections of the Moving Task Time Line that will help you the most at this point:

- "Organizing, Sorting, and Notifying: Weeks 9 to 8"
- "Finalizing Housing Arrangements and Establishing Yourself in Your New Community: Weeks 8 to 6"
- "Making and Confirming Transportation and Travel Plans: Week 6"
- "Uprooting: Weeks 5 to 4"
- "Making and Confirming Moving-Day Plans: Week 3"

You'll find the Moving Task Time Line at the end of this chapter.

PLANNING FOR MOVING DAY

The Professional Move: Some Planning Considerations

- Confirm your move dates and finalize any last contract issues.
- Ask what form of payment movers will accept (check, money order, certified check, traveler's checks) and make necessary arrangements.

The Self-Move: Organizing Volunteers

- Ask friends and relatives to "volunteer" to help you load the truck on moving day.
- Set up shifts, and tactfully let your volunteers know that you are counting on them to arrive on time and stay through their "shift."
- A week or two before moving day, call everyone to remind them.
- Plan on supplying soft drinks and munchies to keep your crew going.

PLANNING CARE FOR YOUR CHILDREN AND PETS

Moving day will be hectic for you and everyone, and possibly dangerous for your young children. Make plans to take younger children and your pets to someone's home or to a care facility.

PLANNING YOUR MOVING-DAY TRAVEL

Driving

- If you will be renting a truck, be prepared to put down a sizable deposit the day you pick up the truck. Some truck rental companies only accept a credit card for this deposit, so go prepared.
- If you belong to an automobile club such as AAA, contact them to obtain maps, suggested routes, alternate routes, rest-stop information, and a trip packet, if they provide this service.
- Visit an online map site such as www.mapblast.com, where you'll find not only a map but also door-to-door driving directions and estimated travel times.
- Find out in advance where you should turn in the truck in your new hometown.

Traveling by Air, Train, or Bus

- Arrange for tickets and boarding passes.
- Speak with the airline to request meals that match dietary restrictions.
- Speak with the airline or the train or bus company to make any special arrangements such as wheelchair accessibility and assistance.

- Plan to dress comfortably.
- If you will be traveling with young children, plan to dress them in bright, distinctive clothing so you can easily identify them in a crowded airport, train station, or bus terminal.

PREPARING TO PACK:
WHAT TO DO WITH THE STUFF YOU HAVE

Moves are complicated, time-consuming, and exhausting. But the process has at least one benefit. A move forces us to consider simplifying our lives by reducing the amount of our personal belongings. If we plan to keep it, we also must pack it, load it, move it, unload it, and unpack it. Here are some suggestions for sifting through your belongings as you prepare for packing.

- Start in one area of your home and go through everything before moving to the next area.
- Ask yourself three questions about each item (sentimental value aside):

  Have we used this in the last year?

  Will we use it in the coming year? For example, if you're moving to a more temperate climate, you might not need all your wool socks and sweaters.

  Is there a place for it in the new home? For instance, if your new home has a smaller living room, you might not have room for your big couch or need all your wall decorations.

If you answer "no" to any or all of these questions, you might want to consider selling the item, giving it away, or throwing it out.

Packing

Here are some tips to help you with one of the most difficult stages of your move—packing.

- Follow a plan. Pack one room at a time. You may find yourself leaving one or two boxes in each room open to receive those items you use right up until the last minute.
- On the outside of each box, describe the contents and room destination. Be as specific as you can, to make unpacking easier.

However, if you are using a professional moving service but doing the packing yourself, consider numbering boxes and creating a separate list of box contents and destinations.

- Put heavy items such as books in small boxes to make them easier to carry.

- Don't put tape on furniture because it may pull off some finish when you remove it.

- As you pack, mark and set aside the items that should go in the truck last (see checklist at the end of this chapter). Mark and set aside your "necessary box" (for a list of items to include in this box, see the checklist at the end of this chapter).

PACKING FRAGILE ITEMS

- When packing breakable dishes and glasses, use boxes and padding made for these items. You may have to pay a little to buy these boxes, but you're apt to save money in the long run because your dishes are more likely to arrive unbroken. Dishes and plates are best packed on edge (not stacked atop each other flat).

- Pad mirrors, pictures, and larger delicate pieces with sheets and blankets.

- Computers fare best if they are packed in their original boxes. If you don't have these, pack your hardware in a large, sturdy box and surround it with plenty of padding such as plastic bubble pack.

- Use plenty of padding around fragile items.

- Mark "FRAGILE" *on the top and all sides* of boxes of breakables so it's easily seen no matter how a box is stacked.

WHAT *NOT* TO PACK

- Don't pack hazardous, flammable, combustible, or explosive materials. Empty your gas grill tank and any kerosene heater fuel as well as gasoline in your power yard tools. These materials are not safe in transit.

- Don't pack valuables such as jewelry, collections, important financial and legal documents, and records for the moving van. Keep these with you in your car trunk or your suitcase.

PACKING AND UNPACKING
SAFELY WITH YOUNG CHILDREN

No matter how well you've kid-proofed your home, that only lasts until the moment you start packing. Then things are in disarray and within reach of youngsters. Here are some tips to keep your toddlers and children safe.

- Items your youngsters have seldom or never seen will pique their curiosity, presenting a potential hazard, so consider what you are packing or unpacking. If you stop packing or unpacking and leave the room even for a moment, take your youngsters with you and close the door or put up a child gate.

- Keep box knives and other tools out of a child's reach.

- As you disassemble or reassemble furniture, keep track of screws, bolts, nuts, and small parts.

- Beware of how and where you temporarily place furniture and other items. (That heavy mirror you just took down off the wall—do you lean it up against the wall until you go get the padding material, inviting a curious youngster to pull or climb on it?) For the same reason, consider how high you stack boxes.

- On arriving at your destination, if you can't find someone to baby-sit, set aside a room in your home where your young children can safely play. Set up the TV and VCR and unpack the kids' videos, books, coloring books and crayons or markers, and some toys and snacks.

- Walk through your new home with children and talk about any potential dangers such as a swimming pool or stairs, establishing your safety rules and boundaries.

MOVING TIP

Take a tape measure and your notebook with you. Measure rooms; sketch your new home and write room measurements on your sketch. Before you move, you'll know whether your current furniture will fit and will have a good idea of how it should be arranged.

- If you have young children who are unaccustomed to having stairs in the home, place a gate at the top and one at the bottom. If your child is walking and over toddler age, walk up and down the stairs together a few times holding the railing until they become accustomed to using the stairs.

Handle with Special Care: Uprooting and Settling the People and Pets in Your Life

The most important advice you can hear is this: Involving children as much as possible will help transform this anxiety-causing, uncertain experience into an exciting adventure. It would take a book to cover this topic comprehensively, but here are some suggestions for making the transition easier:

- *Involve children early.* Ask for their input on decisions and give them age-appropriate tasks such as packing their own belongings and assembling an activity bag to keep them busy while traveling.

- *Don't make empty promises.* Kids can hear the hollow ring when you say, "It'll be just like here. Just give it time," or "You can stay friends with your friends here." That's true, but you know it's not true in the same way, if you're moving a long distance.

- *Deal with fear of the unknown.* If possible, take children with you to look at potential neighborhoods, homes or apartments, and schools. It may be more expensive and require extra effort, but it will ease the transition and help children begin to make the adjustment.

- *Provide as much information as you can.* If it's not possible to take children with you when you visit new neighborhoods, homes or apartments, and schools, take a camera or video recorder. Your children will appreciate the pictures, and the preview will help them begin the transition. You can also use a map to help them understand the new area and the route you will take to get there.

- *Make time to talk with your children about the move.* Especially listen for—and talk about—the anxieties your children feel. By doing so, you will help them through the move (your primary goal)—and you'll deepen your relationship at the same time, which may be more important in the long run.

- *Share your own anxieties with your children—but be sure to keep an overall positive outlook about the move.* Because most aspects of a move are downers, a negative outlook on your part may shed gloom over the whole experience—including its good aspects. On the other hand, a positive outlook on your part may counteract some of your child's emotional turmoil, uncertainty, and fear.
- *Make it fun.* Give older children a disposable camera and ask them to photograph your move. Once you arrive and are settled in, make time together to create the "moving" chapter of your family photo album.

HELPING FAMILY MEMBERS MAINTAIN FRIENDSHIPS

Moving doesn't have to end a friendship.

- Give each child a personal address book and have them write the e-mail address, phone number, and postal mail address for each of their friends.
- Stay in touch. E-mail is an easy way. Establish an e-mail address for every family member (if they don't already have one) before you move so they can give it out to friends. Many Web mail services are free and can be accessed from anywhere you can access the Internet. Examples include *www.msn.com, www.usa.net,* and *www.yahoo.com.*
- Make (and follow through with) plans to visit your old hometown within the first year following your move. Visit friends and drive by your old home, through neighborhoods, and past landmarks. This reconnection with dear friends and fond memories will help your family bring finality to the move.

TRAVELING WITH YOUR PET

- Keep a picture of your pet on your person or in your wallet just in case you get separated from Fido or Fluffy during the move.
- Place identification tags on your pet's collar and pet carrier.

- Take your pet to the vet for an examination just before you move. Ask for advice on moving your particular pet. Specifically ask for advice on how you can help your pet through the move—what you can do before, during, and after the move to help your pet make the transition smoothly.

- Find out if you will need any health certificates for your pet to comply with local regulations in your new home, and obtain them when you visit the vet.

- If your pet is prone to motion sickness or tends to become nervous in reaction to excitement and unfamiliar surroundings, tell your veterinarian, who may prescribe medication for your pet.

- Ask for your pet's health records so you can take them to your new vet.

- If your pet is unusual—say, a ferret or a snake or other reptile—there might be laws in your new city or state regarding the transportation or housing of such an animal. Contact the department of agriculture or a local veterinarian to find out.

- Cats: It's wise to keep your cat indoors for the first two weeks until it recognizes its new surroundings as home.

- Dogs: If appropriate, walk your dog on a leash around your neighborhood to help it become familiar with its new surroundings and learn its way back home.

- If your pet will travel by plane, check with your airline regarding fees and any specific rules and regulations regarding pet transport.

- Your pet will need to travel in an approved carrier (check with your airline regarding acceptable types and sizes).

- Your airline may require a signed certificate of health dated within a certain number of days of the flight. Only your vet can produce this document.

Move Budget-Planning Guide

Housing

Home repairs $ _____

Cleaning supplies and services $ _____

Rental expenses in new city

    Application fees
    (varies—figure $15 to $35 per application) $ _____

    First and last month's rent $ _____

    Damage and security deposit $ _____

    Pet deposit $ _____

    Utility deposits $ _____

    Storage unit rental $ _____

Total. . . . .**$** _____

Moving

Professional moving services or truck rental $ _____

Moving supplies $ _____

Food and beverage for volunteers $ _____

Tips for professional movers; gifts for volunteers $ _____

Moving travel:

    Airline tickets $ _____

    Fuel $ _____

    Tolls $ _____

    Meals: per meal $_____ × _____ meals $ _____

    Hotels: per night $_____ × _____ nights $ _____

Total. . . . .**$** _____

(continues on next page)

(continued from previous page)

Other Expenses

_____	$ _____
_____	$ _____
_____	$ _____
_____	$ _____
_____	$ _____
_____	$ _____
_____	$ _____

Total. . . . .$ _____

GRAND TOTAL. . . . .$ _____

Utilities to Cancel

Utility	Provider name and phone	Cancel date[1]
Water and sewer		
Electricity		
Gas		
Phone		
Garbage		
Cable		
Alarm service		

1. If you are selling your home, the shutoff of essential services (water, electricity, gas) will depend on the final closing and walk-through. Coordinate with your real estate agent.

Utilities to Connect

Utility	Provider name and phone	Service start date	Deposit amount required
Water and sewer			
Electricity			
Gas			
Phone			
Garbage			
Cable			
Alarm service			

Other Services to Cancel, Transfer, or Restart

Service	Provider name and phone	Service end date[1]	Service start date[1]
Subscriptions and Memberships			
Newspaper			
Memberships (health club and so on)			
Internet Service Provider			

1. If applicable

(continues on next page)

(continued from previous page)

Other Services to Cancel, Transfer, or Restart			
Service	**Provider name and phone**	**Service end date**[1]	**Service start date**[1]
Government and School			
Postal mail change of address			
School records			
Voter registration			
Vehicle registration			
Financial			
Bank account[2]			
Direct deposits and withdrawals			
Safe deposit box			
Professional			
Health care (transfer doctors' and dentists' records for each family member) Veterinarian (transfer records) Cleaners (pick up your clothes)			

1. If applicable; 2. Open an account in your new town before closing your existing account.

Checklists

MOVING SUPPLIES

Packing and Unpacking

_____ Tape and tape dispenser. (The slightly more expensive gun-style dispenser is a worthwhile investment because its one-handed operation means you don't need a second person to help you hold the box closed while you do the taping.)

_____ Boxes. (It's worth it to obtain specialty boxes for your dinner-ware, china set, and glasses. Specialty wardrobe boxes that allow your hanging clothes to hang during transport are another big help.)

_____ Padding such as bubble wrap.

_____ Markers.

_____ Scissors or a knife.

_____ Big plastic bags.

_____ Inventory list and clipboard.

_____ Box knife with retractable blade. (Get one for each adult.)

Loading and Moving

_____ Rope. (If nothing else, you'll need it to secure heavy items to the inside wall of the truck.)

_____ Padding blankets. (If you use your own, they may get dirty and you'll need bedding when you arrive. Padding is available for rent at most truck rental agencies.)

_____ Hand truck or appliance dolly. (Most truck rental agencies have them available for rent.)

_____ Padlock for the cargo door.

THE "NECESSARY BOX"

Eating

____ Snacks or food. (Pack enough durable items for right before you depart, your travel, and the first day in your new home— and disposable utensils, plates, cups.)

____ Instant coffee, tea bags, and so on.

____ Roll of paper towels and moistened towelettes.

____ Garbage bags.

Bathing

____ A towel for each person.

____ Soap, shampoo, toothpaste, and any other toiletries.

____ Toilet paper.

Health Items

____ First aid kit including pain relievers.

____ Prescription medicines.

Handy to Have

____ List of contact information. (Make sure you can reach relatives, the moving company, the truck driver's cell phone, and so on.)

____ Small tool kit. (You need to be able to take apart and reassemble items that can't be moved whole.)

____ Reclosable plastic bags to hold small parts, screws, bolts.

____ Spare lightbulbs. (Some bulbs in your new home might be burned out or missing.)

____ Nightlight and flashlight.

OVERNIGHT BAG

_____ Enough clothes for the journey plus the first day or two in your new home.

_____ Personal toiletries.

ITEMS FOR KIDS

_____ Activities for the trip.

_____ Favorite toys and anything else that will help children feel immediately at home in their new room.

Pet Checklist

_____ Food.

_____ A bottle of the water your pet is used to drinking.

_____ Dishes for food and water.

_____ Leash, collar, identification tags.

_____ Favorite toy.

_____ Medicines.

_____ Bed or blanket.

_____ Carrier.

_____ Paper towels in case of accidents.

_____ Plastic bags and a scooper.

_____ Litter and litter box for your cat or rabbit.

Last Items on the Truck

CLEANING

_____ Vacuum cleaner.

_____ Cleaning supplies.

GENERAL

_____ Necessary box.

_____ Setup for kids' temporary playroom.

_____ Other items you'll need the moment you arrive.

New Home Safety Checklist

GENERAL

_____ Watch out for tripping hazards. They will be plentiful until you get everything unpacked and put away, so be careful, and keep a path clear at all times.

HEAT, FIRE, ELECTRICAL

_____ Be sure nothing gets placed too close to heaters.

_____ Test smoke, heat, and carbon monoxide detectors. Find out your fire department's recommendations regarding how many of these devices you should have and where you should place them. If you need more, go buy them (remember to buy batteries) and install them.

_____ Find the fuse or breaker box before you need to shut off or reset a circuit.

WATER

_____ Check the temperature setting on your water heater. For child safety and fuel conservation, experts recommend 120 degrees Fahrenheit.

_____ Locate the water shutoff valve in case of a plumbing problem.

Moving Task Time Line

DECISION MAKING: WEEKS 12 TO 9

_____ Consider your moving options (professional versus self-move) and get quotes.

_____ If you are being relocated by your company, find out what your company covers and what you will be responsible for doing and paying.

_____ Set a move date.

_____ Choose your moving company or truck rental agency and reserve the dates.

If You Own Your Home

_____ Decide whether you want to sell or rent it out.

_____ If you decide to sell, choose a real estate agent and put your home on the market or look into, and begin planning for, selling it yourself.

_____ If you decide to rent out your home, decide whether you want to hire a property management agency or manage the property yourself.

_____ Perform (or hire contractors to perform) home repairs.

If You Currently Rent

____ Notify your landlord of your plans to vacate.

____ Check into cleaning obligations and options.

Tour Your New City or Town

____ Research your new area at the library or online at *www.monstermoving.com.*

____ Contact a real estate agent or property management agency to help you in your search for new lodgings.

____ Go on a school-hunting and house- or apartment-hunting trip to your new town or city.

Additional items:

_____

_____

_____

_____

_____

_____

_____

_____

_____

_____

_____

_____

_____

_____

_____

_____

_____

ORGANIZING, SORTING, AND NOTIFYING: WEEKS 9 TO 8

_____ Obtain the post office's change of address kit by calling 1-800-ASK-USPS or visiting your local post office or *www.usps.gov/moversnet/* (where you'll find the form and helpful lists of questions and answers).

_____ Complete and send the form.

_____ List and notify people, businesses, and organizations who need to know about your move. You may not think of everyone at once, but keep a running list and add people to your list and notify them as you remember them. As you notify them, check them off your list.

_____ Start sorting through your belongings to decide what to keep. Make plans to rid yourself of what you don't want: pick a date for a garage sale; call your favorite charity and set a date for them to come pick up donations; call your recycling company to find out what they will accept.

_____ For moving insurance purposes, make an inventory of your possessions with their estimated replacement value.

_____ If you have high-value items (such as antiques) that you expect to send with the moving company or ship separately, obtain an appraisal.

Additional items:

_____

_____

_____

_____

_____

_____

_____

_____

FINALIZING HOUSING ARRANGEMENTS
AND ESTABLISHING YOURSELF
IN YOUR NEW COMMUNITY: WEEKS 8 TO 6

_____ **Home.** Select your new home and arrange financing; establish a tentative closing date or finalize rental housing arrangements.

_____ **Schools.** Find out school calendars and enrollment and immunization requirements.

_____ **Insurance.** Contact an agent regarding coverage on your new home and its contents as well as on your automobile.

_____ **Finances.** Select a bank, open accounts, and obtain a safe deposit box.

_____ **New Home Layout.** Sketch a floor plan of your new home and include room measurements. Determine how your present furniture, appliances, and decor will fit.

_____ **Mail.** If you haven't found a new home, rent a post office box for mail forwarding.

_____ **Services.** Find out the names and phone numbers of utility providers and what they require from you before they will start service (for example, a deposit, a local reference). (You can list your providers and service start dates on the checklist provided in this chapter.) Schedule service to start a few days before you arrive.

Additional items:

_____

_____

_____

_____

_____

_____

_____

_____

MAKING AND CONFIRMING TRANSPORTATION AND TRAVEL PLANS: WEEK 6

____ Schedule pick-up and delivery dates with your mover.

____ Make arrangements with your professional car mover.

____ If you need storage, make the arrangements.

____ Confirm your departure date with your real estate agent or landlord.

____ Make your travel arrangements. If you will be flying, book early for cheaper fares.

____ Map your driving trip using www.mapblast.com or ask your automobile club for assistance with route and accommodation information.

Additional items:

_____

_____

_____

_____

_____

_____

_____

_____

_____

_____

_____

_____

_____

_____

_____

_____

_____

_____

_____

_____

UPROOTING: WEEKS 5 TO 4

_____ Hold your garage sale, or donate items to charity.

_____ Gather personal records from all health care providers, your veterinarian, lawyers, accountants, and schools.

_____ Notify current utility providers of your disconnect dates and your forwarding address. (You can list your providers and service end dates on the checklist provided in this chapter.)

Additional items:

_____

_____

_____

_____

_____

_____

_____

_____

_____

_____

_____

_____

_____

_____

_____

_____

_____

_____

_____

_____

MAKING AND CONFIRMING MOVING-DAY PLANS: WEEK 3

_____ Make arrangements for a sitter for kids and pets on moving day.

_____ Call moving-day volunteers to confirm move date and their arrival time.

_____ Obtain traveler's checks for trip expenses and cashier's or certified check for payment to mover.

_____ Have your car serviced if you are driving a long distance.

Additional items:

_____

_____

_____

_____

_____

_____

_____

_____

_____

_____

_____

_____

_____

_____

_____

_____

_____

_____

_____

_____

WEEK 2

_____ If you have a pet, take it to the vet for a checkup. For more pet-moving tips, see the section earlier in this chapter on moving with pets.

_____ Arrange for transportation of your pet.

_____ If you are moving into or out of a high-rise building, contact the property manager and reserve the elevator for moving day.

_____ Reserve parking space for the professional moving van or your rental truck. You may need to obtain permission from your rental property manager or from the city.

_____ Drain oil and gas from all your power equipment and kerosene from portable heaters.

Additional items:

_____

_____

_____

_____

_____

_____

_____

_____

_____

_____

_____

_____

_____

_____

_____

_____

_____

_____

MOVING WEEK

_____ Defrost the freezer.

_____ Give away any plants you can't take with you.

_____ Pack your luggage and your necessary box for the trip (see the list provided in this chapter).

_____ Get everything but the day-to-day essentials packed and ready to go.

Additional items:

_____

_____

_____

_____

_____

_____

_____

_____

_____

_____

_____

_____

_____

_____

_____

_____

_____

MOVING DAY

_____ Mark off parking space for the moving van using cones or chairs.

_____ See "Moving Day" section of chapter 5 for further to-do items.

Getting from Here to There: Moving Day and Beyond

This chapter guides you through the next stage in your move: moving day, arriving, unpacking, and settling in. Here you'll find important travel tips for both the self-move and the professional move, information related to a professional car move, and pointers for your first days and weeks in your new home.

The Professional Move

Early on moving day, reserve a large place for the moving truck to park. Mark off an area with cones or chairs. If you need to obtain parking permission from your apartment complex manager or the local government, do so in advance.

GUIDE THE MOVERS

Before work starts, walk through the house with the movers and describe the loading order. Show them the items you plan to transport yourself. (It's best if these are piled in one area and clearly marked, maybe even covered with a sheet or blanket until you're ready to pack them in your car.)

Remain on-site to answer the movers' questions and to provide special instructions.

BEFORE YOU DEPART

Before you hit the road, you will need to take care of some last-minute details:

- Walk through your home to make sure everything was loaded.

- Sign the bill of lading. But first, read it carefully and ask any questions. The bill of lading is a document the government requires movers to complete for the transportation of supplies, materials, and personal property. The mover is required to have a signed copy on hand, and you should keep your copy until the move is complete and any claims are settled.

- Follow the movers to the weigh station. Your bill will be partly based on the weight of your property moved.

UNLOADING AND MOVING IN

Be sure to take care of these details once the movers arrive at your new home:

- Have your money ready. (Professional movers expect payment in full before your goods are unloaded.)

- Check for damage as items are unpacked and report it right away.

- Unless the company's policy prohibits the acceptance of gratuities, it is customary to tip each mover. $20 is a good amount; you may want to tip more or less based on the service you receive.

The Self-Move

The following tips should help you organize and guide your help, as well as make the moving day run more smoothly:

- The day before your move, create a task list. Besides the obvious (loading the truck), this list will include tasks such as disconnecting the washer and dryer and taking apart furniture that can't be moved whole.

- Plan to provide beverages and food for your volunteers. Make it easy on yourself and provide popular options such as pizza or sub sandwiches (delivered), chilled soda pop and bottled water (in an ice chest, especially if you're defrosting and cleaning the refrigerator).

- On moving day, remember, you are only one person. So if you need to defrost the freezer or pack last-minute items, choose and appoint someone who knows your plan to oversee the volunteers and answer questions.

- Be sure you have almost everything packed before your help arrives. Last-minute packing creates even more chaos and it's likely that hastily packed items will be damaged during loading or transit.

- If you end up with an even number of people, it's natural for people to work in pairs because they can carry the items that require two people. If you have an odd number of people, the extra person can rotate in to provide for breaks, carry light items alone, or work on tasks you assign.

- Be sure to match a person's physical ability and health with the tasks you assign.

MOVING TIP

Before you leave, measure your current home and draw a sketch plan, showing room measurements and furniture placement. Take the plan with you, along with a tape measure and notebook, and draw up similar plans for the house or rental unit you're thinking of choosing. Sketches needn't be very detailed at this stage to help you avoid unpleasant surprises— no point in dragging that California King bed across country if it won't fit in the bedroom.

- Appoint the early shift to start on tasks such as disconnecting the washer and dryer and taking apart furniture (such as bed frames) that can't be moved whole.
- Before work starts, walk through the house with your volunteers and describe your loading plan.
- Know your moving truck and how it should be packed for safe handling on the road (ask the truck rental company for directions).
- Load the truck according to the directions your truck rental agency gave you. Tie furniture items (especially tall ones) to the inside wall of the truck. Pack everything together as tightly as possible, realizing that items will still shift somewhat as you travel.

Move Travel

DIRECTIONS TO WASHINGTON, D.C.

Getting to Washington from just about anywhere in the United States is comparatively easy. It's wading through the traffic once you get here that can be the challenge.

Arriving by Car

There are several major interstate highways in and around Washington. The largest is Interstate 95, the major highway that runs from the most northeasterly point in the United States, down along the eastern seaboard to Florida.

I-95 connects to Washington at I-495 in Maryland (the Washington Beltway) and emerges from the Beltway in Virginia headed south.

I-495 is the key roadway to getting around the Washington area. It literally surrounds Washington, running through Maryland and Virginia. Connecting to 495, are several major roadways:

I-395: Cuts across the Virginia suburbs of Arlington and Alexandria and puts a driver back on I-95

I-295: The Baltimore-Washington Parkway connects Washington to Baltimore with a straight and direct route, instead of the rather circuitous Beltway.

I-66: Runs East to West from Washington out into the Virginia suburbs and eventually connects to two of the major cross-country interstates: first, I-81, then I-40, which runs across the lower half of the U.S.

I-270: Runs from the Beltway up through the Maryland suburbs to eventually connect to I-70 the major cross-country roadway that runs across the upper half of the U.S.

The Airports

Three major airports serve the Washington area.

Dulles International Airport is about 25 miles west of Washington and serves as a hub for United Airlines and many international air carriers. It offers shuttle and taxi service to the city and surrounding suburbs. A taxi from Dulles to Washington can cost as much as $45. A shuttle ride, less than $15.

A main advantage to Dulles is that many flights offered from there are nonstop, particularly for cross-country flights.

Ronald Reagan National Airport lies just across the Potomac River from Washington. It is accessible from Washington via the Metro (allow about a half-hour ride from downtown). Taxi rides from Washington to the airport average about $10 to $12.

The airport is served most heavily by Delta, US Airways, Northwest, American, and several regional airlines. It is utilized most by business travelers who take advantage of the Washington to New York and Boston shuttle services of Delta and US Airways.

Because of noise and air-traffic restrictions imposed on the facility, planes cannot leave Reagan National until 7 A.M. and cannot arrive or leave after 10 P.M. Many flights offered from the airport tend to be so-called connector flights, which require at least one stop during the trip and plane transfers.

Baltimore Washington International Airport is about 45 minutes to an hour from downtown Washington and in the past five years has expanded dramatically to meet the needs of Washington travelers and to compete with the two other large regional airports. Its popularity can be attributed, in part, to the fact that many airfares on major carriers are often lower from BWI than from Dulles or Reagan. Another reason: the high-quality and low-cost airline Southwest is based at BWI and offers low fares to just about anywhere in the U.S. from this location.

Shuttle service is available from Washington, Virginia, and Maryland and often costs between $20 to $30 per person. The airport is also accessible from Washington Union Station via Amtrak, which runs a commuter train from D.C. to a stop at BWI on the way to Baltimore.

SELF-MOVE—DRIVING A TRUCK

- A loaded moving truck handles far differently from the typical car. Allow extra space between you and the vehicle you're following. Drive more slowly and decelerate and brake sooner—there's a lot of weight sitting behind you.

- Realize that no one likes to follow a truck. Other drivers may make risky moves to get ahead of you, so watch out for people passing when it's not safe.

- Know your truck's height and look out for low overhangs and tree branches. Especially be aware of filling station overhang height.

- Most accidents in large vehicles occur when backing. Before you back, get out, walk around, and check for obstacles. Allow plenty of maneuvering room and ask someone to help you back. Ask them to stay within sight of your sideview mirror—and talk over the hand signals they should use as they guide you.

- Stop and rest at least every two hours.

- At every stop, do a walk-around inspection of the truck. Check tires, lights, and the cargo door. (If you're towing a trailer, check trailer tires, door, hitch, and hitch security chain.) Ask your truck rental representative how often you should check the engine oil level.
- At overnight stops, park in a well-lighted area and lock the truck cab. Lock the cargo door with a padlock.

IF YOU'RE FLYING OR TRAVELING BY TRAIN OR BUS

- Coordinate with the moving van driver so that you arrive at about the same time.
- Plan for the unexpected such as delays, cancellations, or missed connections.
- Keep in touch with the truck driver (by cell phone, if possible), who may also experience delays for any number of reasons: mechanical problems, road construction, storms, or illness.
- Dress comfortably.
- If you are traveling with young children, dress them in bright, distinctive clothing so you can easily identify them in a crowded airport, train station, or bus terminal.

MOVING TIP

Reserve a large place for the moving truck to park on the day you move out. Mark off an area with cones or chairs. If you need to obtain parking permission from your apartment complex manager or the city, do so in advance.

PROFESSIONAL MOVERS MAY NEED HELP, TOO

Make sure the movers have directions to your new home. Plan your travel so that you will be there to greet them and unlock. Have a backup plan in case one of you gets delayed. It is also a good idea to exchange cell phone numbers with the driver so you can stay in touch in case one of you is delayed.

TIPS FOR A PROFESSIONAL CAR MOVE

A professional car carrier company can ship your car. Alternatively, your moving company may be able to ship it in the van along with your household goods. Ask around and compare prices.

- Be sure that the gas tanks are no more than one-quarter full.
- It's not wise to pack personal belongings in your transported auto, because insurance typically won't cover those items.
- If your car is damaged in transport, report the damage to the driver or move manager and note it on the inventory sheet. If you don't, the damage won't be eligible for insurance coverage.

Unpacking and Getting Settled

You made it. Welcome home! With all the boxes and bare walls, it may not feel like home just yet, but it soon will. You're well on your way to getting settled and having life return to normal. As you unpack boxes, arrange the furniture, and hang the pictures, here are a few things to keep in mind:

- Approach unpacking realistically. It's not necessary (and probably not possible) to unpack and arrange everything on the first day.
- Find your cleaning supplies and do any necessary cleaning.
- Consider your family's basic needs (food, rest, bathing) and unpack accordingly:

    Kitchen: Start with the basics; keep less frequently used items in boxes until you decide your room and storage arrangements.

    Bedrooms: Unpack bedding and set up and make beds.

    Bathroom: Because this tends to be a small room with little space for boxes, unpack the basics early and find a place to store the still-packed boxes until you have a chance to finish.

MAINTAINING NORMALCY . . . STARTING FRESH

During the move and the days following, it's good to keep things feeling as normal as possible. But this can also be a fresh starting point: a time to establish (or reestablish) family rituals and traditions. Beyond the family, this is a time to meet and connect with new neighbors, schoolmates, and your religious or other community.

- Keep regular bedtimes and wake-up times (naps for kids if appropriate).
- If you typically eat dinner together, continue to do this, despite the chaos.
- If you typically have a regular family time—an activity or outing—don't feel bad if you must skip it one week due to move-related chores, but restart this ritual as soon as you can. In fact, your family may appreciate this special time even more in the midst of the upheaval and change.

Rome wasn't built in a day, and neither are friendships. If your move means you have to start over, take heart: persistence and work will pay off over time. Here are a few suggestions for making your first connections with people—individuals and communities of people—in your new area.

- Encourage family members who need encouragement in making new friends.
- Provide opportunities for building friendships from day one. Take a break from unpacking and knock on doors to meet neighbors. (It's not a good idea to start a friendship by asking for help unloading, though!)
- Get involved in activities your family enjoys and make time in your schedule for people, even though moving and resettling is a hectic and busy time.
- Meet and connect with your religious or other community.

DISCOVERING YOUR COMMUNITY

Here you'll find suggestions for getting settled in your new surroundings:

- Be sure every family member gets a feel for the neighborhood and main streets; memorizes your new address; learns (or carries) new home, office, and mobile phone numbers; and knows how to contact local emergency personnel including police, fire, and ambulance.

- Go exploring on foot, bike, mass transit, or by car (turn it into a fun outing) and start learning your way around.
- Locate your local post office and police and fire stations, as well as hospitals and gas stations near your home.
- Scout your new neighborhood for shopping areas.
- Register to vote.
- If you have moved to a new state, visit the Department of Motor Vehicles to obtain your driver's license and register your vehicle (see following).
- If you haven't already done so, transfer insurance policies to an agent in your new community.

MOVING TIP

Draw up a detailed plan of your new home, including scale drawings of each room that show each piece of furniture you plan to take with you. Label furniture and boxes as to where they go in the new home, and have copies of the plan to put in each room there. This will give you at least a chance that most of the work of moving in will only need to be done once.

Useful Phone Numbers

Here is a list of phone numbers that you might find useful as you settle down into your new home and new surroundings.

Animal Control

Alexandria Animal Welfare: (703) 838-4775

Arlington County Animal Welfare: (703) 931-9241

District Animal Control Shelter: (202) 576-6664

Fairfax County Animal Control: (703) 830-3310

Montgomery County Animal Shelter: (301) 217-6999

Prince Georges County Animal Control: (301) 499-8300

Automobiles

American Automobile
   Association (AAA):
   (703) 222-6000

District Department of Motor
   Vehicles: (202) 727-6680

District Booted Vehicles:
   (202) 727-5000

District Abandoned Vehicle
   Removal: (202) 645-4227

Maryland Motor Vehicles
   Administration:
   (301) 948-3177

Virginia Department of Motor
   Vehicles: (703) 761-4655

Health and Medical Care

Emergency: 911

Lead Poisoning Prevention
   Program: (202) 727-9850

Poison Control Center:
   (202) 625-3333

Local Government General Numbers

Alexandria, VA: (703) 838-4000

Arlington County, VA:
   (703) 358-3000

District: (202) 727-1000

Fairfax County, VA:
   (703) 246-2000

Montgomery County, MD:
   (301) 217-6500

Prince George's County, MD:
   (301) 350-9700

Public Schools

Alexandria, VA: (703) 824-6600

Arlington County, VA:
   (703) 358-6000

District: (202) 724-4289

Fairfax County, VA:
   (703) 246-2502

Montgomery County, MD:
   (301) 279-3391

Prince George's County, MD:
   (301) 952-6000

Sanitation

Alexandria Refuse Collection
   and Sanitation:
   (703) 751-5130

Arlington County Refuse
   Removal: (703) 358-6570

District Trash Collection:
   (202) 645-7044

Fairfax County Refuse
   Collection Service:
   (703) 631-1484

Montgomery County Refuse and
   Recycling Collection
   (301) 217-2410

MOVING TIP

Unless company policy prohibits acceptance of gratuities, it is customary to tip each professional mover. $20 is a good amount; you may want to tip more or less based on the service you receive.

If you move yourself, you might also want to give each of your volunteers a gift. Cash or a gift certificate is a nice gesture. Perhaps one of your volunteers is a plant-lover and will cheerfully accept your houseplants as a thank-you gift. It's also a good idea to supply plenty of soft drinks or water and snacks for them!

Transportation

Airports

Baltimore Washington International Airport: (410) 859-7111 or (301) 261-1000

Dulles International Airport: (703) 661-2700

Ronald Reagan National Airport: (703) 419-8000

Buses

Alexandria (VA) DASH: (703) 370-DASH

Fairfax (VA) Connector: (703) 339-7200

MetroBus (Washington, D.C.): (202) 637-7000

Ride On (MD): (301) 217-7433

Subway

Metrorail: (202) 637-7000

Trains

Maryland Rail Commuter (MARC): (800) 325-RAIL

Virginia Railway Express: (703) 497-7777

Utility Emergencies

PEPCO: (202) 833-7500

Virginia Power: (202) 833-1982

Washington Gas: (703) 750-1400

Voter Registration

City of Alexandria:
(703) 838-4050

Arlington County:
(703) 358-3456

District: (202) 727-2525

Fairfax County: (703) 222-0776

Driver's Licensure and Car Registration in Washington, D.C.

The District's Bureau of Motor Vehicles (located at 301 C Street NW—call 202-727-6680 for office hours) is like just about any other big-city motor vehicle office. But many who come from other parts of the country claim that D.C.'s BMV is far worse. So come with lowered expectations and heightened patience.

If you have a valid out-of-state driver's licence, bring it, along with your social security card, or some valid document with your social security number on it, and at least one other original (no photocopies!), valid form of identification that has your legal name and birth date. This could include a passport, school I.D., government I.D. card, or employer I.D.

Residents with a vaild driver's license from out of state have a 30-day grace period to turn in their license. In return, the District waives the written exam. A vision test, though, is mandatory. If you fail to meet the grace period, a written exam is given in the District. You must answer at least 15 of the 20 questions on the exam correctly for a new license (note Maryland and Virginia waive the written exam completely if you have a valid out-of-state license). The cost for a D.C. license is $20.

For car registration: regardless of how new you are to the area, you must have in hand the following: a copy of the car's title, registration (out of state, of course), proof of auto insurance, proof of D.C. residence (since you will need to pay for your registration, a check with your new address on it will serve you doubly well here. Other forms of proof include a signed lease or a utility bill), and your out-of-state plates.

Currently, the D.C. government is considering raising all fees for car registration. At press time, rates were as follows:

$20 for a Washington, D.C., title certificate

$65 registration fee for cars weighing less than 3,500 pounds and $98 for cars weighing more (part of this fee covers the cost of the required auto inspection)

A 6 percent annual excise tax based on the *Blue Book* value of the car weighing less than 3,500 pounds, or 7 percent for cars weighing more

Once you have cleared your paper work, you are required to visit one of the District's auto inspection sites (locations available from BMV and automatic information phone number) within 30 days. It is recommended that you don't wait to visit one of these sites during the last week of the month, when seemingly every procrastinator in town shows up.

Besides your District license and registration, it is also highly recommended that you apply for a residential parking permit for your neighborhood. These allow you to park your car on the street for extended periods where non-residents are limited to two-hours. The cost is $10 per year and in order to receive a sticker (usually applied to the rear bumper), you must present a vaild D.C. car registration, proof of insurance, and proof of residency.

TAKING CARE OF THE
FINANCIAL IMPLICATIONS OF YOUR MOVE

Now that you have arrived, you can take care of some of the financial and tax implications of your move. Here are some things to think about (it's also wise to consult an accountant):

- Some of your moving expenses may be tax-deductible. Prepare for tax filing by collecting receipts from your move. Also contact the Internal Revenue Service to obtain the publication and form you need. Visit *www.irs.gov* or call (800) 829-3676.

- State income tax. If your new state collects income tax, you'll need to file a state income tax form. For help with your relocation-related taxes, visit *www.monstermoving.com* and check out the "Relocation Tax Advisor."

- Other income sources may have tax implications. As you prepare to file, you'll want to consider any other sources of income and whether your new state will tax you on this income. For example, if you are paying federal income tax on an IRA that you rolled over into a Roth IRA and your new state collects income tax, you may also have to pay state income tax on your rollover IRA.

Home at Last

Once the truck is unloaded, the boxes are unpacked, and the pictures are hung, once you're sleeping in a *bed*—instead of on a loose mattress—you'll dream sweet dreams. Tomorrow, with the stress of this move slipping away behind you and the next move not even a faint glimmer on the horizon of your mind, you'll begin to discover the opportunities and savor the possibilities of your new city, new job, new school—your new home.

Getting to Know Your Town

CHAPTER 6

What's Around Town

When it comes to culture, Washington has an over-abundance of riches. Entertainment? The city is a live-wire. Restaurants? More than you could cover in a year of daily dining out. What follows is a list of just about everything you might think of doing for fun, food, and personal enrichment as you begin to venture forth into the nation's capital.

As you peruse the following possibilities, keep in mind that while we've tried to give you a solid overview, this book isn't designed to be a comprehensive city guidebook. Also keep in mind that bars, restaurants, and some smaller entertainment venues are constantly changing hands, closing, and evolving into something different. We've tried to list the more established and well-known sites, but you should also consult more up-to-date sources of information. The ones that almost all residents of the District turn to on a regular basis when they're trying to decide what to do with their free time are:

The Washington Post

www.washingtonpost.com

The most comprehensive weekly source of "what-to-do" information in print and online in the area. The *Post*'s "Weekend" section on Fridays is a must-read, with complete museum, film, nightclub, concert, and restaurant updates. Check out the *Post*'s Web site, too; it's one of the best around.

Washington City Paper

www.washingtoncitypaper.com

Widely available on Thursdays, this is a great source of information on general cultural events, but it's an even better resource than the *Post* when it comes to the more off-beat events in the area, as well as the underground nightclub scene.

CITY FACT

The Washington area's average salary is $36,000. The Washington metro area ranks first in the U.S. in the number of families with income exceeding $100,000.

The Washingtonian

www.washingtonian.com

This magazine is a monthly, but its listings are comprehensive, especially for mainstream arts, exhibits, and films. The restaurant reviews are a tremendous resource, especially online, where all the reviews published in the past few years are accessible. The magazine is also a good way to keep track of upcoming social events, such as big fund-raising dinners. And you might check out the popular personal ads if you're looking for Mr. or Ms. Right.

TicketMaster remains the key resource for tickets to almost all events in and around the city. This is especially true for concerts, big museum exhibits, and sporting events. Keep this in mind when planning your weekends. Call (202) 432-SEAT or (800) 551-SEAT.

Amusement Parks

There are two major amusement parks within easy driving distance of Washington, D.C.

King's Dominion

(804) 876-5000

Located south of Washington down I-95, about a 90- to 120-minute drive, the park features 10 roller coasters with names such as "The Blast," "The Anaconda," and "The Rebel Yell." Included in your entrance fee is admission to a water park with a wave pool and a water-powered fun house. For younger kids, there are shows and attractions featuring popular Nickelodeon TV characters. The park is open daily through September 6; weekends September 11 through October 3. The park opens at 10 A.M. on Saturdays, at 10:30 all other days; closing times range from 8 to 10 P.M. Call to verify hours. Admission: $33.99, $28.99 for seniors, $24.99 for children under age six. Two-day tickets are available.

Six Flags America

Largo, MD
(301) 249-1500

About 30 minutes north of Washington in Largo, Maryland, this theme park, formerly known as Adventure World, opened in the summer of 1999. It features all of the standard amusement park fare: roller coasters, kiddie rides, gift shops, and restaurants. There are also folks dressed up as popular Warner Bros. and DC Comics characters. The park is open daily through September 6. It opens at 10:30 A.M. most days; closing times range from 6 to 10 P.M. The water park closes at 7 P.M. on Sundays. Call to verify hours. Admission: $29.99, $19.99 for seniors, $14.99 for children.

Athletic Clubs and Gyms

Need to work up a sweat that isn't caused by the summer humidity or a grilling before a congressional committee? D.C. has plenty of health clubs. Most are associated with national firms, so it may be fairly easy to transfer a membership you already have. Clubs listed are in Washington, D.C., unless otherwise noted.

Bally's Total Fitness Centers
(800) 695-8111

Numerous locations in the area, call for information.

Chevy Chase Athletic Club
5454 Wisconsin Avenue
(301) 656-8834

Fitness Company at Georgetown
1010 Wisconsin Avenue NW
(202) 625-9100

Results
17th and U Streets NW
(202) 518-0001

Sport and Health Clubs
(703) 556-6550

A number of locations in the area, call for information.

Sport Fit
(202) 887-0760

Numerous locations in the area, call for information.

Washington Sports Club
(202) 332-0100

Numerous locations in the area, call for information.

YMCA
1701 Rhode Island Avenue NW
(202) 232-6700

One of the largest recreational facilities in the area, it's very popular with professionals who can walk here from just about any place downtown.

YWCA Fitness Center
624 9th Street NW
(202) 626-0710

Bars and Nightclubs

Washington has an eclectic mix of bars and nightclubs that should satisfy every taste. From beer halls to retro discos, D.C. knows how to keep its workaholic congressional staffers and just-plain slackers happy. Here's an overview of some of the better-known nightclubs and discos in the District, followed by a list, by neighborhood, of the more popular bars, pubs, and hangouts.

NIGHTCLUBS AND DISCOS

Chief Ike's Mambo Room

1725 Columbia Road NW
(202) 332-2211

It's one of Washington's longstanding nightclubs for dancing and partying the night away. An eclectic mix of regulars hang out at this Adams Morgan spot, which offers a heavy dose of African, Caribbean, and Latin sounds from the speaker system. Patrons generally fall into the 25 to 40 age group; the male-female ratio runs about 2 to 1. Call ahead for live entertainment schedules. Cover charge: $5 on Friday and Saturday nights.

Club Zei

1415 Zei Alley NW
(202) 842-2445

www.zeiclub.com

This classic disco is one of the more popular party places in downtown. It draws young professionals ages 25 to 35; men invariably outnumber women by more than 2 to 1. Thursday is college night; there's live jazz every Friday from 6 to 10 P.M., and women are admitted free on Fridays before 11 P.M.; Saturday is international night. Cover: $10.

MOVING TIP

Pack a "Must Have" box that includes tools to put together furniture, scissors, scotch tape, a flashlight, your address book, and important papers.

Madam's Organ

2003 18th Street NW
(202) 667-5370

Another Adams Morgan stalwart. If you can't find the place, just look for the most outrageous wall mural on the side of a building in all of Washington. The name of the night club says it all. It caters to a crowd of young professionals who want to let their hair down as well as local Adams Morgan residents who treat it as a regular hangout. Good music, stiff drinks, and live entertainment are the draws here. The age range is about 25 to 40, with a male-to-female ratio of about 2 to 1. No cover.

9:30 Club

815 V Street, NW
(202) 393-0930

One Washington's most established nightclubs, it regularly features live music. Lately, the scene has been mostly alternative rock, with a heavy dose of grungers and moshers. The audience falls into the 21 to 30 age group, with an even ratio of men to women. It's a great dance and music scene. The bar in the back is slightly more accessible and quieter, but only by comparison. There's no cover in the back room; cover in the downstairs lounge varies, depending on acts. Call ahead.

Tracks

1111 First Street SE
(202) 488-3320

www.tracks2000.com

One of the largest dance joints in the city, it has three dance floors and eight bars. The crowd is predominantly gay, but the sheer size of the place means there is room for all, and there is usually a pretty diverse mix. Still, the male-to-female ratio runs about 4 to 1. The age range is about 21 to 35, perhaps older. Open Thursday through Sunday; Thursday night is college night. Cover: $5 to $10.

Zanzibar

700 Water Street SW
(202) 554-9100

One of the most diverse and interesting dance clubs in the area. An eclectic mix of African, South American, and Caribbean music makes for a great time whether you want to hit the dance floor or just drink and socialize. The man-woman ratio is about 3 to 1, with ages ranging from 21 to 35. Cover: $10 after 7 P.M. on Friday; $10 after 9 P.M. on Saturday.

BARS

Adams Morgan and U Street

Adams Morgan has long been a D.C. social center, but it has also become a big hassle thanks to traffic and packed bars, restaurants, and clubs. As a result, U Street has taken some of the runoff from the Adams Morgan area. Here are a few places in both neighborhoods to consider for a night out.

The Big Hunt

1345 Connecticut Avenue NW
(202) 785-2333

"The Hunt" isn't in Adams Morgan—it's just below Dupont Circle—but it should be. This is a great bar to spend a few hours on a weekend before moving on to one of the other clubs in the area or catching a cab for the five-minute ride to Adams Morgan.

Café Latrec

2439 18th Street NW

One of Adams Morgan's best-known watering holes—people have been known to dance on the bar when the late-evening crowd really gets going.

Cities

2424 18th Street NW
(202) 328-7194

A great bar and restaurant and a stylish hangout. The menu is eclectic, with a heavy dose of Middle Eastern fare. This is one of the best "date" spots in the city.

CITY FACT

There are 56 lawyers in Washington for every 1,000 people. And almost none of them know how to write a will.

Fox & Hounds Lounge

1533 17th Street NW
(202) 232-6307

Nothing fancy here. Just a good bar with lots of character and a long drinking tradition.

Mille and Al's

2440 18th Street
(202) 387-8131

Miss your college campus frat house with its beer-stained floors, smoky rooms, and ever-present scent of alcohol? Well you'll feel at home at this Adams Morgan standard-bearer, one of the few classic neighborhood dives left in town.

Perry's

1811 Columbia Road NW
(202) 234-6218

One of the great D.C. bar-restaurant institutions, made famous for its singles scene and its rooftop revelers during the spring and summer months. A great bar to spend time with friends on the make, it's also one of the District's great brunch spots for the more staid or settled. It serves good food at comparatively moderate prices.

Republic Gardens

1355 U Street NW
(202) 232-2710

Well known as a hangout with a distinctly South of the Border attitude. The fare is Tex Mex, as are the drinks. A great place to socialize with friends from the office or from the neighborhood—or to make friends over stiff margaritas or Dos Equis.

Stetson's

1610 U Street
(202) 667-6295

Another solid, old-time hangout for the locals. No hanging ferns, nouvelle cuisine here; it's strictly a no-frills shot-and-a-beer joint.

Toledo Lounge

2435 18th Street NW
(202) 986-5416

Rumor has it this bar was started by two sisters from Toledo. So what? A great bar is a great bar. This one is that in spades.

TomTom

2333 18th Street NW
(202) 588-1300.

One of the hipper bar/restaurants in the area, with good Italian food and wine for less than $10 a bottle. It becomes more of nightclub scene after 9 P.M.

U-topia

1418 U Street
(202) 483-7669

A bar and restaurant that takes on a hipper shade of perfection. A lively nightclub scene after 9 P.M. on weekends.

Georgetown

Georgetown is all about bars and restaurants. All of the bars listed below also feature food—although that's not why most people come here on weekends. From Thursday night through Sunday early-mornings, this is the other key singles scene in Washington, D.C., though it is decidedly straight and far less diverse than the Adams Morgan scene. As in the nightclubs and discos, male-to-female ratios tend to be about 2 to 1, with the ages ranging from 18 to 35.

Champions

1206 Wisconsin Avenue
(202) 965-4005

A sports bar with a singles twist; it's a rocking place on weekends.

Clyde's

3236 M Street
(202) 333-9180

A bit more low-key compared to some of the other bars in the area. Better food, too.

Garrett's

3003 M Street
(202) 333-8282

A great college and young professional hangout, with a dining room for burgers on the first floor and a beer-hall atmosphere upstairs.

The Guards

2915 M Street
(202) 965-2350

Another low-key Georgetown hangout, it's a bit more upscale than Clyde's, with more of a clubby feel. If you are 35, on a date, and looking to stop for a nightcap, this is the place to go.

J. Paul's

3218 M Street
(202) 333-3450

A Clyde's knockoff, but very popular, especially on Friday nights.

Martin's Tavern

1264 Wisconsin Avenue
(202) 333-7370

One of the older establishments in Georgetown. Family owned and operated, it offers a bar with character and good food at reasonable prices compared to other places in the area.

Nathan's

3150 M Street
(202) 338-2000

Many years ago there actually was a Nathan who ran this bar and restaurant at the corner of M and Wisconsin. Today that character is gone, but the restaurant-bar is just as lively as ever.

Third Edition

1218 Wisconsin Avenue
(202) 333-3700

Another popular hangout for the college students and young professional on weekend nights.

The Tombs

1226 36th Street
(202) 337-6668

Near the Georgetown University campus, this is more bar than restaurant, but is located near the well-known 1789 restaurant.

Ireland

Yes, Ireland. One of Washington's great cultural quirks is its abundance of Irish bars, with more sprouting up like so many shamrocks. Here are some of the more established as well as ones with a bit of real Irish charm and character.

The Dubliner
4 F Street
(202) 737-3773

The best Irish pub, bar none, in Washington. Good food, good Irish music almost every night of the week, and the best Guinness pourers in town.

Ireland's Four Provinces
3412 Connecticut Avenue
(202) 244-0860

A great neighborhood hangout near the zoo. It's perfect for those dads or moms who need a break after the family outing.

Kelly's Irish Times
14 F Street
(202) 543-5433

Next door to The Dubliner, it's a bigger, louder, rowdier place.

Murphy's
2609 24th Street
(202) 462-7171

A traditional Irish pub with burgers and fish and chips on the menu and Guinness on tap at the bar.

Cinemas

Here is a rundown of District movie theaters. Check the *Washington Post* for current listings.

AMC Union Station
9 Union Station
(202) 998-4262

American Film Institute
John F. Kennedy Center for the Performing Arts
F Street and New Hampshire Avenue NW
(202) 785-4600

Cineplex Odeon Avalon
1¹/₂ blocks south of Chevy Chase Circle
(202) 966-260

Cineplex Odeon Cinema
Near Friendship Heights Metro stop
(202) 966-7248

Cineplex Odeon Dupont Circle 5
1350 19th Street NW
(202) 872-9555

Cineplex Odeon Foundry
1055 Thomas Jefferson Street NW
(202) 333-8613

Cineplex Odeon Inner Circle
2301 M Street NW
(202) 333-3456

Cineplex Odeon Janus 3
1660 Connecticut Avenue NW
(202) 265-9545

Cineplex Odeon Outer Circle
4849 Wisconsin Avenue NW
(202) 244-3116

Cineplex Odeon Tenley
4200 Wisconsin Avenue NW
(202) 363-4340

Cineplex Odeon Uptown
3426 Connecticut Avenue NW
(202) 966-5400

Cineplex Odeon Wisconsin Avenue Cinemas
4000 Wisconsin Avenue NW
(202) 244-0880

Langley IMAX Theater
National Air and Space Museum
6th and Independence Avenue SW
(202) 357-1686

Eugene and Agnes E. Meyer Auditorium
Freer Gallery of Art
12th Street and Independence Avenue SW
(202) 357-3200

Motion Picture Association of America
1600 I Street NW
(202) 293-1966

National Archives Theater
Eighth Street and Pennsylvania Avenue NW
(202) 501-5000

National Gallery of Art East Building Auditorium
Fourth Street at Constitution Avenue NE
(202) 842-6799

National Portrait Gallery Theater
F and 8th Streets NW
(202) 357-2700

Mary Pickford Theater
Library of Congress
1st Street and Independence Avenue SE
(202) 707-5677

Concert Halls

Following are the area's main facilities for musical events such as rock concerts. The venues are in Washington, D.C., unless otherwise noted.

Carter Barron Amphitheater
4850 Colorado Avenue NW
(202) 426-6837

John F. Kennedy Center for the Performing Arts
F Street and New Hampshire Avenue NW
(202) 467-4600

Lisner Auditorium
21 St and H Streets NW
(202) 994-6800

Merriweather Post Pavilion
Located off of I-95
Columbia, MD
(301) 982-1800

USAir Arena
1 North Harry S. Truman Drive
Landover, MD
(301) 350-3400

MOVING TIP

In anticipation of your move, save your newspapers to use in packing smaller items that can be placed in the moving boxes with larger items. This fills in what would normally be unused space in the boxes.

Wolf Trap and The Barns at Wolf Trap
1624 Wolf Trap Road
Vienna, VA
(703) 255-1900

Major Memorial Sites and Locations

Many of the most popular monuments that are synonymous with Washington are centrally located and withing walking distance of one another along the Mall. Addresses for them, as well as others in the D.C. area follow.

Arlington National Cemetery
Memorial Drive (across the Memorial Bridge near the Lincoln Memorial)
Arlington, VA
(703) 692-0931

Jefferson Memorial
15th Street (on the Tidal Basin) SW
Washington, DC
(202) 426-6822

Lincoln Memorial
23rd Street NW (between Constitution and Independence Avenues)
(202) 426-6895

U.S. Capitol
East end of the National Mall
(202) 225-6827

Vietnam Veteran's Memorial
23rd Street and Constitution Avenue NW
(202) 634-1568

Museums/Galleries

Washington has many museums; here is a list of some of the most popular. For information on private art galleries, which are not included in this list, check out *The Washingtonian*, which lists current gallery exhibits. Where admission is not noted, there are "recommended" fees of varying levels. Museums are in Washington, D.C., unless otherwise noted.

Anacostia Museum
1901 Fort Place SE
(202) 287-3369

A black-history museum with a focus on the African-American experience in Washington. Admission: $5.

Arts and Industries Building
900 Jefferson Drive SW
(202) 357-4500

Exhibits focus on the wonders of the Industrial Age, which made America what it is today. Free.

Corcoran Gallery of Art

17th Street and New York Avenue NW
(202) 638-3211

The collection includes European art of the 17th through the 20th centuries and American works from the 18th through the 20th centuries. Offers a number of art classes.

Dolls' House and Toy Museum

5236 44th Street NW
(202) 244-0024

In a tiny house is a museum dedicated to some of the most enjoyable things from childhood. Space is small, but kids of all ages will enjoy this brief sojourn down memory lane. Admission: $4 adults, $2 for children under age 12.

Dumbarton Oaks

1703 32nd Street NW
(202) 338-8278

In the heart of Georgetown, this art museum features Byzantine and Classical works against the backdrop of one of Washington's most beautiful gardens.

Freer Gallery of Art

Jefferson Drive at 12th Street SW
(202) 357-2700

One of the newer Smithsonian museums, it features Asian and Near Eastern art. Free.

Goddard Space Flight Center

Visitor Center, Soil Conservation Road
Greenbelt, MD
(301) 286-8981

Recounts and memorializes America's push for supremecy in space. Free.

Hirschhorn Museum and Sculpture Garden

8th Street and Independence Avenue SW
(202) 357-2700

Modern art of the 19th and 20th centuries. Also sculptures, both indoors and out. Free.

Museum of American History

14th Street and Constitution Avenue NW
(202) 357-2700

One of the great museums in the city, it covers everything from early U.S. history to recent American pop culture. Popular exhibits include Archie Bunker's chair from the TV show "All in the Family" and the set of the TV show "M*A*S*H." Free.

National Air and Space Museum
6th Street and Independence Avenue SW
(202) 357-2700

One of the most popular museums in all of Washington. Also features an IMAX movie theater. Museum free; admission for movies.

CITY
FACT

The *Washington Times* is politically conservative in content, and is owned by the Reverend Sun Muong Moon and the Unification Church. The *Washington Post* is liberal in content and owned by the prominent Graham family. While the *Washington Post* has superior circulation and is a generally superior paper, some people think the *Times* has better coverage of the city than its competitor.

National Gallery of Art—East Wing
4th Street and Constitution Avenue NW
(202) 737-4215

Features 20th-century art and rotating exhibits from all over the world. Free.

National Gallery of Art—West Wing
6th Street and Constitution Avenue NW
(202) 737-4215

European and American art works from the 13th through 19th centuries. Free.

National Museum of African Art
950 Independence Avenue SW
(202) 357-2700

Another new Smithsonian facility, it focuses on African and African-American art. Free.

National Museum of American Art
8th and G Streets NW
(202) 357-2700

America's oldest art collection. Free.

National Museum of Natural History
10th Street and Constitution Avenue NW
(202) 357-2700

This natural science museum is especially popular with kids, thanks to its fossils, dinosaur bones, and insect zoo. Free.

National Museum of Women in Arts
1250 New York Avenue NW
(202) 783-5000

The name says it all. Free, but donations are requested.

National Portrait Gallery
8th and F Streets NW
(202) 357-2700

Portraits and sculptures of American and European descent. Free.

Newseum
1101 Wilson Boulevard
Arlington, VA
(888) 639-7386

This museum covers the news media, past and present. Great interactive exhibits are fun for the kids. Free.

Phillips Collection
1600 21st Street NW
(202) 387-2151

A private collection best known for its French Impressionist, Post-Impressionist, and American Modernist works. Admission: $10.

Renwick Gallery
17th Street and Pennsylvania Avenue NW
(202) 357-2700

Collection of American crafts, paintings, and porcelains. Free.

Arthur M. Sackler Gallery
1050 Independence Avenue SW
(202) 357-2700

Asian art. Free.

Trolley Museum
Northwest Branch Regional Park Bonifant Road, between Layhill Road and New Hampshire Avenue
Wheaton, MD
(301) 384-6088

A musuem dedicated to preserving the heritage of a form of transportation that for the most part no longer exists. Exhibits include many antique trolleys.

U.S. Holocaust Memorial Museum
100 Raoul Wallenberg Place SW (just off 14th Street and Independence Avenue)
(202) 488-0400

As of this writing, it remains the most popular museum in Washington, and also one of the hardest to get into. Even though the exhibits are free, you still need a ticket—and those can be hard to come by unless you plan ahead. Advance tickets are available through TicketMaster, (202) 432-SEAT. A limited number of same-day tickets are available at the museum.

Playhouses/Theaters

Washington has a rich tradition of theater. Here is a current catalogue of the area's professional theater companies as well as some amateur troupes, should you decide to stretch that dream of being an actor a bit further. Included in the following list are some local dinner-theaters. The theaters listed are in Washington, D.C., unless otherwise noted.

PROFESSIONAL

Arena Stage
6th and Maine Streets SW
(202) 488-3300

Ford's Theatre
511 10th Street NW
(202) 638-2941

GALA Hispanic Theater
1625 Park Road NW
(202) 234-7174

John F. Kennedy Center for the Performing Arts
F Street and New Hampshire Avenue NW
(202) 467-4600

The center is the home to the Eisenhower Theater, the Opera House, the Terrace Theater, and the Theater Lab.

National Theater
1321 Pennsylvania Avenue NW
(202) 628-6161

Round House Theatre
12210 Bushey Drive
Silver Spring, MD
(301) 933-9530

Shakespeare Theatre at the Lansburgh
450 7th Street NW
(202) 393-2700

Signature Theatre
3806 South Four Mile Run Drive
Arlington, VA
(703) 820-9771

Source Theatre Company
1835 14th Street NW
(202) 462-1073

Stage Guild
Carroll Hall
924 G Street NW
(202) 529-2084

Studio Theatre
1333 P Street NW
(202) 332-3300

Warner Theatre
13th and E Streets NW
(202) 783-4000

Woolly Mammoth Theatre
1401 Church Street NW
(202) 393-3939

AMATEUR/COMMUNITY THEATER

Actors' Theatre of Washington
(202) 667-5393

Chamber Theatre
(301) 657-2465

Church Street Theater
(301) 738-7073

Clark Street Playhouse
(703) 418-4808

Dominion Stage
(703) 683-0502

Encore Theatre Company of Washington, D.C.
(202) 298-0811

Georgetown Theatre Company
(703) 578-4710

Horizons Theater
(703) 243-8550

INTERACT Theatre Company
(703) 848-2632

Metropolitan Theatrical Company
(301) 530-5211

MetroStage
(703) 548-9044

No Curtain Theatre
(202) 966-3670

Potomac Community Theatre
(301) 299-6803

Prince Georges Publick Playhouse
(301) 277-1710

Reston Community Center Theatre
(703) 476-4500

SCENA Theatre
(703) 549-0002

Smallbeer Theatre Company
(301) 277-8117

Theater J
(202) 883-9665

Theatre Conspiracy
(202) 986-6184

Trumpet Vine Theatre Company
(301) 961-8537

Washington Shakespeare Company
(703) 418-4808

CHILDREN'S THEATER

Adventure Theater
Glen Echo Park
7300 MacArthur Boulevard
Bethesda, MD
(301) 320-5331

Children's Theater of Arlington
2700 South Lang Street
Arlington, VA
(703) 548-1154

Discovery Theatre
Smithsonian Museum of Arts and Industries
900 Jefferson Drive SW
(202) 357-1500

Puppet Company Playhouse
Glen Echo Park
7300 MacArthur Boulevard
Bethesda, MD
(301) 320-6668

DINNER THEATER

Burn Brae
U.S. 29 at Blackburn Road
Burtonsville, MD
(301) 384-5800

Keynote
5 Willowdale Drive
Frederick, MD
(800) 722-7262

Lazy Susan
U.S. 1 at Furnace Road
Woodbridge, VA
(703) 550-7384

West End
4615 Duke Street
Alexandria, VA
(703) 370-2500

Music

As with theater, there are a number of opportunities to enjoy both professional and amateur musical performances in the Washington area. There are also a number of thriving jazz and blues clubs in town. Here's a compilation.

CITY FACT

Almost 70 percent of the residents of Washington, D.C., are African American.

OPERA—PROFESSIONAL

Washington Opera at the Kennedy Center
Opera House, John F. Kennedy Center for the Performing Arts
F Street and New Hampshire Avenue NW
(202) 416-7800; (800) 87-OPERA

OPERA—COMMUNITY

Maryland State Opera Company
(301) 384-4428

Opera Theatre of Northern Virginia
(703) 528-1433

Opera Camerata of Washington
(202) 663-9018

CHORUSES—COMMUNITY

Alexandria Choral Society
(703) 548-4734

Alexandria Harmonizers Barbershop Chorus
(703) 836-0969

Cathedral Choral Society
(202) 537-8980

Choral Arts Society of Washington
(202) 244-3669

Fairfax Choral Society
(703) 642-0862

Gay Men's Chorus
(202) 338-SING

Lesbian and Gay Chorus of Washington
(202) 546-1549

Mormon Choir of Washington
(301) 942-0103

Oratorio Society of Washington
(202) 342-6221

Washington Men's Camerata
(202) 265-8804

Washington Women's Chorus
(202) 244-5925

SYMPHONY ORCHESTRAS—PROFESSIONAL

National Symphony Orchestra
John F. Kennedy Center for the Performing Arts
F Street and New Hampshire Avenue NW
(202) 467-4600

Wolf Trap
1624 Trap Road
Vienna, VA
(703) 255-1868

COMMUNITY ORCHESTRAS

Alexandria Symphony
(703) 845-8005

Arlington Symphony Orchestra
(703) 528-1817

Fairfax Symphony Orchestra
(703) 642-7200

MD—Atlantic Chamber Orchestra
(202) 483-9320

Mount Vernon Orchestra
(703) 799-8229

National Chamber Orchestra
(301) 762-8580

New Columbia Swing Orchestra
(703) 524-4635

Washington Chamber Symphony
(202) 452-1321

JAZZ/BLUES

Blues Alley
1073 Wisconsin Avenue NW
(202) 337-4141

Busara Club
2340 Wisconsin Avenue NW
(202) 337-2340

City Blues Cafe
2651 Connecticut Avenue NW
(202) 232-2300

New Vegas Lounge
1415 P Street NW
(202) 483-3971

Washington Civic Orchestra
(202) 857-0970

MOVING TIP

Make sure the "Must Have" box doesn't end up with all the other boxes, which would defeat the purpose.

One Step Down
2517 Pennsylvania Avenue NW
(202) 331-8863

State of the Union
1357 U Street NW
(202) 588-8810

Takoma Station Tavern
6914 4th Street NW
(202) 829-1999

Video Rentals

If you're not going out, then unpack the VCR first and get to know your local video rental store. Here are a few of the larger ones in D.C.

Blockbuster Video
1751 Columbia Road NW
(202) 462-0100

1639 P Street NW
(202) 232-2682

2332 Wisconsin Avenue NW
(202) 625-6200

6428 Georgia Avenue NW
(202) 722-4700

3519 Connecticut Avenue NW
(202) 363-9500

400 8th Street SE
(202) 546-4044

Hollywood Video
4520 40th Street NW
(202) 364-6490

CITY FACT

While very little about Washington's government works well, traffic-ticket writers are as efficient as they come. They are also swift with the "boot," that locking mechanism that prevents cars from driving off. If you have five unpaid parking tickets, you'll get the boot.

In & Out Video
61 K Street SE
(202) 554-3669

Potomac Video
5185 MacArthur Boulevard NW
(202) 244-8270

4301 Connecticut Avenue NW
(202) 244-0223

4828 MacArthur Boulevard NW
(202) 333-0985

3408 Idaho Avenue NW
(202) 362-4146

3418 Connecticut Avenue NW
(202) 362-6695

5538 Connecticut Avenue NW
(202) 362-5018

Royalle Video
3208 O Street NW
(202) 298-7726

Tapeheadz Video Dupont Circle
1709 17th Street NW
(202) 234-5590

Video Corner
2311 Calvert Street NW
(202) 232-1599

Video Entertainment
905 H Street NE
(202) 547-6400

Video King
1845 Columbia Road NW
(202) 483-8801

Video Plus
3222 North Street NW
(202) 298-8470

Video Unlimited of Georgetown
1653 Wisconsin Avenue NW
(202) 342-1106

Video Warehouse
4300 Connecticut Avenue NW
(202) 237-0700

Washington Video
2012 South Street NW
(202) 265-1141

1647 Wisconsin Avenue NW
(202) 342-0574

401 M Street SW
(202) 646-0830

Restaurants

Washington is a town that likes to dine out. Often times it's on an expense account. But there are plenty of restaurants in the city that thrive on the little guy and gal who are looking for a tasty but reasonably priced meal or for a dining adventure.

There are plenty of dining guides and restaurant listings to help you decide where to eat out. Here we're listing some of the more affordable eateries in Washington, D.C., along with some of the city's most special restaurants. Unless otherwise noted by a (★) symbol, a meal should not cost more than $20. Restaurants designated with a (★) symbol are highly rated and of exceptional value or quality.

For more detailed information about the restaurants listed here, and the many more that are in Washington, we recommend the *Washington Post* and its online edition (*www.washingtonpost.com*) and the *Washingtonian* magazine and Web site (*www.washington-ian.com*). Both offer restaurant reviews as well as the latest news on the local restaurant scene. Bon appétit!

America Restaurant

Union Station
50 Massachusetts Avenue NE
(202) 682-9555

A huge menu that includes regionally well-known meals from all over the country, from steak, meatloaf, and ribs to many kinds of fish.

Archibald's

1520 K Street NW
(202) 638-5112

Nothing fancy, just sandwiches and burgers.

Armand's Chicago Pizzeria

226 Massachusetts Avenue NE
(202) 547-6600

One of Washington's most popular deep-dish, Chicago-style pizza joints.

B. Smith's ★

Union Station
50 Massachusetts Avenue NE
(202) 289-6188

The Washington cousin of this well-known New York restaurant. It features new Southern cuisine.

Bertolini's Authentic Trattoria

801 Pennsylvania Avenue NW
(202) 638-2140

Italian food served in comfortable surroundings.

Big Hunt

1345 Connecticut Avenue NW
(202) 785-2333

Burgers and beers are always on tap.

Bistro Bis ★

Bellevue Hotel
15 E Street NW
(202) 638-0900

One of the new French restaurants in the city and one of the best. Bistro fare served in high-end surroundings.

Bistro Francais

3128 M Street NW
(202) 338-3830

An old-line French bistro in the heart of Georgetown.

Blackie's House of Beef ★

1217 22nd Street NW
(202) 333-1100

Want a slab of prime rib or a hunk of steak and mid-range prices? This may be the spot.

Brickskeller Inn

1523 22nd Street NW
(202) 293-1885

More than 100 different kind of beers to pick from and burgers to go along with them.

Cafe Mozart

1331 H Street NW
(202) 347-5732

One of the few German restaurants in the city.

Cafe On M

2350 M Street NW
(202) 429-0100

Sandwiches and traditional American fare.

The Capital Grille ★

601 Pennsylvania Avenue NW
(202) 737-6200

Steak, steak, and more steak at one of the premier power lunch spots in town. Call ahead for reservations.

Capitol City Brewing Co.

1100 New York Avenue NW
(202) 628-2222

One of Washington's more popular brew pubs.

Chadwicks—Friendship Heights

5247 Wisconsin Avenue NW
(202) 362-8040

Chadwicks—Georgetown

3205 K Street NW
(202) 333-2565

Burgers and beer at both locations.

Ciao Baby Cucina

1736 L Street NW
(202) 331-1500

Casual Italian fare.

Citronelle ★

The Latham Hotel
3000 M Street NW
(202) 625-2150

One of the most expensive and best nouveau French restaurants in America.

Clyde's of Georgetown

3236 M Street NW
(202) 333-9180

One of Washington's most popular burger and beer joints at night and brunch spots on weekends.

Comedy Cafe

1520 K Street NW
(202) 638-5653

Comedy club serves up laughs and pub food in equal quantities.

Dancing Crab

4611 Wisconsin Avenue NW
(202) 244-1882

Bring an appetite and be prepared to get your hands dirty working through steamed and spiced crabs and shrimp.

Dar Es Salam

3056 M Street NW
(202) 337-6680

Middle Eastern fare in an elegantly casual venue.

Dixie Grill

518 10th Street NW
(202) 628-4800

Down home diner food.

MOVING TIP

Put heavier items (books, kitchen equipment) in smaller boxes and make sure they are packed last and unloaded first. It will make the unloading job seem that much easier.

The Dubliner Pub

Phoenix Park Hotel
520 North Capitol Street NW
(202) 737-3773; (800) 824-5419

Pub food on higher scale. Burgers and beers, as well as a top-flight sheperd's pie, lamb chops, and stew for dinner.

El Bodegon

1637 R Street NW
(202) 667-1710

Spanish with a flare.

Fanatics Sports Bar & Grill

1520 K Street NW
(202) 638-6800

Sports bar with all the side orders you'd want.

Felix Restaurant & Lounge

2406 18th Street NW
(202) 483-3549

One of the best big band/swing bands in town, the Eric Felten Orchestra, performs here regularly. Martinis and bistro fare.

Filomena Ristorante ★

1063 Wisconsin Avenue NW
(202) 338-8800

Upscale Italian.

Franklyn's Coffeehouse/Cafe

2000 18th Street NW
(202) 319-1800

Traditional coffeehouse with breakfast and light lunch fare.

Fran O'Brien's Steak House

Capital Hilton
1001 16th Street NW
(202) 783-2599

An upscale sports bar with fine steaks and chops.

Galileo ★
1110 21st Street NW
(202) 293-7191

This Italian restaurant is consistently one of the highest-rated restaurants in the city.

Garden Terrace ★
Four Seasons Hotel
2800 Pennsylvania Avenue NW
(202) 342-0444

The in-house dining room for one of Washington's nicest hotels.

Garrett's
3003 M Street NW
(202) 333-1033

More of a drinking establishment than a restaurant, but burgers and pub fare are always on the menu.

Georgetown Seafood Grill ★
3063 M Street NW
(202) 333-7038

Top flight seafood, from the regional favorites like crabs and oysters to fish from around the world.

Georgia Brown's ★
950 15th Street NW
(202) 393-4499

Upscale southern cuisine in casual setting. Great fried chicken. A favorite of the Clinton White House.

Fleet Street Bar
1101 17th Street NW
(202) 296-8075

New bar and burger joint in downtown, formerly the Ha'Penny Lion.

Hard Rock Cafe
999 E Street NW
(202) 737-7625

The national chain's Washington outlet.

Hogate's
800 Water Street SW
(202) 484-6300; (800) 424-9169

An old-line Washington seafood restaurant. Popular with tourists and locals alike on the waterfront.

Hunan Chinatown
624 H Street NW
(202) 783-5858

One of the few old-time Chinese restaurants in Chinatown.

I Matti Trattoria
2436 18th Street NW
(202) 462-8844

Casual Italian.

Il Radicchio

1211 Wisconsin Avenue NW
(202) 337-2627

1509 17th Street NW
(202) 986-2627

Operated by the owner of the upscale Galileo, these Italian trattoria's are casual, affordable, and very popular.

J. Paul's

3218 M Street NW
(202) 333-3450

Similar in style and substance to other restaurant bars in Georgetown, like Clyde's.

Japan Inn ★

1715 Wisconsin Avenue NW
(202) 337-3400

Upscale Japanese fare.

Jockey Club ★

Fairfax Hotel, Washington, D.C.
2100 Massachusetts Avenue NW
(202) 293-2100; (800) 241-3333

One of the best known hotel restaurants, a hangout for the Washington elite, and the restaurant where Al Gore dined as a child when his family lived in the hotel.

Kinkead's ★

2000 Pennsylvania Avenue NW
(202) 296-7700

One of Washington's best and most popular restaurants. Specializes in seafood. A perfect restaurant for a special occasion.

La Chaumiere ★

2813 M Street NW
(202) 338-1784

One of the last traditional, old-line Washington French restaurants.

La Colline ★

400 North Capitol Street NW
(202) 737-0400

Another old-line Washington French restaurant. Popular with Capitol Hill's most influential personalities.

La Fonda Restaurant

1639 R Street NW
(202) 232-6965

Great Spanish food.

Le Rivage

1000 Water Street SW
(202) 488-8111

Popular French nouveau dining spot.

Legal Sea Foods ★
2020 K Street NW
(202) 496-1111

The Washington outlet to this legendary Boston seafood restaurant.

Lucky U Bar
1221 Connecticut Avenue NW
(202) 466-2336

More bar than restaurant. Burgers and appetizers are on the menu.

Lulu's New Orleans Cafe
1217 22nd Street NW
(202) 861-5858; (800) 538-9828

Want the flavors of the Big Easy? This is the place.

Martin's Tavern
1264 Wisconsin Avenue NW
(202) 333-7370

An old-time Georgetown bar and restaurant. A great brunch spot.

Miss Saigon Vietnamese Cuisine
1847 Columbia Road NW
(202) 667-1900

The name says it all.

The Monocle on Capitol Hill ★
107 D Street NE
(202) 546-4488

Traditional American fare in one of the power-lunch spots on The Hill.

Morrison-Clark Inn ★
11th and Massachusetts Avenue NW
(202) 898-1200; (800) 332-7898

One of Washington's most popular spots for modern American cooking.

Morton's of Chicago ★
3251 Prospect Street NW
(202) 342-6258

Besides the Palm, Washington's best-known steak and power spot.

Murphy's
2609 24th Street NW
(202) 462-7171

An Irish pub with burgers and assorted sandwiches.

Notte Luna
809 15th Street NW
(202) 408-9500

Casual Italian fare.

The Occidental Grill ★

1475 Pennsylvania Avenue NW
(202) 783-1475

A historic restaurant near the White House. Great for a meal or an after-work cocktail.

Old Ebbitt Grill

675 15th Street NW
(202) 347-4801

A power breakfast and lunch spot across the street from the White House and Treasury building.

Old Glory Barbecue

3139 M Street NW
(202) 337-3406

A comparatively new addition to the BBQ scene in Washington.

Palm Restaurant ★

1225 19th Street NW
(202) 293-9091

The premier power lunch and dinner spot in all of Washington. Steaks, lobsters, and Italian food are a must.

Paolo's ★

1305 Wisconsin Avenue NW
(202) 333-7353

Popular, modern Italian spot that is well-known as much for its social scene as its food.

Papa Razzi

1064-66 Wisconsin Avenue NW
(202) 298-8000

Casual Italian.

Pesce Fish Market & Bistro Cafe ★

2016 P Street NW
(202) 466-3474

Good seafood with an Italian twist.

Pizzeria Uno

3211 M Street NW
(202) 965-6333

Part of the national Chicago-style pizza chain in the heart of Georgetown.

Prime Rib ★

2020 K Street NW
(202) 466-8811

For beef and service, one of the finest restaurants in Washington.

The Restaurant at the Jefferson ★

Jefferson Hotel
1200 16th Street NW
(202) 833-6206

The power breakfast spot in D.C.

River Club ★

3223 K Street NW
(202) 333-8118

A luxurious and special seafood restaurant near the Potomac River.

Rocklands—Washington's Barbeque & Grilling Co.

2418 Wisconsin Avenue NW
(202) 333-2556

Another fine BBQ joint. Try the BBQ lamb sandwhich if it's on the menu.

Ruth's Chris Steak House ★

1801 Connecticut Avenue NW
(202) 797-0033

Part of the national steakhouse chain. Its oulet in Bethesda is getting better reviews.

Sam & Harry's ★

1200 19th Street NW
(202) 296-4333

Another good steak and lobster house.

Sbarro

Union Station
50 Massachusetts Avenue NE
(202) 289-0767

Italian fast food.

Sea Catch Restaurant

1054 31st Street NW
(202) 337-8855

Casual seafood.

Sequoia Restaurant ★

3000 K Street NW
(202) 944-4200

Another high-end seafood and new American cuisine.

Sesto Senso ★

1214 18th Street NW
(202) 785-9525

Expensive Italian in the heart of downtown.

1789 Restaurant ★

1226 36th Street NW
(202) 965-1789

One of the most romantic restaurants in Washington. Great food, too.

Sfuzzi of Washington

50 Massachusetts Avenue NE
(202) 842-4141

Modern Italian, part of the national chain.

Sholl's Colonial Cafeteria

1990 K Street NW
(202) 296-3065

A Washington institution. Cafeteria food for the masses in downtown.

Spirit Cruises ★
6th and Water Streets SW, Pier #4
(202) 554-8000

Take a cruise on the Potomac at sunset and enjoy a good meal to boot.

MOVING TIP

Packing dishes by wrapping them in paper and stacking them actually gives you a higher risk of breakage. Instead, wrap plates and platters in bubble wrap and pack them on their edge.

State of the Union
1357 U Street NW
(202) 588-8810

A great bar with food as an afterthought.

Tabard Inn
1739 N Street NW
(202) 785-1277

Modern American cuisine in one of the prettiest settings in Washington. In spring and summer ask about seating on the patio.

Taberna del Alabardero
1776 I Street NW
(202) 429-2200

One of Washington's better known Spanish restaurants.

Terrace Cafe at the National Gallery of Art
4th and Constitution Avenue NW
(202) 347-9401

Take in the great art and then have a bite. Light luncheon fare.

The Tombs
1226 36th Street NW
(202) 337-6668

More of a bar than a restaurant. But good burgers and traditional pub fare.

Tony Cheng's Mongolian Restaurant
619 H Street NW, 1st floor
(202) 842-8669

Create your own meal the Mongolian way.

Uptown Bakers
3313 Connecticut Avenue NW
(202) 362-6262

Great breads make for great sandwiches for picnics and visits to the zoo.

Vidalia ★

1990 M Street NW

(202) 659-1990

One of Washington's best moderan American restaurants.

Wall Street Deli

1201 Pennsylvania Avenue NW

(202) 783-4035

Takeout salads and sandwiches.

West End Cafe

1 Washington Circle NW

(202) 293-5390; (800) 424-9671

Casual luncheon fare.

Zed's Ethiopian Cuisine

3318 M Street NW

(202) 333-4710

For a change of pace, take a chance on this restaurant, which serves traditional Ethiopian food.

Shopping Centers

The following is a list of the region's major malls and shopping centers.

Ballston Common Mall

4238 Wilson Boulevard

Arlington, VA 22203-1823

(703) 243-5363

Chevy Chase Pavilion

5335 Wisconsin Avenue NW

Washington, DC 20015

(202) 686-5335

Crystal City Shops

1664 Crystal Square Arcade

Arlington, VA 22202

(703) 920-3930

Fair Lakes Center

I-66 and Fairfax County Parkway

Fairfax, VA 22033

Fair Oaks

11750 Fair Oaks

I-66 and Route 50 W

Fairfax, VA 22033

Fashion Centre at Pentagon City

1100 South Hayes Street

Arlington, VA 22202

(703) 415-2400

Frederick Towne Mall

U.S. Route 40 W and Waverly
Drive
Frederick, MD 21701

The Gallery at Harbourplace

200 E. Pratt Street
I-95, I-83, I-70, and U.S. 40
Baltimore, MD 21202

Georgetown Park

3222 M Street NW
Washington, DC 20007
(202) 342-8190

Lake Forest

701 Russell Avenue
at Montgomery Village and
Frederick Avenues
Gaithersburg, MD 20877

Landmark Mall

5801 Duke Street
Duke Street and I-395
Alexandria, VA 22304

Landover Mall

Capitol Beltway and Landover
Road
Landover, MD 20785

Martinsburg Mall

800 Foxcroft Avenue
I-81 (Exits 12 and 13)
Martinsburg, WV 25401

Mazza Gallerie

5300 Wisconsin Avenue NW
Washington, DC 20015
(202) 966-6114

Montgomery Mall

7101 Democracy Boulevard
Bethesda, MD 20817
(301) 469-6000

Old Post Office Pavilion

1100 Pennsylvania Avenue NW
Washington, DC 20004
(202) 289-4224

Potomac Mills Mall

2700 Potomac Mills Circle
Prince William, VA 22192
(800) VA-MILLS

St. Charles Town Center

5000 Route 301 South
Route 301 and Smallwood Drive
Waldorf, MD 20603

Shops at National Place

529 14th Street NW
Washington, DC 20045
(202) 783-9090

Spotsylvania Mall

137 Spotsylvania Mall
I-95 and Route 3
Fredericksburg, VA 22407

Springfield Mall
6500 Springfield Mall
Franconia Road and I-95
Springfield, VA 22150

Torpedo Factory Art Center
105 North Union Street
Alexandria, VA 22314
(703) 838-4199

Tysons Corner Center
1961 Chain Bridge Road
McLean, VA 22102-4562
(703) 893-9400, (703) 847-3089

Tysons Galleria
2001 International Drive
McLean, VA 22102
(703) 827-7700

Union Station
50 Massachusetts Avenue
Washington, DC 20002
(202) 289-1908; (800) 527-2554

Wheaton Plaza
6500 Springfield Mall
University Boulevard West and
Veirs Mill Road
Wheaton, MD 20902

White Flint Mall
11301 Rockville Pike
North Bethesda, MD 20895-1021
(301) 468-5777

Sports

PROFESSIONAL SPORTS

When it comes to Washington sports, it's feast or famine. The professional basketball team in town, the NBA Washington Wizards, have been so bad for so long, people have given up on them. But now that Michael Jordan is a partial owner, it may be worth the price of a ticket to watch his team walk through another season of futility.

The same cannot be said for the local professional football team, the Washington Redskins, and the professional hockey team, the Washington Capitals, both winners by any standard. Washington's professional soccer team, the DC United, have won several championships; tickets to their matches are among the best bargains in town.

And then there's major league baseball. The Baltimore Orioles are a touchy subject inside the Beltway. While many baseball fans root for the boys in Baltimore, Washingtonians has been lobbying hard for a baseball team they can call their own.

For current schedules for all of the professional teams, consult the *Washington Post* or *Washington Times* sports section.

Baseball

The Baltimore Orioles play on one of the finest ball fields in the country, Oriole Park at Camden Yards. The season runs from late March to early October (or later if they are winning). The Orioles are a popular team and sell out regularly. For general information about tickets, call the ticket office at (410) 685-9800. To order tickets, call TicketMaster at (202) 432-SEAT or (410) 481-SEAT.

Basketball

The Wizards play their "unique" brand of ball at the new, spacious MCI Center in downtown D.C. For schedule and game information, call (301) NBA-DUNK. To order tickets, call TicketMaster at (202) 432-SEAT or (410) 481-SEAT.

Football

With the Redskins, you either love them or hate them. Whichever camp you're in, you've got lots of company. Tickets to games at the new FedEx Field in Landover, Maryland, are tough to come by, especially when the team is winning. Still, tickets can be had, especially for preseason games. The team recently announced it would be moving its training camp to Northern Virginia. Call (202) 546-2222 for more information.

Hockey

The Capitals, usually called the "Caps" for short, are one of the NHL's premier teams. Like the Wizards, they play at MCI Center. For tickets call TicketMaster at (202) 432-SEAT or (410) 481-SEAT.

Soccer

The DC United have won three Major League Soccer championships in four years and are one of the most entertaining teams in the area to watch. Tickets are inexpensive, making it possible for a family to go out and enjoy high-quality professional sports played in one of America's premier sports facilities, Robert F. Kennedy Stadium, for a reasonable amount of money. For tickets, call TicketMaster at (202) 432-SEAT or (410) 481-SEAT.

Horse Racing

There are three major race tracks in the Washington area. Most are open year-round, offering off-track betting and broadcasts from other tracks from around the country when no on-site races are scheduled.

Laurel Race Course
Route 198 and Race Track Road
Laurel, MD
(301) 725-0400

Pimlico Race Course
Hayward and Winner Avenues
Baltimore, MD
(410) 542-9400

Rosecroft Raceway
6336 Rosecroft Drive
Fort Washington, MD
(301) 567-4000

CITY FACT

For the cheapest haircuts in the city ($8), check out the basements of most Senate and House office buildings.

COLLEGE SPORTS

There are a number of fine college athletic programs in the area, especially if you are a fan of Division I college basketball. Here is the low-down on most of the major teams.

Basketball

Georgetown is in the Big East league with national powers University of Connecticut, Syracuse, St. John, and Seton Hall. The team plays many of its games at the MCI Center. For tickets call (202) 687-4692.

George Washington University's Colonials play their games on campus at the Smith Center. Look for Basketball Hall of Fame coach Red Auerbach and CNN news celebrity Wolf Blitzer in the stands. For tickets call (202) 994-6650.

The University of Maryland Terrapins play in the highly competitive Atlantic Coast Conference, against such teams as North Carolina, Duke, and Virginia. The Terps play their home games at Cole Field House. For tickets call (301) 314-8587.

Football

The University of Maryland Terrapins play their home games in Byrd Stadium. For tickets call (301) 314-8587.

U.S. Naval Academy games are played in Annapolis at the Navy-Marine Memorial Stadium. For tickets call (410) 268-6060.

PARTICIPANT SPORTS

Local recreation and parks departments maintain parks, trails, and lakes, as well as tennis courts, basketball courts, and other sports and recreational facilities. For information on leagues or organizing a team, contact:

District of Columbia: Department of Recreation, (202) 673-7660

Alexandria: Department of Recreation Parks and Cultural Activities, (703) 838-4345

Arlington: County Department of Parks Recreation and Community Resources, (703) 358-4710

Montgomery County: Department of Recreation, (301) 217-6790

Maryland: National Capital Park and Planning Commission, (301) 699-2400

Bicycling

Bicycling is a popular family activity in the Washington area, probably because there are so many open areas with bike paths: the C&O Canal Towpath, Mount Vernon Trail, and Rock Creek Park, to name a few (see "Parks and Green Spaces," on page 259). If you want more information about area biking opportunities or would like to join up with others who are serious about their peddling, contact one of the following groups:

Arlington Cycling Club
Arlington, VA
(202) 543-6546

Bike the Sites, Inc.
Washington, DC
(202) 966-8662

Potomac Pedallers Touring Club
Washington, DC
(202) 363-TOUR

If you don't own a bike, but want to stretch those legs, get some sun, and see the city from a different perspective, the following shops offer bike rentals. They are in the District unless otherwise noted.

Big Wheel Bikes
1034 33rd Street NW
(202) 337-0254

2 Prince Street
Alexandria, VA
(703) 739-2300

City Bikes
2501 Champlain Street NW
(202) 265-1564

Metropolis Bike & Scooter, Inc.
709 8th Street SE
(202) 543-8900

Hiking

There are numerous trails in and around the Washington area, especially if you are willing to drive west to Shenandoah National Park in the Blue Ridge Mountains. If you want a simple hike without a long drive, try Great Falls National Park (see "Parks and Green Spaces," on page 259) or Carderock, on the Maryland side of the Potomac. A number of area groups organize outdoor excursions for hikers and nature lovers.

Appalachian Mountain Club
(202) 298-1488

Northern Virginia Hiking Club
(703) 440-1805

Potomac Appalachian Trail Club
(703) 242-0965

Potomac Backpackers
(703) 524-1185

Sierra Club
(202) 547-2326

Washington Women Outdoors
(301) 864-3070

Horseback Riding

When you have that urge to get in the saddle and ride off into the sunset, visit one of the region's several large horse-riding facilities.

MOVING TIP

If you don't buy mover's pads, use older blankets and quilts to protect large pieces of finished furniture. And don't use tape that might ruin the finish on tables, sofas, and chairs.

Cavallo Farm
Highway 659
Chantilly, VA
(703) 327-6431

Meadowbrook Stables
Meadowbrook Lane and East-West Highway
Chevy Chase, MD
(301) 589-9026

Rock Creek Park Horse Centre
5100 Glover Road NW
Washington, DC
(202) 362-0117

Swimming

There are plenty of public and private swimming pools in the area that can help you escape the heat and humidity that bears down on Washington in the summer. Public high schools in the city that have pools are open to the public during the summer months. In surrounding areas, contact parks departments for more information.

District of Columbia, (202) 576-6436

Alexandria, (703) 838-4343

Arlington County, (703) 358-6262

Fairfax County, (703) 246-5601

Montgomery County, (301) 217-6840

Prince Georges County, (301) 249-7200

YOUTH SOCCER LEAGUES

Soccer is the big sport in this area for kids. For an overview of local soccer programs, contact the Metropolitan D.C.-Virginia-Maryland Soccer Association (703-321-7254), which can give you current information on leagues, coaching seminars, and the like. Local Kiwanis Clubs are regular sponsors of some leagues. Here is a list of local soccer groups that can serve as resources:

Alexandria Soccer Association, Inc.
Alexandria, VA
(703) 684-5425

Annandale Boys Club Inc.
Annadale, VA
(703) 941-4410

Arlington Soccer
Arlington, VA
(703) 532-2088

Bethesda Soccer Club
Bethesda, MD
(301) 871-2268

Fairfax Police Youth Club
Fairfax, VA
(703) 591-3792

Gaithersburg Parks and Recreation Soccer
Gaithersburg, MD
(301) 258-6350

National Capital Soccer League Inc.
(703) 385-1608

Springfield Youth Club
Springfield, VA
(703) 455-8554

Stoddert DC Club
Washington, DC
(202) 965-4625

Parks and Green Spaces

Despite the urban feel of Washington, the city and the surrounding areas offer lots of green and open space. Thanks to the city's history and numerous moratoriums on construction, many of the parks and open lands that in other cities might have long disappeared remain free and clear for people to enjoy.

For information about Washington-area parks, contact:

District of Columbia, Department of Park and Recreation, (202) 673-7660

Arlington County, Department of Parks, Recreation, and Community Resources, (703) 358-4747

City of Alexandria, Department of Recreation, Parks, and Cultural Activities, (703) 838-4343

Fairfax County Park Authority, (703) 324-8700

Montgomery County Department of Parks, (301) 495-2525

National Park Service, National Capital Region, (202) 619-7222

Northern Virginia Regional Park Authority, (703) 352-5900

Following is a list of the major parks and open spaces in the Washington area. Admission is free unless otherwise noted.

C&O Canal Towpath

The path runs 23 miles from Georgetown to Seneca, Maryland, and is open to bikers, joggers, and fishermen.

Dumbarton Oaks Gardens

1703 32nd Street NW
(202) 339-6400

This is one of Washington's great gardens. Admission: $2 for adults and $1 for seniors and children 12 and under.

East Potomac Park

(202) 426-6765

This park, better known as Haines Point, is the site of the huge, half-buried sculpture, *The Awakening*.

Great Falls

This is actually two parks: one in Maryland and, across the way from the falls, one in Virginia. The water fall is spectacular, and the hiking trails are some of the best in the area.

National Arboretum

3501 New York Avenue NW
(202) 245-2726

Acres upon acres of greenery.

National Mall

(202) 619-7222

The Abraham Lincoln memorial, the Korean Conflict memorial, and the memorial for the Veterans of the Vietnam War are all found on the mall.

Rock Creek Park

(202) 282-1063

This is the largest green space in Washington, D.C., proper. Besides rolling hills and shady walkways, it has recreational facilities such as bike paths, tennis courts, playgrounds, and picnic areas. Beach Drive, between Broad Branch Road and Ross Drive, is closed to cars and open to bicycles and roller skaters on weekends (7 A.M. Saturday to 7 P.M. Sunday). The Nature Center (5200 Glover Road NW, 202-426-6828) offers guided nature walks.

Theodore Roosevelt Island

Along the Potomac River, the island is accessible from the George Washington Parkway in Virginia or a bridge from Rosslyn. It's a pleasant hike to a large memorial to Teddy Roosevelt, a man revered for his love of the outdoors and all things natural.

West Potomac Park

(202) 376-6695

The park encompasses several of the national memorials including the Jefferson and Roosevelt sites.

Zoos and Aquariums

National Aquarium

Department of Commerce Building
4th Street and Constitution Avenue NW
(202) 482-2825

National Zoological Park

3000 Connecticut Avenue NW
(202) 673-4800; (202) 673-4717

The zoo covers acres and is home to more than 5,000 animals. Unfortunately, the last of two major attractions, the pandas, died in 1999. The zoo and China have reached accord on "renting" two more within the next couple of years. Free.

Calendar of Events

Here is a quick recap of the major events in Washington. Almost all are marked with activities that are free to the public and receive advance attention in publications such as the *Washington Post,* the *Washington Times, The City Paper,* and *Washingtonian.* Keep your eyes peeled and mark your calendars.

January

Martin Luther King Jr.'s Birthday Observance, Lincoln Memorial

February

Chinese New Year Parade, Chinatown, (202) 724-4091

Abraham Lincoln's Birthday Observance Concert, Lincoln Memorial

George Washington's Birthday Parade, Old Town Alexandria, (703) 838-4200

George Washington's Birthday Celebration, Washington Monument

Black History Month Exhibition, Smithsonian Institution, (202) 357-2700 and Martin Luther King Memorial Library, (202) 727-1211

March

Alexandria St. Patrick's Day Parade, Old Town Alexandria

Washington St. Patrick's Day Parade, Constitution Avenue, (202) 673-7660

April

National Cherry Blossom Festival and Parade, Constitution Avenue

White House Easter Egg Roll, White House, (202) 456-2200

Smithsonian Kite Festival, Washington Monument grounds, (202) 357-3030

International Film Fest D.C., at various area theaters, (202) 724-5613

Goddard Space Flight Center Community Day, Goddard Space Center, Greenbelt, Maryland, (301) 286-2000

White House Spring Garden Tours, (202) 456-2200

May

Annapolis Waterfront Arts Festival, Annapolis Harbor

Virginia Gold Cup (horses), The Plains, Virginia

School Safety Patrol Parade, Constitution Avenue

Chesapeake Bay Bridge Walk, Chesapeake Bay Bridge

Preakness Horse Race Celebration, Pimlico Raceway, Baltimore (410) 542-9400

Memorial Day Ceremonies, at various area memorials

Memorial Day Weekend Concert, West Lawn, U.S. Capitol, (202) 619-7222

June

Kemper Open Golf Tournament, Tournament Players Club, Avenel, Potomac, Maryland, (301) 469-3737

Capital Jazz Fest, Nissan Pavilion, Manassas, Virginia

Wolf Trap Jazz and Blues Festival, Wolf Trap, Vienna, Virginia, (703) 255-1800

Festival of American Folklife, National Mall

July

Fourth of July Celebration, National Mall, (202) 619-7222

Legg-Mason Tennis Classic, William H.G. Fitzgerald Tennis Center

Chincoteague Pony Swim, Chincoteague Island, Maryland

August

Georgia Avenue Day, Banneker Park, (202) 723-5166

Maryland Renaissance Festival, Crownsville, Maryland

September

Maryland Seafood Festival, Sandy Point State Park, Maryland

Adams Morgan Day, Columbia Road, (202) 332-3292

October

Fells Point Fun Festival, Baltimore

Taste of D.C., Pennsylvania Avenue, (202) 724-5000

International Gold Cup Steeplechase Races, the Plains, Virginia

Marine Corps Marathon, throughout Washington and Virginia

Columbus Day Ceremonies, Union Station, (202) 619-7222

White House Fall Garden Tours, South Lawn, (202) 456-2200

November

Veterans' Day, ceremonies at various locations

December

Christmas Walk, Alexandria, Virginia

White House Christmas Tours, the White House

National Christmas Tree Lighting, the Ellipse

U.S. Botanic Garden's Christmas Poinsettia Show,
(202) 226-4082

Transportation

As you plan a move to the Washington, D.C., area, it's important to consider the transportation options available in the District and in the region. More so than in some other cities, where you live may well determine how you get from home to work or school and back again.

This is due, in part, to the fact that Washington was a comparatively old city before its Metro system was constructed. While subway and commuter lines were built in conjunction with the city itself in many other places, the D.C. Metro service was constructed around a city that was already more than 150 years old. The bulk of the Metro system was completed in 1976, a time when the communities outside of D.C. proper were just beginning to see real growth and development. Instead of being designed for city dwellers, the

MOVING TIP

Save some money on storing a bunch of junk and decide whether or not some of your possessions might not be better used by the Salvation Army or Goodwill. Either in your hometown, or in Washington, there are a number of charities that would willingly haul away suitable items.

D.C. Metro system was built for daily commuters from the Virginia and Maryland suburbs. As a result, a few of the more popular District neighborhoods don't have a convenient Metro station.

Complicating matters further, some neighborhoods that don't have Metro service *do* have severe on-street and off-street parking limitations, making owning a car a problem, too.

THE METRO

The D.C. Metro system consists of four complete lines and one line that's incomplete. Three lines—the Orange, Yellow, and Blue lines— run from Virginia across D.C. and into Maryland. The Red Line services the Maryland suburbs, running through the District and then back into Maryland. A fifth line, the Green Line, is operational, but remains under construction. In all, there are about 76 Metro stops in the D.C. area. Many stations are underground, with escalator and elevator service. In general, the stations are safe and clean.

Trains run from 5:30 A.M. until midnight on weekdays, and from 8 A.M. until midnight on weekends. At press time the Metro system was experimenting with a 1 A.M. or 2 A.M. shutdown time on Saturday and Sunday to make it easier for riders to enjoy the city's nightlife, but no permanent change in the schedule has been made.

Fares during rush hour are based on distance; one-way fares can cost as much as $2.10. Off-peak one-way fares are a flat $1.10. If you purchase a fare card for $20 you receive a 10-percent discount, thus saving you a couple of bucks on your commute each week.

City FACT

When riding up or down Metro escalators, never block the left lane. Those are reserved for the high-powered types who can't waste the time just going along for the ride.

None of the Metro lines travel in a straight, north-south or east-west route. Instead they run through and around neighborhoods and communities that were deemed to be in need of a Metro stop back in 1976, or that the planners felt might need Metro service in the future. The growth of the suburbs in Virginia and Maryland in the past 20 years validates the planners' decisions.

Metro stations are identified on street level by tall brown kiosks, with bands of color on top representing the Metro lines that run through the station. Trains are identified by their final destination. For example, if you board an Orange Line train to Vienna, you've caught the train traveling west through D.C. into Virginia.

If you move to Washington without a car and you'd rather not commute by bike, the Metro line and its ever-expanding connections via bus routes may be your best and cheapest mode of transportation in and around Washington. What follows is a closer look at each line and the communities it serves.

The Red Line

The Red Line serves one of the two busiest commuter corridors in the Washington area. It is shaped like a "U," beginning north of Washington in Montgomery County, Maryland. The county has one of the nation's fastest growing high-tech communities, and quite a few apartment buildings and condo and townhouse complexes have built up around the Metro stops. The Red runs north through Rockville, the county seat, through Bethesda, and then into Washington, D.C.

The Red Line runs along perhaps the most popular and desirable living areas in Washington—the Wisconsin Avenue/Connecticut Avenue corridor. The line then travels from the Shady Grove Metro stop in Germantown, Maryland, downtown, through the business centers, and then back up north through Takoma Park and eventually to suburban Wheaton, Maryland.

The Orange Line

The Orange is probably the second most heavily traveled line in the system. It runs a comparatively straight east-west route across the heavily populated Northern Virginia suburbs, through D.C., and into Maryland.

The line starts out in Vienna, Virginia, which 20 years ago was an underdeveloped, almost rural, area. Today, townhouses surround the Metro station and Vienna is a thriving community, in great part because of the Metro.

From Vienna, the train runs through Arlington and Rosslyn, both communities with extensive housing possibilities, before crossing under the Potomac to D.C., Capitol Hill, and points east in Maryland.

The Blue/Yellow Lines

The Blue runs parallel to the Orange Line for much of Washington, but splits off once it crosses the Potomac River into Virginia. The Blue line services the Virginia suburbs that run south along the river, including Alexandria and its surrounding neighborhoods.

The Blue Line provides transportation to three major employment centers: Rosslyn, which is a corporate headquarters for such companies as Gannett; the Pentagon, one of the largest employers in all of Washington; and Crystal City, essentially an extension of the Pentagon, but with corporate offices, apartments and rental homes, and numerous restaurants and shops. The Blue Line also has a convenient stop inside the newly refurbished Ronald Reagan National Airport.

The Yellow Line services downtown D.C. and is a direct link to the Pentagon and Alexandria. For commuters there, it is the quickest route because from Washington, it bypasses several of the stops made by the Blue Line in D.C. and Virginia.

The Green Line

Currently undergoing expansion, the Green Line is a newer Metro line that covers D.C. and some Maryland suburbs that have seen explosive growth in the past 10 years and that were underserved. While several of these suburbs are mentioned in the book, for your purposes the Green Line is simply another color in the Metro's rainbow.

TAXI CABS

Cabs in Washington, D.C., can be a cheap and convenient means of transportation, if you don't mind riding in 20-year-old cars that have seen little to no maintenance in many years. That said, there are always plenty of cabs to be had, especially in areas where there is nightlife and heavy foot traffic or major residential areas where morning and evening commuters are looking for a lift.

Cabs in Washington don't have meters, instead they use a zone system. This can save you money, given the heavy gridlock that hits the city during morning and evening commutes.

At press time D.C. had announced plans to require meters in cabs but, as with many things in the District, bureaucratic battling is holding up that proposal. The reason for the meter proposal is that cabs in both Virginia and Maryland operate on meters—$1.25 to start, then a quarter for each quarter mile.

MOVING TIP

When packing your computer gear, color code your cables and wires. To avoid any risk of losing data, back up your hard drive on diskettes and pack them separately from the rest of your computer. Just don't pack those disks with your magnet collection.

D.C. law prohibits Virginia and Maryland cabs from picking up passengers hailing them on the streets. Still, if you care about such things, the suburban cabs are generally cleaner, more courteous, and more reliable than D.C. cabs, especially during rainy or snowy weather. D.C. cabbies are notorious for charging unofficial rain or snow "fees" that can add as much as $10 to a fare.

The following are the area's most reliable cab companies.

D.C.

Capitol Cab, (202) 546-2400

Diamond Cab, (202) 387-6200

Yellow Cab, (202) 544-1212

MOVING TIP

Remember local charities when picking through your attic and basement before your move. What's junk to you might be useful to them—and you get a small tax write-off.

Virginia

Blue Top Cab, (703) 243-8294

Red Top Cab, (703) 522-3333 (regularly voted best cab company in the area)

Yellow Cab, (703) 522-2222

Maryland

Barwood Cab, (301) 984-1900

CHAPTER 7

What's Out of Town

Washington, D.C., is within easy driving distance of Virginia, Maryland, West Virginia, North Carolina, Delaware, and Pennsylvania. So there are numerous opportunities for day trips, weekend getaways, and quick vacations from the daily grind. (Or, if you haven't quite settled into the daily grind, speedy escapes from all of those boxes in your living room waiting to be unpacked.) After only an hour or so in the car, you can hit the beach, climb a mountain, or experience the somber realities of war at a Civil War battleground.

Because the Washington, D.C., area is one of the country's top tourist destinations, we're not going to devote a lot of space to the kind of travel information you can readily get from other sources. The *Washington Post* (*www.washingtonpost.com*), for example, offers a superb Weekend section as well as detailed information on day trips and other recreational opportunities. It's one of the best resources for planning trips and other weekend activities. Another good resource is one of the finest city magazines in America, *The Washingtonian* (*www.washingtonian.com*). It provides lots of ideas about where to go for fun and frolic inside Washington and out. There are also numerous guidebooks to turn to for additional information; check any bookstore or newsstand in the area.

Here are some suggestions for getting away from whatever it is you are trying to escape. We've highlighted three of the biggest draws in the area, and provided a few thumbnail sketches of others.

Annapolis

Nothing in the Washington area is more prized than the gastronomic and recreational bounty that is the Atlantic Ocean shoreline. And when it comes to travel, nothing in the area exceeds the destinations that lie near the water. One of the most popular of these destinations is the town of Annapolis, the community that many consider the jewel of the Mid-Atlantic region.

About an hour's drive from D.C. as the seagull flies, Annapolis is a comparatively small community filled with history, culture, and food, all of which can be devoured in a day or weekend visit. To get here take I-495 to U.S. 50 to Exit 24 (Rowe Boulevard). For a more scenic journey, take rural Route 450.

Annapolis is the state of Maryland's capital, and history and/or architecture buffs will want to pay a visit to the statehouse. By the way, you might find some free parking at the statehouse; otherwise it's meters and pay lots. Compared to D.C., though, parking in Annapolis isn't terribly expensive. At press time the going rate was about a $1 an hour, with the first hour free in most lots.

At one time, people came to Annapolis for the politics. Today, they come for the scenery and the food. Start your journey at City Dock and Market House, a dieter's nightmare of a building. Here you'll find plenty of what Annapolis and the surrounding area is known for: seafood. There are oysters, boiled shrimp, crab cakes, and blue crabs—in the shell or with the backfin meat separated. During some of the winter and spring months, one of the great delicacies of the region can be found all over town: soft-shell crabs. These are crabs that have outgrown their shells and have been caught before new ones harden. There is nothing finer than a soft-shell crab sandwich (pan-fried, with nothing but a bit of butter on a plain hamburger bun) and a schooner of beer on a warm April afternoon.

Follow Maryland Avenue up a ways to the U.S. Naval Academy, one of America's most historic and tradition-soaked institutions of higher learning. The men and women enrolled here have committed themselves to four years of intense mental and physical training to defend our country on sea, in the air, and on land. Stop by the Armel-Leftwich Visitor Center to arrange a walking tour of the campus, which are given year-round. For more information on Annapolis and the surrounding area contact the Annapolis and Anne Arundel County Visitors Bureau at (410) 268-8687 or visit the Web site, *www.visit-annapolis.org.*

Williamsburg

Many Washington residents consider Williamsburg the area's number one tourist attraction. The reason is simple. Williamsburg offers something for everyone: history, architecture, recreation, shopping, dining, and entertainment.

Williamsburg is the focal point of the area known as the "historic triangle." It encompasses Colonial Williamsburg, a seat of power during the Revolutionary War; the settlement of Jamestown, where America's history began; and Yorktown Battlefield, where the Revolutionary War ended with the British surrender.

Colonial Williamsburg is in many ways a grown-up's amusement park. It is a living, breathing "wayback" machine, a place

MOVING TIP

Double-box your computer hardware. Seal it in a box, wrap the box with bubble wrap, and then place it in a bigger box. Or put the smaller box in a larger box filled with packing peanuts.

where visitors can step into Virginia as it was in the 1700s. Here the people dress in authentic period costume and the shops sell 18th-century products. The guides, who give tours of the compound every hour on the hour, speak of Williamsburg in the present tense—only they maintain that the present is the year 1770. In addition to preserved historic buildings and museums, Colonial Williamsburg has several fine restaurants and shops selling high-quality souvenirs and products made of pewter, silver, and handmade paper.

For information about Colonial Williamsburg, call (800) 447-8679 or log-on to its Web site, *www.history.org.* The basic admission ticket, which is good for one day and does not include all attractions and tours within the colonial museums, costs $30. Admission for children ages six to 17 is $18 for up to seven consecutive days.

If it's 'hot and you're traveling with kids, you'll probably want to visit one (or both!) of the larger amusement parks in the region: Busch Gardens and its sister park, Water Country USA. Both parks have staffs that are extremely helpful and dedicated to making your visit worth the price of admission, which is saying something. Admission to Busch Gardens is $33 for adults and $26 for children ages three to six Water Country admission is $25.50 for adults, $17.95 for ages three to six Look for discount coupons for admission in the *Washington Post*—they appear often. Both parks are open daily Memorial Day through Labor Day and on weekends in May and September. For more information call (800) 343-7946 or (757) 253-3350.

If shopping is what you want to do, Williamsburg has that, too. Route 60 in "downtown" Williamsburg offers mile upon mile of outlet shops. Check the Williamsburg Pottery Factory at (757) 564-3326. It doesn't sell just pottery, but everything—literally—from soup to nuts.

If you're heading out of Washington on a Friday afternoon or evening, expect a long drive to Williamsburg. It's best to turn the trip into a long weekend by leaving Thursday evening instead. Take I-395 out past the Beltway to I-95 South, then take I-295 South to I-64 East to the Williamsburg–Camp Peary exit. Plan on a three- to four-hour trip.

Baltimore

Known as "Charm City," Baltimore lives up to its nickname. While some people think Washington is too antiseptic, Baltimore has character to spare. It's a great day-trip or weekend-getaway destination because without traveling very far you still feel as though you've gone someplace very different from D.C.

You'll want to start at the Inner Harbor, among the first of the major "downtown rehab" projects undertaken in U.S. cities in the mid-1970s and early 1980s. The Inner Harbor's focal point is Harborplace, a gussied-up shopping mall and tourist attraction. It has restaurants and unusual shops and serves as the gateway to a number of attractions within easy walking distance.

To one side of Harborplace is Oriole Park at Camden Yard, the original "retro" ballpark. Just as the Inner Harbor and similar projects changed the way city centers are designed, this ballpark changed the way baseball stadiums are designed and built. On game days you'll need a ticket to take advantage of some of the bars and shops that are in the old railroad building that serves as the park's backdrop. But on days when there's no game, the park is open on a limited basis to tourists who just want to see where the great Cal Ripkin played peer-less ball. Baseball fans will also want to stop in at the Baltimore Orioles Museum at 216 Emory Street, (410) 727-1539.

But even if you are not a sports fanatic, there is much in Baltimore to keep you interested and entertained. The National Aquarium (410-576-3800) is one of the finest in America, with exhibits on the delicate ecosystem that surrounds it in the Chesapeake Bay. Admission is $11.50 for adults, $9.50 for seniors, $7.50 for children age three and over.

Next to the aquarium is the Baltimore Maritime Museum, featuring tours of the submarine *U.S.S. Torsk,* the ship *Chesapeake,* and the *U.S.S. Constellation.* Also in the Inner Harbor area is the Maryland Science Center (410-685-5225). It has lots of exhibits that will appeal to kids, as well as an IMAX theater. Admission is $8.50 for adults, $6.50 for kids four to 17.

City Fact

On average, an escalator ride at a Metro station takes one-and-three-quarter minutes. The longest Metro escalator ride is said to be at the Wheaton station, although the escalators at Dupont Circle and Bethesda could be just as long.

A quick walk from Inner Harbor is the exclusive neighborhood of Federal Hill, full of trendy shops, restaurants, and beautiful homes. When you've had your fill of the high life, head over to Fells Point, where everyone else likes to hang out in the bars, restaurants, art galleries, and unique shops. This neighborhood often appeared in the now-defunct Baltimore-based crime TV show, *Homicide, Life on the Street.* Walk the cobbled streets and check out all the action, then head over to Brown's Wharf, where several restaurants offer great seafood as well as Italian and Mexican fare. If you like mussels, you have to stop by the Baltimore institution, Bertha's (410-327-5795).

From Fells Point, walk to the neighborhood next door, Baltimore's Little Italy. It features a number of great Italian restaurants, bakeries, and shops selling gelato and Italian ice.

MOVING TIP

If your move is do-it-yourself, call around to shopping club warehouses and ask for some of their larger boxes. Most will be happy to give them away.

To get to Baltimore, take the Beltway to I-95 North and look for the exits. Or take the Baltimore-Washington Parkway until it becomes Russell Street; take a right on Russell at the Inner Harbor and look for parking. Amtrak trains leave from Washington's Union Station; tickets are $22 round-trip. On weekdays only, MARC commuter trains run regularly between Washington and Baltimore ($9.50 round trip).

For more information, call the Baltimore Area Convention and Visitors Association at (800) 282-6632 or go to *www.baltimore.org* online.

Other Trips

Here are a few more excursions in the area. Some can be done in a day; others you will want to devote a bit more time to.

SHENANDOAH NATIONAL PARK, VIRGINIA

In the Washington area, the fall has come to be known as "foliage season." Even local newscasts provide viewers with daily updates on when the colors of the leaves will be the most vibrant.

In this part of the country, the place to see the spectacular fall colors at their best is Shenandoah National Park in Virginia. The park is beautiful any time of year, but fall and spring are when it really shines.

You can take in the sights of the park from your car by traveling along the scenic Skyline Drive that runs through the area. Shenandoah National Park is about a 90-minute drive from Washington; take I-66 to U.S. Route 340. For more information about the park and the surrounding area, call (800) 999-4714.

CHARLOTTESVILLE, VIRGINIA

First and foremost, Charlottesville, Virginia, is known as the site of Monticello, the home and plantation of Thomas Jefferson. But Washington locals keep going back for a number of different reasons.

There is the University of Virginia main campus, designed and founded by Jefferson, which anchors the town of Charlottesville. Both the football and basketball teams have storied pasts, and a football game here is a great way to enjoy a Saturday afternoon in autumn.

Charlottesville has also become a center for brew pubs and a favorite spot for talented chefs looking to open their own restaurants on limited budgets. The result is an eclectic mix of dining choices and numerous entertainment options.

Admission to Monticello is $8. For information on special events here, call (804) 293-6789.

Also in the area is the home of another American founding father, James Monroe. He and Jefferson were practically neighbors. Monroe's farm, Ash Lawn, can be toured for $7. Call (804) 293-9539 for more information.

Charlottesville is a two-hour drive from Washington, D.C.: take I-66 West to U.S. Route 29 South, which will take you straight into the historic district. For more information, call the Charlottesville Convention and Visitors Center at (804) 977-1783 or log-on to *www.charlottesvilletourism.org*.

FREDERICKSBURG AND RICHMOND, VIRGINIA

By driving south down I-95, you can visit two great Southern towns where history is everywhere and antiquing has become *the* weekend pastime.

Your first stop is Fredericksburg, a town about 50 miles south of Washington. In the past five years, Fredericksburg has been transformed from a sleepy hamlet to a thriving tourist stop, in part because artists, small-business owners, and restaurateurs have discovered that the Victorian downtown historical district is a pleasant—and more affordable—alternative to Washington.

If you don't want to drive, Amtrak (800-872-7245) has train service to Fredericksburg; round-trip fares are $28 to $38. Virginia Railway Express (703-684-0400) operates commuter trains between Washington and Fredericksburg; round-trip tickets are $13.40. For more information, contact the Fredericksburg Visitors Center at (800) 678-4748.

If you get back on I-95 and drive another 50 miles south, you'll arrive at Richmond, Virginia, the state capital and the capital of the Confederacy during the Civil War. Be sure to drive down Monument Boulevard, with its statues of famous soldiers, politicians, and native sons (in recent years tennis great Arthur Ashe was memorialized with a statue here).

Richmond is also accessible by train; contact Amtrak at (800) 872-7245 for fare information. But the train station is not in town, so it's best to drive. For more information, call the Richmond Convention and Visitors Bureau at (800) 365-7272 or check out *www.virginia.org*.

CITY FACT

While many Washingtonians are rabid Redskin football fans, there are just as many devoted fans from other NFL cities who live in the Washington area. As a result, many bars offer Sunday specials for fans of such teams as the Buffalo Bills, the Miami Dolphins, the Philadelphia Eagles, the Dallas Cowboys, and the Chicago Bears. Check out the Washignton *City Paper* for advertisements about parties, or contact your team's local fan club for further information.

HARPERS FERRY, WEST VIRGINIA

Made famous as the site of abolitionist John Brown's attempt to capture the United States Armory and incite a rebellion to free the slaves of what was then part Virginia, Harpers Ferry, West Virginia, is today a national park known as much for its natural attributes as for its history. This is where the Shenandoah and Potomac Rivers meet the Blue Ridge Mountains, and the scenery here is spectacular.

Begin your visit to Harpers Ferry National Park (304-535-6298) at the Cavalier Heights Visitors Center, off Route 340 ($5 parking). From there you can walk or take a shuttle bus to the lovely and interesting restored "Lower Town." Shuttles run every 10 minutes.

Harpers Ferry's biggest attractions, however, are its natural wonders. Within walking distance of the Lower Town is Jefferson's Rock, which provides a stunning overview of the valley. Or you can take a walk along the Appalachian Trail by crossing the Potomac River Bridge to the C&O Canal towpath.

Harpers Ferry is 55 miles from D.C. via I-270 to Frederick, then I-70 West to Route 340 South. Contact the Harpers Ferry Visitor Center at (304) 535-6298 or *www.nps.gov/hafe* for more information.

ST. MICHAELS, MARYLAND

There is scenic beauty to spare here, mostly on the water. You can spend a day sailing, then feast on crabs for lunch or dinner. Or skip the sailing and just eat crabs for lunch *and* dinner.

To take it all in, tour the harbor on *The Patriot* (410-745-3100) or the *Princess II*, which gives eco-tours of the area. If you're a do-it-yourselfer, you can rent a boat at the Town Dock Marina (410-745-2400). Or you can explore on land by renting a bike for about $4 an hour.

St. Michaels is about 100 miles from D.C. Take the Beltway to U.S. Route 50 across the Bay Bridge. Turn right on Route 322 and right again on Route 33 East. Call (410) 822-4606 or visit the Web site at *www.talbotchamber.org* for more information about the area.

CHINCOTEAGUE, VIRGINIA

This island is best known for its Chincoteague horses, a herd of wild ponies that swim across Assateague Channel annually in July. It's a sight to behold and a major event in the area.

Aside from the horses, which you can come across regularly year-round, the island features the Chincoteague National Wildlife Refuge. It offers several large nature trails and beaches and is home to more than 300 species of birds, including ospreys and peregrine falcons.

Chincoteague is about a four-hour drive from the District. Take I-495 to U.S. Route 50 across the Bay Bridge and south to Salisbury to U.S. Route 13 and then Route 175 east to the island. For more information, call the Chincoteague Chamber of Commerce at (757) 336-6161, the Chincoteague National Wildlife Refuge at (757) 336-6122), or go to the Web site *www.chincoteaguechamber.com.*

CITY FACT

The best shoeshine in the city can be had in the basement of the Mayflower Hotel. Price: $5.

CIVIL WAR SITES: ANTIETAM, MARYLAND, AND GETTYSBURG, PENNSYLVANIA

Within easy driving distance of Washington are two of the nation's major Civil War battle sites—"must sees" if you love history.

Closest to home is Antietam, Maryland. Here, Confederate General Robert E. Lee, who was coming off an epic victory over the North at Manassas, Virginia, and had taken siege in Sharpsburg, Maryland, near Antietam Creek. His battle plans fell into the hands of the Union Army, and General George McClellan attempted to catch Lee in one of the bloodiest battles of the war. Today you can tour the Antietam battlefield on foot, on bike, or by car.

Antietem is little more than an hour drive from Washington: take I-270 North to I-70 West to Exit 29 and continue for about 10 miles. The park visitors center is open 8:30 A.M. to 6 P.M. daily; admission is $2 per person, $4 for a family. For more information call the Antietam National Battlefield at (301) 432-5124.

Farther north on I-270 is Gettysburg, Pennsylvania, the site of the best-known battle of the Civil War. While the national park is the centerpiece of the area, there are other things to see and do. Downtown Gettysburg has a historic district that's full of shops selling antiques, Civil War–era memorabilia, and arts and crafts. You can also tour the farm that President Dwight D. Eisenhower retired to after his years in the White House.

For more information about Gettysburg, call (717) 334-6274 or log on to the Web site *www.gettysburg.com.*

THE SHORE: REHOBOTH, DEWEY, AND BETHANY, DELAWARE

When summer hits Washington, the town seems to clear out. From about late June through August, rush-hour traffic seems to disappear and downtown streets seem a bit more wide-open. It's because everyone is at the beach.

When they want to enjoy the sun and surf, most Washingtonians drive to one of Delaware's three better beaches: Rehoboth, Dewey, and Bethany.

Rehoboth is the most developed of the three, with lots of fast-food chain restaurants, an outlet shopping mall, and lots of motels and condo buildings for summer visitors. Rehoboth is popular with families and college kids (many of who take on summer jobs here). It is also a favorite of the gay community, which has a large presence here throughout the summer. The diverse mix makes for a rollicking and raucous time on the shore.

If you are looking for something a little more restful, you might want to venture to Dewey Beach. There you will find a more tranquil beach (this is compared to Rehoboth—the place is still jam-packed with people) and other sites. Delaware Seashore State Park (302-227-2800), which has boating and camping facilities, is located here.

Bethany is perhaps the quietest of the big three. It is more family-oriented, but still features plenty of fast-food joints and late-night bars. It also has some nicer restaurants—a plus for those adults who can take a break from the kids and enjoy a quiet night out on the town.

Without summer traffic, Rehoboth is a little more than three hours from Washington—on a Friday night in July, the trip can take four to five hours. From the Beltway take U.S. Route 50 over the Bay Bridge to U.S. Route 404 East and into downtown Rehoboth. Dewey and Bethany can be reached essentially the same way.

CHAPTER 8

Volunteer and Community Involvement

With its politics-is-everything attitude and its bureacratic approach to life, Washington, D.C., has been accused of being a cold and heartless town. In fact, nothing could be further from the truth. Washington is filled to the gills with do-gooders. There seem to be a dozen charity fund-raisers each night of the week, and members of Washington's large activist community make protests a familiar sight.

But the volunteer scene here is not limited to wealthy philanthropists or dedicated protestors. If you really want to spend some time helping people, animals, the community you live in, or the world at large, there are no better places to live than Washington, D.C., and its surrounding suburbs. Because of the region's diverse community, extensive amount of green space, and numerous historic sites that require care, there are many opportunities for a willing person to lend a helping hand.

What follows is a list of some local organizations in need of volunteers, as well as resources that can help you find a program that suits your interests. Note that some organizations that have offices outside of Washington may have programs or volunteer opportunities in the city as well as in their own communities.

General Volunteer Organizations

Alexandria Volunteer Bureau
(703) 836-2176

Arlington County Volunteer Office
(703) 228-5811

Catholic Charities
(703) 841-2531

One of the largest resources for volunteer programs in Washington and the area. Runs volunteer and outreach programs that assist families, children, seniors, the homeless, and others in need.

D.C. Jewish Community Center
(202) 518-9400

This is a great resource for anyone looking to volunteer. The program is open to everyone, and the organization's reach has extended far beyond the areas its name implies. The J.C.C. can link you to any number of programs, private and public, including ones that it runs for families, the elderly, children, and the homeless.

Greater D.C. Cares
(202) 289-7378

Connects volunteers with social-service agencies and programs in D.C.—everything from homeless shelters, food kitchens, and child-care centers to community cleanups and senior citizen services. This is a great resource if you are new to the area and looking to get involved in the community.

Lutheran Social Services
(202) 232-6380

This is another religious organization that does work in the Washington community. You don't have to be Lutheran to participate.

Montgomery County Volunteer and Community Service Center
(301) 777-2600

Prince Georges Voluntary Action Center
(301) 779-9444

Salvation Army
(202) 829-0100

The organization with the familiar name is in need of all kinds of volunteer assistance, from help in picking up donations to people to stand by the Christmas buckets during the holiday season.

Washington Urban League
(202) 829-7334

YMCA
(202) 232-6700

MOVING TIP

A month before your move, make sure your medical, legal, and school records are transferred to the appropriate people in your new city. Remember, for all of Washington's appeal, city government, from the BMV to the school system, is still very much a disorganized mess. You cannot trust that what you expect to be done will, in fact, be done.

YWCA
(202) 626-0700

Animals

Animal Rescue of Montgomery County
(301) 279-1823

Animal Welfare League of Arlington County
(703) 931-9241

Washington Humane Society

(202) 333-4010

Volunteers care for animals in shelters. The society also runs animal adoption projects throughout the area.

Arts and Museums

Business Volunteers for the Arts

(202) 638-2406

Popular with young professionals looking to provide a service while also making business and social contacts.

Friends of the Kennedy Center

(202) 416-8000

One of the largest arts groups in the area, it has fund-raising and volunteer programs for one of the premier performing arts centers in America.

Smithsonian Institution

(202) 357-2700

Volunteers are always needed—as tour guides, support staff, fund-raisers, etc.—at the many Smithsonian sites in Washington, D.C.

Children

Boys and Girls Clubs of Greater Washington

(301) 587-4315

Nationally recognized organizations that offer educational and recreational opportunities for kids.

Children's Defense Fund

(202) 628-8787

Volunteers for this well-known advocacy group work with kids in urban centers and/or get involved on the political front on Capitol Hill.

Higher Achievement Program

(202) 842-5116

Education and job-training programs.

MOMS (Mothers Offering Maternal Support)

(301) 424-0656.

Matches teen mothers or pregnant girls with volunteer mothers, who teach parental skills and offer additional support.

Secret Santa Program

(703) 228-5811

An Arlington County–sponsored program that anonymously links a volunteer with an "adopted" family. The volunteers provide "their" family with Christmas gifts, toys, and a holiday meal. Children are encouraged to participate, either alone or with their parents.

CITY FACT

Unless you are a masochist, never drive into Georgetown on a Friday or Saturday night. Take a cab instead.

The Environment

Arlingtonians for a Clean Environment

(703) 358-6427

The group sponsors some of the largest and most popular eco-events in the area, including the annual Potomac River Cleanup, as well as Adopt-a-Stream and Adopt-a-Highway programs.

Chesapeake Wildlife Sanctuary

(301) 390-7010

Friends of the National Zoo

(202) 673-4955

One of the most popular groups in the area, FONZ offers programs for adults and children inside one of the best zoos in the country, perhaps the world.

**Garden Resources of
Washington (GROW)**
(202) 234-0591

**Patuxent Environmental
Science Center**
(301) 497-5833

National Park Service
(202) 619-7077

Sierra Club
(202) 547-2326

Gay and Lesbian Organizations/AIDS Outreach

Food and Friends
(202) 488-8278

Volunteers provide meals and companionship to homebound
patients with AIDS.

Gay and Lesbian Activists Alliance
(202) 667-5139

Provides services and support to the Washington gay and lesbian
community.

Whitman Walker Clinic
(202) 797-3576

One of the nation's most prominent AIDS organizations, it pio-
neered fund-raising for AIDS. It also offers health education, outreach programs, free HIV testing, and related services.

Health

American Cancer Society
(202) 483-2600

American Red Cross
(202) 737-8300

The Hungry and the Homeless

Covenant House
(202) 610-9600

Provides food, clothing, and shelter to homeless and at-risk kids.
Volunteers work directly with the youths, providing mentoring, job
training, education, and recreation. This is an especially appealing
program for people in their 20s and early 30s, and volunteers in
those age groups are very much in demand at Covenant House.

Habitat for Humanity
(202) 563-3411

This national organization
works to build housing and find
shelter for those who can't afford
it. The group has offices in
Washington and Virginia.

Hand to Hand
(301) 983-HAND

This group prepares meals and
delivers them to Washington
shelters for homeless people.

MOVING TIP

One month before your expected move,
start your relocation process by completing change-of-address cards for all of your
important contacts: banks, credit card
companies, utilities, in-laws.

Martha's Table
(202) 328-6608

Serves hungry low-income and homeless people living near 14th and
W Streets NW. It also operates McKenna's Wagon, a mobile soup
kitchen. Volunteers cook food in their homes that is then distributed
to people in need. The organization also runs a summer camp for
kids.

Meals on Wheels
(202) 723-5617

This national organization provides meals to homebound seniors
and to some area homeless shelters.

SOME (So Others Might Eat)

(202) 797-8806; (202) 797-7562

The highly visible Washington project offers volunteer opportunities for adults and children.

Washington Area Gleaning Network

(703) 370-0155

The organization gathers produce from local farms after harvest and distributes it to homeless people in the city.

Literacy

Literacy Volunteers of America

(202) 387-1772

Washington Literacy Council

(202) 387-9029

People with Disabilities

Columbia Lighthouse for the Blind

(202) 462-2900

Volunteers assist blind children and adults through reading, transportation, and day-camp programs.

Disabled American Veterans

(202) 554-3501

National Center for Therapeutic Riding

(202) 362-4537

You don't have to have a horse to join this group. Members bring joy to children and adults who are seeking to expand their horizons beyond their physical limitations through horseback riding.

Recording for the Blind
(202) 244-8990

The organization offers an extensive reading program for blind people in the area.

Seniors

In addition to those listed below, the organizations described under "General Volunteer Organizations" have programs for the elderly: Catholic Charities, D.C. Jewish Community Center, Greater D.C. Cares, Lutheran Social Services, Salvation Army, Washington Urban League, YMCA, and YWCA.

American Red Cross Volunteer Shoppers Program
(301) 588-2515

Iona Senior Services
(202) 966-1055

IONA.org

A nonprofit organization providing a number of services to senior citizens in the Washington area, including home visits, grocery shopping, and transportation. It also runs a day-care program for seniors.

Special Olympics
(202) 441-7770

One of the most popular volunteer programs for teenagers. They help organize local and national sporting events for developmentally disabled children and adults.

CITY FACT

The fastest way to get from downtown to Georgetown isn't by way of M Street. Take K Street to the Whitehurst Freeway. Even in rush hour it will save you 10 to 20 minutes.

Finding the Essentials

CHAPTER 9

Important Places to Know

Getting adjusted to a new city and a new neighborhood can take time. The following section provides the names and phone numbers of some important and useful resources, including local merchants that can make your life a little easier.

Cleaners/Laundries

Aaron's Cleaners
1813 Benning Road NE
(202) 399-2105

Ackerman's
1823 Columbia Road NW
(202) 232-6110

American Valet
4100 Massachusetts Avenue NW
(202) 686-7190

Artistic Valet
1837 Columbia Road NW
(202) 462-1666

Barr Cleaners
910 17th Street NW
(202) 785-1155

Bergmann's Laundry
1301 E Capitol Street SE
(202) 547-0418

Best Cleaners
4608 Wisconsin Avenue NW
(202) 362-2705

Brandywine Valet Shop
4545 Connecticut Avenue NW
(202) 237-0588

Canal Cleaners
5118 MacArthur Boulevard NW
(202) 363-8009

CITY
FACT

The nicest and most underrated park in
the city to sit in and just relax is
McPherson Square.

Capitol Towers Cleaners
210 Massachusetts Avenue NE
(202) 543-6352

Cathedral Custom Cleaners
3000 Connecticut Avenue NW
(202) 234-1288

Chevy Chase Circle Cleaners
5708 Connecticut Avenue NW
(202) 237-5850

Cleveland Park Valet
3303 Connecticut Avenue NW
(202) 966-6574

Colberts Cleaners
2129 Rhode Island Avenue NE
(202) 529-6088

Columbia Cleaners
2130 Ward Place NW
(202) 331-8414

Diamond Square Cleaners
1815 Wisconsin Avenue NW
(202) 337-0112

Diplomat Cleaners
4483 Connecticut Avenue NW
(202) 363-9631

Dorchester Cleaners
2480 16th Street NW
(202) 667-4003

Downtown Cleaners
2000 L Street NW
(202) 223-4330

Embassy Cleaners
4215 Connecticut Avenue NW
(202) 966-1118

11 M Cleaners
1131 11th Street NW
(202) 842-3328

Embassy Row Cleaners
1509 17th Street NW
(202) 232-7063

Esteem Cleaners
2100 Pennsylvania Avenue NW
(202) 429-0591

Express Cleaners
603 48th Street NE
(202) 396-6462

Georgetown Cleaners
1070 1-2 31st Street NW
(202) 965-9655

Georgetown Market & Dry Cleaners
201 Massachusetts Avenue NE
(202) 543-4222

Georgetown Valet
2401 Pennsylvania Avenue NW
(202) 296-2966

601 Pennsylvania Avenue NW
(202) 628-5029

2031 Florida Avenue NW
(202) 319-2024

1655 Q Street NW
(202) 462-4335

1613 Foxhall Road NW
(202) 333-3338

Gold Star Cleaners
2201 Wisconsin Avenue NW
(202) 333-4881

2140 L Street NW
(202) 466-4881

Jins Dry Cleaners
1944 New Hampshire Avenue
(202) 328-0132

Kilroys Cleaners
826 Upshur Street NW
(202) 723-5742

Kims Cleaners
1726 20th Street NW
(202) 328-4722

1797 Lanier Place NW
(202) 232-2576

Lafayette Cleaners
1120 20th Street NW
(202) 463-8991

Lamont Cleaners
3173 Mount Pleasant Street NW
(202) 387-2555

Le Valet Cleaners
1012 Pennsylvania Avenue SE
(202) 544-1150

2311 M Street NW
(202) 466-7122

Mayflower Valet
1101 Vermont Avenue NW
(202) 842-2352

McColloughs Try Me Cleaners
817 S Street NW
(202) 986-7492

Metro Cleaners
307 5th Street NE
(202) 543-9033

4620 14th Street NW
(202) 723-3311

Michigan Park Cleaners
3928 12th Street NE
(202) 526-8209

Mid City Cleaners
1601 14th Street NW
(202) 462-5320

Midtown Cleaners
2605 P Street NW
(202) 333-1331

Minas Dry Cleaners
419 6th Street NW
(202) 637-9355

Miracle Cleaners
1212 13th Street NW
(202) 347-1962

Paramount Cleaners
608 8th Street NE
(202) 547-5604

Park Drive Cleaners
4901 Wisconsin Avenue NW
(202) 244-9808

Park Hill Cleaners
601 Massachusetts Avenue NE
(202) 547-6755

Parkland Cleaners
3811 McKinley Street NW
(202) 966-2411

Parklane Cleaners
4304 Connecticut Avenue NW
(202) 363-5510

Parkplace Cleaners
3504 Connecticut Avenue NW
(202) 966-4717

Parks Cleaners & Shoe Repair
New York Avenue and
H Street NW
(202) 371-0777

Royal Cleaners
418 4th Street SW
(202) 488-2886

1990 K Street NW
(202) 223-8544

Russells Cleaners
5121 Georgia Avenue NW
(202) 882-5775

Sargent II Cleaners
2420 Wisconsin Avenue NW
(202) 333-5667

Scot Cleaners
5004 Benning Road SE
(202) 584-1470

Swift Cleaners
138 7th Street NE
(202) 543-1922

1700 R Street NW
(202) 667-5330

Tash Cleaners
1921 Benning Road NE
(202) 396-4617

Techworld Cleaners
800 K Street NW
(202) 408-3309

Terrace Valet Tailors & Cleaners
5824 Georgia Avenue NW
(202) 726-5192

The Capitol Hill
301 1st Street NE
(202) 543-3140

The Cleaner of Cleaners
300 E Street SW
(202) 488-7882

Tip Top Cleaners
3423 M Street NW
(202) 333-8138

MOVING TIP

Two weeks before your move, make appointments or arrangements to have all of your utilities shut off the day *after* your move. This way, should something go wrong, you're not left high and dry (not to mention dark and cold).

TLC Cleaners
2121 L Street NW
(202) 463-3515

Tonys One Hour Martinizing
6143 Georgia Avenue NW
(202) 882-7725

Tower Cleaners & Launderers
*2026 Martin Luther
King Jr. Avenue*
(202) 678-9875

Towers Valet
4201 Cathedral Avenue NW
(202) 537-5023

True Cleaners
700 Kennedy Street NW
(202) 726-0055

Tuckerman Valet
1205 Tuckerman Street NW
(202) 291-0686

Twelfth Street Cleaners
3525 12th Street NE
(202) 526-7836

21 K Street Valet
909 21st Street NW
(202) 822-0864

Uptown 1 Hour Cleaners
3333 Connecticut Avenue NW
(202) 363-5050

Grocery Stores/Supermarkets

Colonnade Food and Wine
2801 New Mexico Avenue NW
(202) 338-0414

D.C. Super Market
539 8th Street NE
(202) 543-0488

Federal Market
1215 23rd Street NW
(202) 293-0014

Foggy Bottom Grocery
2140 F Street NW
(202) 337-4652

Georgetown Market
3405 M Street NW
(202) 965-3732

Glover Park Market
2411 37th Street NW
(202) 333-4030

Ivy Market
1900 Capital Avenue NE
(202) 526-8277

J & R Market
500 Irving Street NW
(202) 829-1034

K & D Food Market

1201 S Street NW

(202) 387-8880

L Street Market

700 L Street SE

(202) 546-3023

Lees Market

1025 7th Street NE

(202) 544-2446

McKinley Market

321 I Street NE

(202) 832-7377

Metro K Supermarket

1864 Columbia Road NW

(202) 483-6100

Palisades Market

4554 MacArthur Boulevard NW

(202) 333-1700

Quincy Market

114 Quincy Place NE

(202) 635-1048

Safeway Food and Drug Stores

2550 Virginia Avenue NW

(202) 338-3628

6500 Piney Branch Road NW

(202) 723-5644

4310 Connecticut Avenue NW

(202) 244-0180

MOVING TIP

Two weeks before your move, arrange for your utilities to be turned on the day *before* you arrive in your new home. Allow for the fact that the local utilities—Pepco, Bell Atlantic, and Virginia Power—all require about a half-hour of your time while processing your new accounts.

5545 Connecticut Avenue NW

(202) 244-6097

401 M Street SW

(202) 554-9155

645 Milwaukee Place SE

(202) 561-4656

3830 Georgia Avenue NW

(202) 882-1140

4203 Davenport Street NW

(202) 364-0290

1701 Corcoran Street NW

(202) 667-6825

301 Rhode Island Avenue NW
(202) 234-6012

415 14th Street SE
(202) 547-4333

1747 Columbia Road NW
(202) 667-0774

1800 20th Street NW
(202) 483-3908

322 40th Street NE
(202) 397-2802

Super Fresh
4330 48th Street
(202) 362-4208

Tenley Market
4326 Wisconsin Avenue NW
(202) 363-8683

Towers Market
4201 Cathedral Avenue NW
(202) 363-7600

West End Market
2424 Pennsylvania Avenue NW
(202) 659-5000

Hospitals

Children's Hospital
111 Michigan Avenue NW
(202) 745-5000

Columbia Hospital for Women
2425 L Street NW
(202) 293-6500

D.C. General Hospital
1900 Massachusetts Avenue SE
(202) 675-5000

George Washington University Medical Center
901 23rd Street NW
(202) 994-1000

Georgetown Hospital
3800 Reservoir Road NW
(202) 687-2000

Howard University Hospital
2041 Georgia Avenue NW
(202) 865-6100

Medlink Hospital at Capitol Hill
700 Constitution Avenue NE
(202) 546-5700

Providence Hospital
1150 Varum Street NE
(202) 269-7000

Sibley Memorial Hospital
5255 Loughboro Road NW
(202) 537-4000

Suburban Hospital
8600 Old Georgetown Road
Bethesda, MD
(301) 896-3100

Washington Adventist Hospital
7600 Carroll Avenue
Takoma Park, MD
(301) 891-7600

Washington Hospital Center
110 Irving Street NW
(202) 877-7000

Pharmacies

Center Pharmacy
4900 Massachusetts Avenue NW
(202) 363-9240

Chevy Chase Pharmacy
3812 Northampton Street NW
(202) 966-8600

Columbia Heights Professional Pharmacy
3316 14th Street NW
(202) 232-1455

CVS
1028 19th Street NW
(202) 659-3280

Dumbarton Pharmacy
3146 Dumbarton Avenue NW
(202) 338-1020

Foers Pharmacy
818 18th Street NW
(202) 775-4400

City Fact

If you want to take a tour of Capitol Hill, try to arrange it through a congressional staffer, who can get you or your visitors special access to areas regular folks can't get into.

Foers Pharmacy
650 Pennsylvania Avenue SE
(202) 544-4583

McLean Drugs
4900 Massachusetts Avenue NW
(202) 966-6424

MOVING TIP

If your mover is driving into the Washington area, do what you can to ensure he or she spends as little time as possible on the I-495 Beltway, especially if you are paying by the hour on the day of delivery and unloading. Traffic can cut a good hour or two from your schedule.

Morgan Pharmacy
3001 P Street NW
(202) 337-4100

Mount Pleasant Pharmacy
3169 Mount Pleasant Street NW
(202) 387-3100

North Capitol Pharmacy
1418 North Capitol Street NW
(202) 265-0314

Resource Pharmacy
1160 Varnum Street NW
(202) 832-2200

Robinsons Apothecary
922 East Capitol Street NW
(202) 544-1600

Rodmans Discount Drug
5100 Wisconsin Avenue NW
(202) 363-1041

Rite Aid Pharmacies
1306 U Street NW
(202) 328-8761

1306 U Street NW
(202) 328-8763

Foxhall Square
(202) 966-0267

Places of Worship

BAPTIST

Bethesda First Baptist Church
5033 Wilson Lane
Bethesda, MD
(301) 654-4159

Canaan Baptist Church
1607 Monroe Street NW
(202) 234-5330

**First Baptist Church of
Alexandria**
2932 King Street
Alexandria, VA
(703) 684-3720

**First Baptist Church of
Chesterbrook**
1740 Kirby Road
McLean, VA
(703) 356-7088

**Saint Stephen's Baptist
Church**
628 M Street NW
(202) 289-1665

BUDDHIST

**Buddhist Congregational
Church of America**
5401 16th Street NW
(202) 829-2423

Buddhist Vihara Society Inc.
5017 16th Street NW
(202) 723-0773

Ekoji Buddhist Temple
8134 Old Keene Mill Road
Springfield, VA
(703) 569-2311

Nipponzan Myohoji Inc.
4900 16th Street NW
(202) 291-2047

**Zen Buddhist Center of
Washington, D.C., Inc.**
7004 9th Street NW
(202) 829-1966

EPISCOPAL

All Saints' Church
3 Chevy Chase Circle
Bethesda, MD
(301) 654-2488

Saint Francis Episcopal Church
9220 Georgetown Pike
Great Falls, VA
(703) 759-2082

Saint James Episcopal Church
11815 Seven Locks Road
Potomac, MD
(301) 1762-8040

Saint John's Episcopal Church—Georgetown Parish
3240 O Street NW
(202) 338-1796

Truro Episcopal Church
10520 Main Street
Fairfax, VA
(703) 273-1300

Washington National Cathedral
Wisconsin and Massachusetts Avenues NW
(202) 537-6200

HINDU

Golden Lotus Temple
4748 Western Avenue
Bethesda, MD
(301) 229-3871

ISLAMIC

Ahmadiyya Movement in Islam
15000 Good Hope Road
Silver Spring, MD
(301) 879-0110

Islamic Education Center
7917 Montrose Road
Potomac, MD
(301) 340-2070

Masjid Muhammad
1519 4th Street NW
(202) 483-8832

Moorish Science Temple of America
732 Webster Street NW
(202) 726-5025

JEHOVAH'S WITNESSES

Jehovah's Witnesses Kensington Congregation
11235 Newport Mill Road
Kensington, MD
(301) 933-2119

Jehovah's Witnesses Northern Virginia Congregation
6 East Masonic View Avenue
Alexandria, VA
(703) 836-6030

Jehovah's Witnesses Spring Valley
2950 Arizona Avenue NW
(202) 966-1705

MOVING TIP

Remember: Large trucks are not allowed on I-66 at any time inside the Beltway. The same goes for the George Washington Parkway.

JEWISH

Conservative

Adas Israel Congregation
Connecticut Avenue and Porter Street NW
(202) 362-4433

Agudas Achim Congregation Northern Virginia
2908 Valley Street
Alexandria, VA
(703) 998-6460

B'nai Israel Congregation
6301 Montrose Road
Rockville, MD
(301) 881-6550

Congregation Beth El of Montgomery County
8215 Old Georgetown Road
Bethesda, MD
(301) 652-2606

Fairfax Jewish Congregation
2920 Arlington Boulevard
Arlington, VA
(703) 979-4466

Ohr Kodesh Congregation
8402 Freyman Drive
Chevy Chase, MD
(301) 589-3880

Olam Tikva
3800 Glenbrook Road
Fairfax, VA
(703) 425-1880

Tifereth Israel Congregation
7701 16th Street NW
(202) 882-1605

Orthodox

Beth Sholorn Congregation and Talmud Torah
11825 Seven Locks Road
Potomac, MD
(301) 279-7010

Congregation Ahavat Israel
9401 Mathy Drive
Fairfax, VA
(703) 764-0239

Georgetown Synagogue— Kesher Israel Congregation
2801 North Street NW
(202) 337-2337

Ohev Sholorn Talmud Torah Congregation
7712 16th Street NW
(202) 882-7225

Southeast Hebrew Congregation
10900 Lockwood Drive
Silver Spring, MD
(301) 593-2120

Reform

Beth Ami
800 Hurley Avenue
Rockville, MD
(301) 340-6818

Beth El Hebrew Congregation
3830 Seminary Road
Alexandria, VA
(703) 370-9400

Hebrew Congregation
3935 Macomb Street NW
(202) 362-7100

Northern Virginia Hebrew Congregation
1441 Wiehle Avenue
Reston, VA
(703) 437-7733

Rodef Shalom
2100 Westmoreland Street
Falls Church, VA
(703) 532-2217

Temple Emanuel
10101 Connecticut Avenue
Kensington, MD
(301) 942-2000

Temple Micah
2829 Wisconsin Avenue NW
(202) 342-9175

Temple Sinai
3100 Military Road NW
(202) 363-6394

LUTHERAN

Bethany Lutheran Church
2501 Beacon Hill Road
Alexandria, VA
(703) 765-8255

Christ Lutheran Church of Bethesda
8011 Old Georgetown Road
Bethesda, MD
(301) 652-5160

Georgetown Lutheran Church
1556 Wisconsin Avenue NW
(202) 337-9070

Saint Paul's Lutheran Church
4900 36th Street NW
(202) 966-5489

Zion Evangelical Lutheran Church
7410 New Hampshire Avenue
Takoma Park, MD
(301) 434-0444

METHODIST

Ashbury Methodist Church
1 I and K Streets NW
(202) 628-0009

Congress Heights United Methodist Church
421 Alabama Avenue SE
(202) 562-0600

Great Falls United Methodist Church
10100 Georgetown Pike
Great Falls, VA
(703) 759-3705

Mount Olivet United Methodist Church
1500 North Glebe Road
Arlington, VA
(703) 527-3934

CITY FACT

The waiting list for Washington Redskins season tickets now stands at 20,000. Some people have been on the list since 1975.

Saint Paul's United Methodist Church
10401 Armory Avenue
Kensington, MD
(301) 933-7933

Wesley United Methodist Church
8412 Richmond Avenue
Alexandria, VA
(703) 780-5019

ORTHODOX CHRISTIAN

Greek Orthodox Church of Saint George
7701 Bradley Boulevard
Bethesda, MD
(301) 469-7990

Saint George's Antiochian Orthodox Christian Church
4335 16th Street NW
(202) 723-5335; (301) 816-9541

Russian Orthodox Church of Saint Nicholas
3500 Massachusetts Avenue NW
(202) 333-5060

PRESBYTERIAN

Arlington Presbyterian Church
3507 Columbia Pike
Arlington, VA
(703) 920-5660

Heritage Presbyterian Church
8503 Fort Hunt Road
Alexandria, VA
(703) 360-9546

Chevy Chase Presbyterian Church
1 Chevy Chase Circle NW
(202) 363-2202

National Presbyterian Church
4101 Nebraska Avenue NW
(202) 537-0800

Fifteenth Street Presbyterian Church
1701 15th Street NW
(202) 234-0300

Potomac Presbyterian Church
10301 River Road
Potomac, MD
(301) 299-6007

Takoma Park Presbyterian Church
310 Tulip Avenue
Takoma Park, MD
(301) 270-5550

ROMAN CATHOLIC

Basilica of the National Shrine of the Immaculate Conception
Michigan Avenue and 4th Street NE
(202) 526-8300

Holy Trinity Catholic Church
1000 Potomac Street NW
(202) 337-2840

Our Lady of Perpetual Help
1600 Morris Street SE
(202) 678-4999

Saint Augustine
1419 V Street NW
(202) 265-1470

Saint Bartholomew's Church
7212 Blacklock Road
Bethesda, MD
301-229-7933

Saint Dominic's Church
630 E Street SW
(202) 554-7863

Saint Thomas Apostle
2665 Wooley Road NW
(202) 234-1488

Shrine of the Most Blessed Sacrament
6001 Western Avenue NW
(202) 966-6575

MOVING TIP

If moving into Arlington County or upper Northwest Washington, make sure your mover has explicit and clear directions to your home. Many neighborhoods in both areas have complicated street layouts, deadends, one-block streets that stop and start for several miles, etc.

SEVENTH-DAY ADVENTIST

Capital Memorial Seventh-Day Adventist Church
3150 Chesapeake Street NW
(202) 362-3668

Capitol Hill Seventh-Day Adventist Church
914 Massachusetts Avenue SE
(202) 543-1344

Emmanuel Temple Seventh-Day Adventist Church
2707 DeWitt Avenue
Alexandria, VA
(703) 836-6673

Fourth Street Friendship Seventh-Day Adventist Church
1611 4th Street NW
(202) 1797-9255

UNITARIAN

Universalist National Memorial Church
1810 16th Street NW
(202) 387-3411

Post Offices

327 7th Street SE
(202) 547-6191

2 Massachusetts Avenue NE
(202) 523-2628

300 A Street SW
(202) 523-2144

458 L'Enfant Plaza SW
(202) 523-2103

45 L Street SW
(202) 635-5302

3401 12th Street NE
(202) 635-5315

2650 Naylor Road NE
(202) 635-5307

600 Pennsylvania Avenue SE
(202) 523-2173

5921 Georgia Avenue NW
(202) 523-2392

1921 Florida Avenue NW
(202) 232-7613

1145 19th Street NW
(202) 523-2506

1110 20th Street NW
(202) 523-2410

1423 Irving Street NW
(202) 523-2397

2300 18th Street NW
(202) 483-5042

3430 Connecticut Avenue NW
(202) 523-2395

1215 31st Street NW
(202) 523-2406

2336 Wisconsin Avenue NW
(202) 965-2000

4005 Wisconsin Avenue NW
(202) 635-5305

1145 9th Street NW
(202) 523-2506

CITY FACT

If you want to see political hotshots, hang out at the bars and restaurants on the Hill: La Colline and the Monocle are the most popular for elected officials.

2512 Virginia Avenue NW
(202) 965-2730

3050 K Street NW
(202) 523-2406

7400 Wisconsin Avenue NW
(301) 941-2664

5910 Connecticut Avenue NW
(301) 941-2792

Shopping

APPLIANCE STORES

Applianceland
10801 Baltimore Avenue
Beltsville, MD
(301) 595-7360

866 Rockville Pike
Rockville, MD
(301) 762-5544

Bargain Spot
936 Rhode Island Avenue NE
(202) 529-1192

Best Buy
1201 Hayes Street
Arlington, VA
(703) 414-7090

Bray and Scarff
7924 Wisconsin Avenue NW
(301) 654-4150

Murrell's Electronics
2140 Wisconsin Avenue NW
(202) 338-7730

BEDDING AND LINENS

MOVING TIP

A good, moderately priced local beer to reward friends or strangers for helping with your move is Old Dominion.

Bed Bath & Beyond
12270 Rockville Pike
Rockville, MD
(301) 231-7637

5716 Columbia Pike
Falls Church, MD
(703) 578-3374

Linens 'N Things
Call (800) LNT-8765 for locations.

BOOKSTORES

The two big chains in the area are listed below. But Washington has some great independent booksellers, with a wide variety of publications on the shelves. Check out the list and give them a try before going to the big boys.

Barnes & Noble
30th and M Streets NW
(202) 965-9880

Borders Books & Music
1800 L Street NW
(202) 466-4999

11301 Rockville Pike
Rockville, MD
(301) 816-1067

5871 Crossroads Center Way
Bailey's Cross Roads, VA
(703) 998-0404

1201 South Hayes Street
Arlington, VA
(703) 418-0166

11054 Lee Highway
Fairfax, VA
(703) 359-8420

Kramerbooks
1517 Connecticut Avenue NW
(202) 387-1400

One of the great bookstores in Washington, it also features a nice coffee shop.

Lambda Rising
1625 Connecticut Avenue NW
(202) 462-6969

This Dupont Circle bookstore carries gay and lesbian fiction and non-fiction titles.

Politics & Prose
5015 Connecticut Avenue NW
(202) 364-1919

The name says it all. It also features a used-book shop.

Vertigo Books
1337 Connecticut Avenue NW
(202) 429-9272

A good, all-purpose bookshop.

DEPARTMENT STORES

Bloomingdales

Tysons Corner Mall
Dolley Madison Boulevard and
Leesburg Pike
McLean, VA
(703) 556-4600

White Flint Mall
11301 Rockville Pike
(301) 984-4600

This high-end New York chain is competing against Macy's and Nordstrom's. Bloomies is popular not only for its fashions, but also for its furniture: they sell some of the nicest sofas in town. There isn't a store in Washington, but there are a number of anchoring malls in the suburbs.

CITY
FACT

If you live in Washington you will share the city with more than 20 million new neighbors each year. They are called tourists.

Hecht's

Metro Center
12th and G Streets NW
(202) 628-6661

701 North Glebe Road
Arlington, VA
(703) 524-5100

Montgomery Mall
7135 Democracy Boulevard
Bethesda, MD
(301) 469-6800

Tysons Corner Mall
Dolley Madison Boulevard and
Leesburg Pike
McLean, VA
(703) 893-4900

Owned by the May Company, one of the largest department store and shopping mall companies in the country, this is a basic department store that is popular in the area.

Macy's

Pentagon City
1000 South Hayes Street
Arlington, VA
(703) 418-4488

Tysons Galleria
1651 International Drive
McLean, VA
(703) 556-0000

It's perhaps the most famous department store in America.

Nordstrom
Montgomery Mall
7111 Democracy Boulevard
Bethesda, MD
(301) 365-4111

Pentagon City
1000 South Hayes Street
Arlington, VA
(703) 415-1121

Tysons Corner Mall
1961 Chainbridge Road
McLean, VA
(703) 761-1121

The arrival of this West Coast retailer just a decade ago shook up the Washington market. Nordstrom is known for quality and service. Its sales staff is actually helpful—a trait previously almost unknown in these parts. Nordstrom carries well-made clothing, cosmetics, toiletries, and accessories. It started as a shoe store and the shoe department still carries a wide range of styles and sizes.

Saks Fifth Avenue
5555 Wisconsin Avenue
Chevy Chase, MD
(301) 657-9000

Tysons Galleria
2051 International Drive
McLean, VA
(703) 761-0700

Two locations for this high-end retailer.

FURNITURE

IKEA
Potomac Mills Outlet Mall
Dale City, VA
(703) 494-4532

outside of Baltimore
(410) 931-5400

This Swedish home store offers stylish and moderately priced housewares and furniture (some assembly may be required). If you're looking for bargains, IKEA is worth the trip.

MOVING TIP

Most apartment buildings in Washington allow moves only on Saturdays and Sundays. Make sure you notify your landlord about your arrival time and reserve an elevator for that time. Landlords are sticklers about these things.

Marlo Furniture

With a number of outlets in the Washington area, this large, discount furniture seller always seems to be having a sale. Check local papers for the latest deal.

MATTRESSES

Dial-A-Mattress
9385 Washington Boulevard
Laurel, VA
800-MATTRES

Mattress Discounters

The chain has more than 30 locations in the Washington

Pottery Barn
5335 Wisconsin Avenue NW
(202) 244-9330

Tysons Galleria
McLean, VA
(703) 821-8504

Storehouse
Congressional Plaza
1601 Rockville Pike
Rockville, MD
(301) 231-7310

6700 Wisconsin Avenue
Bethesda, MD
(301) 654-6829

7505-J Leesburg Pike
Falls Church, VA
(703) 821-5027

809 South Washington Street
Alexandria, VA
(703) 548-6934

Solid, moderately priced furniture is the draw here.

area. Check your phone book or the *Washington Post* for weekly sales and advertisements.

Mattress Warehouse

Call (301) 230-BEDS for area locations.

CHAPTER 10

Local Schools and Colleges

Selecting a school—whether for your child or yourself—is one of the most important decisions you'll make in your lifetime. The Washington, D.C., area makes the decision-making process easier in that it has so many high-quality institutions to choose from. But, on the other hand, Washington makes the decision tougher because there are so many options to consider!

Like that in any urban area, D.C.'s public school system has its problems. Lots of them, in this case. Many schools are in disrepair, and some have even been shut down by the city's own health department. That said, Washington, D.C., public schools are working to make improvements. And like any city school system, where you decide to live can determine the quality of the school your child enrolls in. As noted in the overview of the city's neighborhoods in chapter 1, areas within the Northwest and parts of the Northeast quadrants of Washington, D.C., have a number of high-quality public schools. Further along in this chapter we discuss private schools in D.C. as well as in Maryland and Virginia.

Metro Area Public School Districts

Washington, D.C., (202) 724-4289

Alexandria, VA, (703) 824-6600

Arlington County, VA, (703) 358-6000

Fairfax County, VA, (703) 246-2502

Montgomery County, MD, (301) 279-3391

Prince Georges County, MD, (301) 952-6000

Enrolling in Washington, D.C., Public Schools

What follows is quick primer on public school enrollment for families moving into the area. The policies of the Washington, D.C., Public Schools (DCPS) are no different from those of most other big-city public education departments. Still, it's helpful to have a sense of what to expect.

 CITY FACT

There are more cabs per capita in Washington than in any other city in America.

TUITION

The Washington, D.C., Public Schools (DCPS) are taxpayer-funded. Washington residents do not pay tuition, although certain special programs may require a small fee for such things as teaching supplies. Students who do not reside in the District must pay tuition to attend DCPS schools. Tuition fees vary depending on the program in which the student is enrolled. For more information, contact the Division of Student Residency.

Division of Student Residency
DCPS
825 North Capitol Street NE, Room 7115
Washington, DC 20002
(202) 442-5125

REGISTRATION

In order to register children in Washington, D.C., elementary school, middle school, junior high school, or senior high school, parents must contact the school they want their children to attend. Students are guaranteed enrollment in their neighborhood schools, but if parents wish to enroll their child in a different school within their district or in another school district, they must receive permission from the principal of the school they wish the child to attend.

If you are moving into the area during the school year, and you want to enroll your child in a school outside your district, you should contact the DCPS. The school system sets deadlines regarding when a student may be enrolled in an out-of-district school. The dates vary from year to year, but generally the deadlines are a month before the fall and spring semesters begin. Transfers are allowed on a space-available basis.

If you are transferring a child from a school outside the Washington school district, and you know where you will be residing, contact the DCPS to determine which neighborhood schools your children should be enrolled in. This way, you can ask your present school system to forward all records to the new school before you actually register your children.

When you go to register your child, bring the following items with you:

- Proof of the child's birth date
- Legal proof of residency
- Immunization records

Residency Requirements

Washington, D.C., requires that you provide three separate documents to confirm your residency in the city. The school will keep these on file for reference. Any of the following are acceptable:

- Proof of payment of D.C. personal income tax during the last tax period
- A current tax-withholding statement that contains the applicant's name
- A valid D.C. driver's license or non-driver's identification card
- Vehicle registration
- Valid, unexpired lease, rent, or mortgage receipts
- A D.C. voter registration card
- Utility bills from within the last two months, along with cancelled checks or receipts indicating that they have been paid

Immunization Requirements

At the time of registration, your child must have had the following immunizations:

- DPT (Diphtheria/Pertussis/Tetanus)
- OPV (Oral Polio Vaccine)
- MMR (Measles/Mumps/Rubella)
- HIb (Hemophilus Influenza type b)
- HepB (Hepatitis B)
- Varicella (if the child has not had chicken pox)

Note: The hepatitis B and varicella requirements have been added within the last few years. Older students may not have received these immunizations; if your child is in the fifth grade or older, check to see if they are on his or her record. All students in the fifth grade or older should also have a tetanus/diphtheria booster shot, unless it has been less than five years since a previous immunization. Call the DCPS Office of Student Health at (202) 442-5141 if you require additional information.

Washington, D.C., Public Schools

What follows is a list of Washington, D.C., public schools by district. Elementary schools include pre-kindergarten (pre-K) through Grade 6. Middle schools include Grades 6 through 8. Junior high schools run from Grades 7 through 9. Senior high schools run from Grades 9 through 12.

DISTRICT 1

Elementary Schools

Ada Elementary School
2020 19th Street NW
Washington, DC 20009
(202) 673-7311

Bancroft Elementary School
1755 Newton Street NW
Washington, DC 20010
(202) 673-7280

Bruce-Monroe Elementary School
3012 Georgia Avenue NW
Washington, DC 20001
(202) 576-6215

Cleveland Elementary School
1825 8th Street NW
Washington, DC 20001
(202) 673-7290

H. D. Cooke Elementary School
2525 17th Street NW
Washington, DC 20009
(202) 673-7294

MOVING TIP

If you are renting a van or truck and relocating from out of the area, keep in mind that there are few truck drop-off lots actually in Washington. You may have to drop your truck off in a Virginia or Maryland suburb. Find out the closest lot to ensure you don't get stuck with a late drop-off charge.

Gage-Eckington Elementary School
2025 3rd Street NW
Washington, DC 20001
(202) 673-7305

Meyer Elementary School
2501 11th Street NW
Washington, DC 20001
(202) 673-7259

Oyster Elementary School
300 Bryant Street NW
Washington, DC 20001
(202) 671-0081

CITY
FACT

The Washington Beltway is 67 miles long.

Park View Elementary School
3560 Warder Street NW
Washington, DC 20010
(202) 576-6222

Tubman Elementary School
3101 13th Street NW
Washington, DC 20010
(202) 673-7285

Middle Schools

Garnet-Patterson Middle School
2001 10th Street NW
Washington, DC 20001
(202) 673-7329

Lincoln Middle School
3101 16th Street NW
Washington, DC 20010
(202) 673-7345

High Schools

Banneker Senior High School
800 Euclid Street NW
Washington, DC 20001
(202) 673-7322

Bell Multicultural Senior High School
3145 Hiatt Place NW
Washington, DC 20010
(202) 673-7314

Cardozo Senior High School
1300 Clifton Street NW
Washington, DC 20009
(202) 673-7385

DISTRICT 2

Elementary Schools

Amidon Elementary School
401 I Street SW
Washington, DC 20024
(202) 724-4867

Bowen Elementary School
101 M Street SW
Washington, DC 20024
(202) 724-4871

Ellington School of the Arts
1698 35th Street NW
Washington, DC 20007
(202) 282-0123

Garrison Elementary School
1200 S Street NW
Washington, DC 20009
(202) 673-7263

Hyde Elementary School
3219 O Street NW
Washington, DC 20007
(202) 282-0170

Montgomery Elementary School
421 P Street NW
Washington, DC 20001
(202) 673-7245

Ross Elementary School
1730 R Street NW
Washington, DC 20009
(202) 673-7200

Seaton Elementary School
1503 10th Street NW
Washington, DC 20001
(202) 673-7215

Stevens Elementary School
1050 21st Street NW
Washington, DC 20036
(202) 724-4852

Thoon Elementary School
1200 L Street NW
Washington, DC 20005
(202) 724-4910

Walker-Jon Elementary School
100 L Street NW
Washington, DC 20001
(202) 535-1222

Middle School

Hardy Middle School
1819 35th Street NW
Washington, DC 20007
(202) 282-0057

Junior High Schools

Francis Junior High School
2425 N Street NW
Washington, DC 20037
(202) 724-4841

Jefferson Junior High School
801 7th Street SW
Washington, DC 20024
(202) 724-4881

Shaw Junior High School
925 Rhode Island Avenue NW
Washington, DC 20001
(202) 673-7203

R. H. Terrell Junior High School
1000 1st Street NW
Washington, DC 20001
(202) 535-2000

High School

School Without Walls Senior High School
2130 G Street NW
Washington, DC 20037
(202) 724-4889

DISTRICT 3

Elementary Schools

Eaton Elementary School
3301 Lowell Street NW
Washington, DC 20008
(202) 282-0103

Hearst Elementary School
3950 37th Street NW
Washington, DC 20008
(202) 282-0106

Janney Elementary School
4130 Albemarle Street NW
Washington, DC 20016
(202) 282-0110

Key Elementary School
5001 Dana Place NW
Washington, DC 20016
(202) 282-0113

Lafayette Elementary School
5701 Broad Branch Road NW
Washington, DC 20015
(202) 282-0116

Mann Elementary School
4430 Newark Street NW
Washington, DC 20016
(202) 282-0126

Murch Elementary School
4810 36th Street NW
Washington, DC 20008
(202) 282-0130

Stoddert Elementary School
4001 Calvert Street NW
Washington, DC 20007
(202) 282-0143

High School

Wilson Senior High School
3950 Chesapeake Street NW
Washington, DC 20016
(202) 282-0120

DISTRICT 4

Elementary Schools

Barnard Elementary School
430 Decatur Street NW
Washington, DC 20011
(202) 576-6231

Brightwood Elementary School
1300 Nicholson Street NW
Washington, DC 20011
(202) 576-6199

Clark Elementary School
4501 7th Street NW
Washington, DC 20011
(202) 576-6219

LaSalle Elementary School
501 Riggs Road NE
Washington, DC 20011
(202) 576-6120

Powell Elementary School
1350 Upshur Street NW
Washington, DC 20011
(202) 576-6247

Raymond Elementary School
915 Spring Road NW
Washington, DC 20010
(202) 576-6236

Paul Robeson School
3700 10th Street NW
Washington, DC 20010
(202) 576-5151

Rudolph Elementary School
5200 2nd Street NW
Washington, DC 20011
(202) 576-6186

Shaed Elementary School
301 Douglas Street NE
Washington, DC 20002
(202) 576-6052

Shepherd Elementary School
7800 14th Street NW
Washington, DC 20012
(202) 576-6140

Takoma Elementary School
7010 Piney Branch Road NW
Washington, DC 20012
(202) 576-6127

Trudell Elementary School
800 Ingraham Street NW
Washington, DC 20011
(202) 576-6202

Whittier Elementary School
6201 5th Street NW
Washington, DC 20011
(202) 576-6156

Middle School

Macfarland Middle School
4400 Iowa Avenue NW
Washington, DC 20011
(202) 576-6207

Junior High School

Deal Junior High School
3815 Fort Drive NW
Washington, DC 20016
(202) 282-0100

High Schools

Coolidge Senior High School
6315 5th Street NW
Washington, DC 20011
(202) 576-6143

Roosevelt Senior High School
4301 13th Street NW
Washington, DC 20011
(202) 576-6130

DISTRICT 5

Elementary Schools

Brookland Elementary School
1150 Michigan Avenue NE
Washington, DC 20017
(202) 576-6082

Bunker Hill Elementary School
1401 Michigan Avenue NE
Washington, DC 20017
(202) 576-6095

Burroughs Elementary School
1820 Monroe Street NE
Washington, DC 20018
(202) 576-6039

J. F. Cook Elementary School
30 P Street NW
Washington, DC 20001
(202) 673-7221

Emery Elementary School
1720 1st Street NE
Washington, DC 20002
(202) 576-6034

Langdon Elementary School
1900 Evarts Street NE
Washington, DC 20018
(202) 576-6048

Malcolm X Elementary School
1401 Brentwood Road NE
Washington, DC 20002
(202) 698-3888

Marshall Elementary School
3100 Fort Lincoln Drive NE
Washington, DC 20018
(202) 576-6900

Noy Elementary School
2725 10th Street NE
Washington, DC 20018
(202) 576-6071

Slowe Elementary School
1404 Jackson Street NE
Washington, DC 20017
(202) 576-6075

Taft Elementary School
1800 Perry Street NE
Washington, DC 20018
(202) 576-6101

Webb Elementary School
1375 Mount Olivet Road NE
Washington, DC 20002
(202) 724-4543

Wheatley Elementary School
1299 Neal Street NE
Washington, DC 20002
(202) 724-4555

Young Elementary School
820 26th Street NE
Washington, DC 20002
(202) 724-4569

MOVING TIP

If you're moving into an older Washington home, try to get door and hallway dimensions before the moving day so you can compare the measurements to your furniture dimensions. Many older D.C. homes have narrow doors and hallways that can stall an otherwise smooth move.

Middle School

Backus Middle School
5171 South Dakota Avenue NE
Washington, DC 20017
(202) 576-6110

Junior High School

Browne Junior High School
850 26th Street NE
Washington, DC 20002
(202) 724-4547

High Schools

Dunbar Senior High School
1301 New Jersey Avenue NW
Washington, DC 2000
(202) 673-7233

Moore Academy Senior High School
1001 Monroe Street NE
Washington, DC 20017
(202) 576-7005

Spingarn Senior High School
2500 Benning Road NE
Washington, DC 20002
(202) 724-4525

DISTRICT 6

Preschool

Reggio Preschool
425 C Street NE
Washington, DC 20002
(202) 698-3283

Elementary Schools

Brent Elementary School
330 3rd Street SE
Washington, DC 20003
(202) 698-3363

Gibbs Elementary School
500 19th Street NE
Washington, DC 20002
(202) 724-4573

Ketcham Elementary School
1919 15th Street SE
Washington, DC 20020
(202) 698-1122

Ludlow-Taylor Elementary School
659 G Street NE
Washington, DC 20002
(202) 698-3244

Maury Elementary School
1250 Constitution Avenue NE
Washington, DC 20002
(202) 698-3838

Miner Elementary School
601 15th Street NE
Washington, DC 20002
(202) 724-4565

Orr Elementary School

2200 Minnota Avenue SE
Washington, DC 20020
(202) 645-3288

Payne Elementary School

305 15th Street SE
Washington, DC 20003
(202) 698-3262

Peabody Elementary School

425 C Street NE
Washington, DC 20003
(202) 698-3277

Tyler Elementary School

1001 G Street SE
Washington, DC 20003
(202) 698-3577

Van-Ness Elementary School

1150 5th Street SE
Washington, DC 20003
(202) 698-3818

Watkins Elementary School

420 12th Street SE
Washington, DC 20003
(202) 698-3355

J. O. Wilson Elementary School

660 K Street NE
Washington, DC 20002
(202) 698-4733

Middle Schools

Kramer Middle School

1700 Q Street SE
Washington, DC 20020
(202) 698-1188

Stuart-Hobson Middle School

410 E Street NE
Washington, DC 20002
(202) 698-4700

CITY FACT

The city of Washington, D.C., is only 26 square miles, but the Washington, D.C. metro area is 6,000 square miles.

Junior High Schools

Eliot Junior High School

1830 Constitution Avenue NE
Washington, DC 20002
(202) 673-8666

Hine Junior High School
335 8th Street SE
Washington, DC 20003
(202) 698-3330

Eastern Senior High School
1700 East Capitol Street NE
Washington, DC 20003
(202) 698-4500

High Schools

Anacostia Senior High School
1601 16th Street SE
Washington, DC 20020
(202) 645-3000

DISTRICT 7

Elementary Schools

Aiton Elementary School
533 48th Place NE
Washington, DC 20019
(202) 724-4627

Beers Elementary School
3600 Alabama Avenue SE
Washington, DC 20020
(202) 645-3240

Benning Elementary School
100 41st Street NE
Washington, DC 20019
(202) 724-4586

Burrville Elementary School
801 Division Avenue NE
Washington, DC 20019
(202) 724-4598

Davis Elementary School
4430 H Street SE
Washington, DC 20019
(202) 645-3220

Drew Elementary School
5600 Eads Street NE
Washington, DC 20019
(202) 724-4922

C. W. Harris Elementary School
301 53rd Street SE
Washington, DC 20019
(202) 645-3188

Houston Elementary School
1100 50th Place NE
Washington, DC 20019
(202) 724-4622

Kenilworth Elementary School
1300 44th Street NE
Washington, DC 20019
(202) 724-4643

Kimball Elementary School
3375 Minnesota Avenue SE
Washington, DC 20019
(202) 645-3150

Merritt Elementary School
5002 Hay Street NE
Washington, DC 20019
(202) 724-4618

Nalle Elementary School
219 50th Street SE
Washington, DC 20019
(202) 645-7300

Plummer Elementary School
4601 Texas Avenue SE
Washington, DC 20019
(202) 645-3179

Randle Highlands Elementary School
1650 30th Street SE
Washington, DC 20020
(202) 645-3282

River Terrace Elementary School
420 34th Street NE
Washington, DC 20019
(202) 724-4589

Shadd Elementary School
5601 East Capitol Street SE
Washington, DC 20019
(202) 645-3155

Smothers Elementary School
4400 Brooks Street NE
Washington, DC 20019
(202) 724-4640

Thomas Elementary School
650 Anacostia Avenue NE
Washington, DC 20019
(202) 724-4593

Middle Schools

Ronald H. Brown Middle School
4800 Meade Street NE
Washington, DC 20019
(202) 724-4632

Evans Middle School
5600 East Capitol Street NE
Washington, DC 20019
(202) 724-4727

Sousa Middle School
3650 Ely Place SE
Washington, DC 20019
(202) 645-3170

High School

H. D. Woodson Senior High School
5500 Eads Street NE
Washington, DC 20019
(202) 724-4500

DISTRICT 8

Elementary Schools

Birney Elementary School
2501 Martin Luther King
Avenue SE
Washington, DC 20020
(202) 698-1133

Draper Elementary School
908 Wahler Place SE
Washington, DC 20032
(202) 645-3309

Ferebee-Hope Elementary School
3999 8th Street SE
Washington, DC 20032
(202) 645-3100

Garfield Elementary School
2435 Alabama Avenue SE
Washington, DC 20020
(202) 698-1600

Green Elementary School
1500 Mississippi Avenue SE
Washington, DC 20032
(202) 645-3470

Hendley Elementary School
425 Chesapeake Street SE
Washington, DC 20032
(202) 645-3450

King Elementary School
3200 6th Street SE
Washington, DC 20032
(202) 645-3440

Leckie Elementary School
4200 Martin Luther King
Avenue SW
Washington, DC 20032
(202) 645-3330

McGogney Elementary School
3400 Wheeler Road SE
Washington, DC 20032
(202) 645-3320

Moten Elementary School
1565 Morris Road SE
Washington, DC 20020
(202) 698-1144

Patterson Elementary School
4399 South Capitol Terrace SW
Washington, DC 20032
(202) 645-3477

Savoy Elementary School
2400 Shannon Place SE
Washington, DC 20020
(202) 698-1515

Simon Elementary School
401 Mississippi Avenue SE
Washington, DC 20032
(202) 645-3360

Stanton Elementary School
2701 Naylor Road SE
Washington, DC 20020
(202) 645-3255

Terrell Elementary School
3301 Wheeler Road SE
Washington, DC 20032
(202) 645-3740

Turner Elementary School
3264 Stanton Road SE
Washington, DC 20020
(202) 698-1155

Wilkinson Elementary School
2330 Pomeroy Road SE
Washington, DC 20020
(202) 698-1111

Middle School

Hart Middle School
601 Mississippi Avenue SE
Washington, DC 20032
(202) 645-3420

MOVING TIP

If you can get your D.C. cable installed in advance, do so. D.C. Cable is notoriously slow about installation and setup. Most apartment buildings will let them in before you move in.

Junior High School

Johnson Junior High School
2600 Douglass Road SE
Washington, DC 20020
(202) 698-1570

High School

Ballou Senior High School
3401 4th Street SE
Washington, DC 20032
(202) 645-3390

Metro Area Private Schools

Here's a list of private schools in Washington, D.C., as well as in the Maryland and Virginia suburbs. The tuition fees listed are as of fall 1999; fees are per school year unless otherwise noted.

WASHINGTON, D.C.

Aidan Montessori School
2700 27th Street NW
Washington, DC 20008
(202) 387-2700

www.aidan1.com

1¹/₂ years–12 years

$2,700–$9,650

Annunciation School
3825 Klingle Place NW
Washington, DC 20016
(202) 362-1408

K–Grade 8

$3,400

Archbishop Carroll High School
4300 Harewood Road NE
Washington, DC 20017
(202) 529-0900

www.ee.cua.edu/~carroll/

Grades 9–12

$5,250 (Catholic), $5,500 (non-Catholic)

Beauvoir, the National Cathedral Elementary School
3500 Woodley Road NW
Washington, DC 20016
(202) 537-6492

www.beauvoir.cathedral.org

Pre-K–Grade 3

$13,368

Blessed Sacrament School
5841 Chevy Chase Parkway NW
Washington, DC 20015
(202) 966-6682

www.blsed-sacrament.com

K–Grade 8

$3,400 (parishioners), $6,000 (non-parishioners)

British School of Washington
7775 17th Street NW and 4715 16th Street NW
Washington, DC 20012
(202) 829-3700

www.britishschool.org

Pre-K–Grade 8

$9,500

Capitol Hill Day School

210 South Carolina Avenue SE
Washington, DC 20003
(202) 547-2244

www.chds.org

Pre-K–Grade 8

$10,500–$11,300 (Pre-K–K),
$11,450 (Grades 1–5), $11,865
(Grades 6–8)

Children's House of Washington

3133 Dumbarton Street NW
Washington, DC 20007
(202) 342-2551

3–5 years

$4,200–$5,200

Edmund Burke School

2955 Upton Street NW
Washington, DC 20008
(202) 362-8882

www.eburke.org

Grades 6–12

$14,700

Field School

2126 Wyoming Avenue NW
Washington, DC 20008
(202) 232-0733

www.fieldschool.com

Grades 7–12

$15,009

Georgetown Day School

4530 MacArthur Boulevard NW
Washington, DC 20007
(202) 333-7727

www.gds.org

Pre-K–Grade 8

$14,657–$16,495

Georgetown Day School

4200 Davenport Street NW
Washington, DC 20016
(202) 966-2666

www.gds.org

Grades 9–12

$16,632–$16,767

Georgetown Montessori School

1041 Wisconsin Avenue NW
Washington, DC 20007
(202) 337-8058

$1^{1}/_{2}$–6 years

$3,900–$7,000

Holy Trinity School of Georgetown

1325 36th Street NW
Washington, DC 20007
(202) 337-2339

Pre-K–Grade 8

$6,600–$7,600 (Pre-K–K),
$5,000–$6,500 (Grades 1–8)

CITY FACT

The famous Capitol Steps comedy troupe got its name from former congressman John Jenrette's sexual liaison on the actual Capitol steps.

Jewish Primary Day School

2850 Quebec Street NW
Washington, DC 20008
(202) 362-4446

www.jpds.org

K–Grade 6

$7,644

Kinderhaus

3400 Lowell Street NW
Washington, DC 20016
(202) 686-3570

5307 Connecticut Avenue NW
Washington, DC 20015
(202) 244-0719

www.kinderhaus.org

2 months–5 years

$660–$900 a month

Little Flower Montessori School

3029 16th Street NW
Washington, DC 20009
(202) 667-6803

$2^{1}/_{2}$–6 years

$450–$550 per month

Lowell School

1640 Kalmia Road NW
Washington, DC 20012
(202) 577-2000

www.lowellschool.org

Pre-K–Grade 5

$7,250–$11,500 (Pre-K), $11,875 (K–Grade 5)

Maret School

3000 Cathedral Avenue NW
Washington, DC 20008
(202) 939-8800

www.maret.org

K–Grade 12

$13,800–$16,510

Midtown Montessori School

33 K Street NW
Washington, DC 20001
(202) 789-0222

2–6 years

$23.55 per day

Montessori School of Chevy Chase

5312 Connecticut Avenue NW
Washington, DC 20015
(202) 362-6212

2^1/$_2$–6 years

$4,200 (half day), $5,900 (full day)

Montessori School of Washington

1556 Wisconsin Avenue NW
Washington, DC 20007
(202) 338-1557

2–6 years

$3,600–$5,900

National Presbyterian School

4121 Nebraska Avenue NW
Washington, DC 20016
(202) 537-7500

www.nps/dc.org/school

Pre-K–Grade 6

$6,202–$11,770

Nativity Catholic Academy

6008 Georgia Avenue NW
Washington, DC 20011
(202) 723-3322

Pre-K–Grade 8

$2,800

Naylor Road School

2403 Naylor Road SE
Washington, DC 20020
(202) 584-5114

Pre-K–Grade 8

$3,850–$5,000

Our Lady of Victory School

4755 Whitehaven Parkway NW
Washington, DC 20007
(202) 337-1421

www.olv.pvt.k12.dc.us

Nursery–Grade 8

$3,000–$3,900

Parkmont School

4842 16th Street NW
Washington, DC 20011
(202) 726-0740

www.parkmont.org

Grades 6–12

$14,500

Randall-Hyland Private School

4339 Bowen Road SE
Washington, DC 20019
(202) 582-2966

2–5 years

$240 biweekly

Rock Creek International School

1550 Foxhall Road NW
Washington, DC 20007
(202) 387-0387

Pre-K–Grade 5

$7,515–$12,000

Sheridan School

4400 36th Street NW
Washington, DC 20008
(202) 362-7900

K–Grade 8

$12,700–$14,630

Sidwell Friends School

3825 Wisconsin Avenue NW
Washington, DC 20016
(202) 537-8111

www.sidwell.edu

Pre-K–Grade 12

$14,180–$16,400

Note: The Clintons and the Gores sent their children here.

St. Ann's Academy

4404 Wisconsin Avenue NW
Washington, DC 20016
(202) 363-4460

Pre-K–Grade 8

$1,800 (pre-K), $3,600 (K–Grade 8)

St. John's College High School

2607 Military Road NW
Washington, DC 20015
(202) 363-2316

www.stjohns-chs.org

Grades 7–8 boys only; Grades 9–12 co-ed

$6,300–$7,200

St. John's Episcopal Preschool

3240 O Street NW
Washington, DC 20007
(202) 338-2574

$3,000–$5,000

St. Patrick's Episcopal Day School

4700 Whitehaven Parkway NW
Washington, DC 20007
(202) 342-2805

www.stpatricks.washington.dc.us

Nursery–Grade 6

$6,975–$13,110

St. Peter's Interparish School

422 3rd Street SE
Washington, DC 20003
(202) 544-1618

www.stpetersinterparish.org

Pre-K–Grade 8

$3,470–$4,120

Washington Ethical High School

7750 16th Street NW
Washington, DC 20012
(202) 829-0088

www.members.aol.com/
wehs/wehs.html

Grades 9–12

$12,800

Washington Hebrew Congregation Early Childhood Center

3935 Macomb Street NW
Washington, DC 20016
(202) 895-6334

$1^1/_2$–5 years

$1,210–$4,830 (temple members), $1,510–$5,605 (nonmembers)

Washington International School

3100 Macomb Street NW
Washington, DC 20008
(202) 243-1800

www.wis.edu

Pre-K–Grade 12

$7,000–$16,000

MARYLAND

Abingdon Montessori School

5144 Massachusetts Avenue
Bethesda, MD 20816
(301) 320-3646

2–6 years

$5,500–$7,000

Apple Montessori School

11815 Seven Locks Road
Potomac, MD 20854
(301) 340-2244

$2^1/_2$–6 years

$2,780–$5,560

Aspen Hill Montessori School

3820 Aspen Hill Road
Wheaton, MD 20906
(301) 871-1364

2–6 years

$412–$665 per month

Melvin J. Berman Hebrew Academy

13300 Arctic Avenue
Rockville, MD 20853
(301) 962-9400

2 years–Grade 12

$1,965–$8,840

Berwyn Baptist School
4720 Cherokee Street
College Park, MD 20740
(301) 474-1561

3 years–Grade 6

$990–$3,470

MOVING TIP

If you're driving a truck through downtown Washington, avoid Connecticut Avenue and K Street. Both are difficult to make left turns on and are seemingly always busy with traffic.

Bethesda Community School
7500 Honeywell Lane
Bethesda, MD 20814
(301) 652-0117

2–6 years

$150–$840 per month

Bethesda Country Day School
5615 Beech Avenue
Bethesda, MD 20814
(301) 530-6999

Pre-K–K

$200–$700 per month

Bethesda Montessori School
7611 Clarendon Road
Bethesda, MD 20814
(301) 986-1260

www.Bethesdamontsori.com

2–6 years

$4,500–$7,600

Julia Brown Montessori Schools
1300 Miltone Drive
Silver Spring, MD 20904
(301) 622-7808

2 years–Grade 3

$315–$645 per month

Bullis School
10601 Falls Road
Potomac, MD 20854
(301) 299-8500

www.bullis.org

Grades 3–12

$12,000–$16,000

Butler School
15951 Germantown Road
Darnestown, MD 20874
(301) 977-6600

Pre-K–Grade 8

$4,200–$6,850

Calvary Lutheran School

9545 Georgia Avenue
Silver Spring, MD 20910
(301) 589-4001

www.celcs.org

K–Grade 7

$3,800

Charles E. Smith Jewish Day School

11710 Hunter Lane
Rockville, MD 20852
(301) 881-1404

www.cjds.org

Grades 7–12

$11,260 (Grades 7–11), $5,820
(Grade 12)

Christ Episcopal School

109 South Washington Street
Rockville, MD 20850
(301) 424-6550

www.c-rockville.org

Pre-K–Grade 8

$1,580–$6,880

Concord Hill School

6050 Wisconsin Avenue
Chevy Chase, MD 20815
(301) 654-2626

3 years–Grade 3

$7,000–$10,000

French International School

9600 Fort Road
Bethesda, MD 20814
(301) 530-8260

Pre-K–Grade 12

$6,783–$8,820

Geneva Day School

11931 Seven Locks Road
Potomac, MD 20854
(301) 340-7704

www.genevadayschool.org

2 years–K

$1,320–$6,700

German School, Washington, D.C.

8617 Chateau Drive
Potomac, MD 20854
(301) 365-4400

www.germanschool.org/home

Pre-K–College prep

$3,500–$4,800

Grace Episcopal Day School

9411 Connecticut Avenue
Kensington, MD 20895
(301) 949-5860

www.geds.org

Grades 1–6

$8,732–$8,845

Hebrew Day School of Montgomery County
1401 Arcola Avenue
Silver Spring, MD 20902
(301) 649-5400

K–Grade 6

$5,630 (K), $6,280 (Grades 1–6)

Holden Montessori Day School
5450 Massachusetts Avenue
Bethesda, MD 20816
(301) 229-4024

2–6 years

$2,995–$6,100

Holy Redeemer School
9715 Summit Avenue
Kensington, MD 20895
(301) 942-3701

www.hrs-ken.org

K–Grade 8

$2,650 (parishioners), $3,750 (non-parishioners)

Laurel Baptist Academy
701 Montgomery Street
Laurel, MD 20725
(301) 498-5060

www.laurelbaptistacademy.org

K–Grade 12

$3,200

Little Flower School
5601 Massachusetts Avenue
Bethesda MD 20816
(301) 320-3273

www.c-a.org

Pre-K–Grade 8

$2,700–$3,960

Lone Oak Montessori School
10201 Democracy Boulevard
Potomac, MD 20854
(301) 469-4888

2–3 years and Grades 1–6

$2,300–$5,750 (toddler), $6,500 (elementary)

Lone Oak Montessori School
10100 Old Georgetown Road
Bethesda, MD 20814
(301) 469-4888

3–5 years

$4,985–$6,875

Manor Montessori School
11200 Old Georgetown Road
Rockville, MD 20852
(301) 299-7400

2–6 years

$4,900–$8,050

Manor Montessori School
10500 Oaklyn Drive
Potomac, MD 20854
(301) 299-7400

Ages 2–8

$4,900–$8,050

Norwood School
8821 River Road
Bethesda, MD 20817
(301) 365-2595

www.norwood.pvt.k12.md.us

K–Grade 8

$12,700–$13,800

Our Lady of Good Counsel High School
11601 Georgia Avenue
Wheaton, MD 20902
(301) 942-1155

www.gchs.com

Grades 9–12

$7,950

Our Lady of Lourdes School
7500 Pearl Street
Bethesda, MD 20814
(301) 654-5376

www.c-a.org

Pre-K–Grade 8

$2,950 (parishioners), $3,700 (non-parishioners)

MOVING TIP

Taking only weather into consideration, the worst months to move into Washington are December, January, and February (snow and rain), and July and August (heat and humidity).

Primary Day School
7300 River Road
Bethesda, MD 20817
(301) 365-4355

Pre-K–Grade 2

$6,300–$9,300

St. Andrew's Episcopal School
8804 Postoak Road
Potomac, MD 20854
(301) 983-5200

www.sa.org

Grades 6–12

$15,200–$16,170

St. Elizabeth School

917 Montrose Road
Rockville, MD 20852
(301) 881-1824

K–Grade 8

$2,940–$3,347 (parishioners),
$5,582 (non-parishioners)

St. Francis Episcopal Day School

10033 River Road
Potomac, MD 20854
(301) 365-2642

Pre-K–Grade 5

$3,050–$9,300

St. Vincent Pallotti High School

113 Street Mary's Place
Laurel, MD 20707
(301) 725-3228

www.pallotti.pvt.k12.md.us

Grades 9–12

$6,650

Takoma Academy

8120 Carroll Avenue
Takoma Park, MD 20912
(301) 434-4700

www.ta.edu

Grades 9–12

$480–$610 per month

Thornton Friends School

13925 and 11612 New Hampshire
Avenue
Silver Spring, MD 20904
(301) 384-0320

www.intr.net/tfup/

Grades 6–12

$11,495–$12,295

Walden Montessori Academy

7730 Bradley Boulevard
Bethesda, MD 20817
(301) 469-8123

2–6 years

$2,000–$7,500

Washington Christian Academy

1820 Franwall Avenue
Silver Spring, MD 20902
(301) 649-1070

www.wca1.org

3 years–Grade 12

$5,324–$6,568

Washington Episcopal School

5600 Little Falls Parkway
Bethesda, MD 20816
(301) 652-7878

www.w.pvt.k12.md.us

Nursery–Grade 8

$6,100–$13,580

Washington Hebrew Congregation Early Childhood Center
11810 Falls Road
Potomac, MD 20854
(301) 279-7505

18 months–Grade 2

$855–$7,350 (temple members),
$1,025–$8,100 (nonmembers)

Woods Academy
6801 Greentree Road
Bethesda, MD 20817
(301) 365-3080

www.woodsacademy.org

Pre-K (Montessori)–Grade 8

$5,825–$8,390

VIRGINIA

Academy of Christian Education
11480 Sunset Hills Road, 10E
Reston, VA 20190
(703) 471-2132

www.ace-academy.com

Pre-K–Grade 6

$6,000–$7,000

Alexandria Country Day School
2400 Russell Road
Alexandria, VA 22301
(703) 548-4804

www.alexandriacountryday.org

K–Grade 8

$8,800–$10,500

Aquinas Montessori School
8334 Mount Vernon Highway
Alexandria, VA 22309
(703) 780-8484

2$^{1}/_{2}$–13 years

$5,355–$7,155

Arlington Montessori House
3809 North Washington Boulevard
Arlington, VA 22201
(703) 524-2511

3–5 years

$3,285

Bethlehem Baptist Christian Academy
4601 West Ox Road
Fairfax, VA 22030
(703) 631-1467

www.bethlehembaptist.net

3 years–Grade 12

$3,200–$4,100

Bishop Ireton High School

201 Cambridge Road
Alexandria, VA 22314
(703) 751-1453

www.ireton.org

Grades 9–12

$6,100–$9,100

Bishop Denis J. O'Connell High School

6600 Little Falls Road
Arlington, VA 22213
(703) 237-1400

www.ee.cua.edu/oconnell

Grades 9–12

$5,100 (Arlington diocese members), $5,950 (non-diocesan Catholics), $6,700 (non-Catholics)

Blessed Sacrament Grade School and Early Childhood Center

1417 West Braddock Road
Alexandria, VA 22302
(703) 998-4170

Pre-K–Grade 8

$2,060–$2,580

Brooksfield School

1830 Kirby Road
McLean, VA 22101
(703) 356-5437

2 years–Grade 3

$5,030–$10,154

Browne Academy

5917 Telegraph Road
Alexandria, VA 22310
(703) 960-3000

www.browneacademy.org

3 years–Grade 8

$3,493–$11,520

Burgundy Farm Country Day School

3700 Burgundy Road
Alexandria, VA 22303
(703) 960-3431

www.burgundyfarm.org

Pre-K–Grade 8

$11,000–$12,000, transfers extra

Calvary Road Christian School and Preschool

6811 Beulah Street
Alexandria, VA 22310
(703) 971-8004

www.crcs.org

3 years–Grade 8

$5,250 (Pre-K), $3,150 (K–Grade 8)

Chesterbrook Montessori School

3455 North Glebe Road
Arlington, VA 22207
(703) 241-8271

$2^{1}/_{2}$–6 years

$3,600–$3,800

Children's House of Montessori
3335 Annandale Road
Falls Church, VA 22042
(703) 573-7599

2¹/₂–6 years

$3,535 (half day) –$5,940 (full day)

Christ Church School
Route 33
Christ Church, VA 23031
(804) 758-2306; (800) 296-2306

www.christchurchva.com

Grades 8–12; boys' boarding school, co-ed day school

$8,850 (day), $21,250 (boarding)

Congressional Schools of Virginia
3229 Sleepy Hollow Road
Falls Church, VA 22042
(703) 533-9711

www.congrsionalschools.org

6 weeks–Grade 8

$8,700–$11,000

Corpus Christi Elementary School
7506 Street Phillip's Court
Falls Church, VA 22042
(703) 573-4570

3301 Glen Carlyn Road
Falls Church, VA 22041
(703) 820-7450

www.corpuschristischool.org

Grades 1–8

$2,255 (parishioners), $4,015 (non-parishioners), $4,345 (non-Catholics)

MOVING TIP

If you can deal with the intense heat and humidity, July and August are not such bad times to move to Washington, since many of the city's residents seem to disappear during those months, easing traffic and parking concerns.

Episcopal High School
1200 North Quaker Lane
Alexandria, VA 22302
(703) 933-3000

www.episcopalhighschool.org

Grades 9–12, boarding school

$23,100

CITY FACT

Warren Beatty and his sister Shirley McLaine, along with fellow actor Sandra Bullock, all attended the same high school in Arlington, Virginia. But not at the same time.

Flint Hill School
10409 Academic Drive
Oakton, VA 22124
(703) 242-0705
www.flinthill.org

Pre-K–Grade 12

$8,855–$13,878

Grace Episcopal School
3601 Russell Road
Alexandria, VA 22305
(703) 549-5067

Pre-K–Grade 5

$1,920–$7,560

Hope Montessori
4614 Ravensworth Road
Annandale, VA 22003
(703) 941-6836

2$^{1}/_{2}$–6 years

$320 per month

Hunter Mill Country Day School
2021 Hunter Mill Road
Vienna, VA 22181
(703) 281-4422

Preschool

$581 per month

Hunter Mill Montessori
2709 Hunter Mill Road
Oakton, VA 22124
(703) 938-7755

2$^{1}/_{2}$–5 years

$4,815 (half day)–$6,795 (full day)

Immanuel Lutheran School
109 Belleaire Road
Alexandria, VA 22301
(703) 549-7323

K–Grade 8

$2,700 (congregants), $3,600 (non-congregants)

Jewish Day School of Northern Virginia

8900 Little River Turnpike
Fairfax, VA 22031
(703) 978-9789

K–Grade 7

$6,830 (K–Grade 1), $7,525 (Grades 2–6), $9,000 (Grade 7)

Langley School

1411 Balls Hill Road
McLean, VA 22101
(703) 356-1920

www.langley.edu.net

Pre-K–Grade 8

$7,765–$13,630

Montessori School of Alexandria

6300 Florence Lane
Alexandria, VA 22310
(703) 960-3498

2¹/₂–12 years

$4,500–$6,850

Montessori School of Cedar Lane

3035 Cedar Lane
Fairfax, VA 22031
(703) 560-4379

2¹/₂–6 years

$3,804 (half-day), $5,749 (full-day)

Montessori School of Northern Virginia

6820 Pacific Lane
Annandale, VA 22003
(703) 256-9577

www.nv.org

2–9 years

$2,420–$6,190

Our Savior Lutheran School

825 South Taylor Street
Arlington, VA 22204
(703) 892-4846

www.osva.org

K–Grade 8

$2,900

Paul VI Catholic High School

10675 Lee Highway
Fairfax, VA 22030
(703) 352-0925

www.paulvinet.com

Grades 9–12

$5,490 (diocesan), $7,210 (non-diocesan)

Potomac School

1301 Potomac School Road
McLean, VA 22101
(703) 356-4101

www.potomacschool.org

Pre-K–Grade 12

$8,925–$15,960

Queen of Apostle School

4409 Sano Street
Alexandria, VA 22312
(703) 354-0714

K–Grade 8

$2,750 (parishioners), $3,450
(Catholic non-parishioners),
$4,200 (non-Catholics)

St. Clement Episcopal School

1701 North Quaker Lane
Alexandria, VA 22302
(703) 998-8795

www.saintclement.org

Pre-K–K

$315 per month (half-day), $825
(full day)

St. Leo the Great School

3704 Old Lee Highway
Fairfax, VA 22030
(703) 273-1211

www.stleoschool.pvt.K12.va.us

Pre-K–Grade 8

$100–$175 per month (half-day
Pre-K); other grades $2,250
(parishioners), $3,200 (non-
parishioners), $3,550 (non-
Catholics)

St. Luke's Catholic School

7005 Georgetown Pike
McLean, VA 22101
(703) 356-1508

K–Grade 8

$2,950 (parishioners), $3,950
(non-parishioners), $5,565
(non-Catholics)

MOVING TIP

Washington is filled with political tran-
sients: people who every two, four, or six
years lose their jobs and leave town. That
means lots of available housing, particularly on Capitol Hill, where many congressional staffers reside. If you are looking
to relocate, keep the "Election Year
Factor" in mind. After elections, almost
everyone in town knows someone who is
moving out.

St. Rita's School

3801 Russell Road
Alexandria, VA 22305
(703) 548-1888

www.saintrita-school.org

K–Grade 8

$2,500 (parishioners), $2,800
(non-parishioners), $3,250
(non-Catholics)

St. Stephen's and St. Agnes Schools

400 Fontaine Street
Alexandria, VA 22302
(703) 212-2705

Pre-K–Grade 12, St. Stephen's
for boys, St. Agnes for girls

$9,990–$13,480 (Pre-K–Grade
5), $14,190 (Grades 6–8),
$15,000 (Grades 9–12)

Thornton Friends School

3830 Seminary Road
Alexandria, VA 22304
(703) 461-8880

Grades 9–12

$12,395

Town and Country School of Vienna

9525 Leesburg Pike
Vienna, VA 22182
(703) 759-3000

3 years–Grade 6

$4,750 (half-day pre-K), $7,900
(all others)

Vienna Adventist Academy

340 Courthouse Road
Vienna, VA 22180
(703) 938-6200

K–Grade 12

$2,300–$4,400

Westminster School

3819 Gallows Road
Annandale, VA 22003
(703) 256-3620

K–Grade 8

$7,900–$9,600

Colleges, Universities, and Professional Schools

The Washington, D.C., area features one of the largest selections of academic options in the country. Here is a list of colleges, universities, and professional schools that offer job-training, with their phone numbers and Web addresses, where you can find additional information and enrollment procedures.

AccuTech Business Institute
(301) 694-0211
www.accutechtraining.com

American University
(202) 885-1470; (202) 885-1000
www.american.edu

Anne Arundel Community College
(410) 647-7100
www.aacc.cc.md.us

Bowie State University
(301) 464-3000
www.bowiestate.edu

Capitol College
(301) 369-2800; (800) 950-1992
www.Capitol-College.edu

Catholic University of America
(202) 319-5000
www.cua.edu/

Charles County Community College
(800) 933-9177
www.charles.cc.md.us

Columbia Union College
(301) 891-4000; (800) 835-4212
www.cuc.edu

Computer Learning Centers
(703) 823-0300
www.GetTheSkills.com

Florida Institute of Technology
(703) 751-1060
www. segs.fit.edu

Frederick Community College
(301) 846-2431
www.fcc.cc.md.us

Gallaudet University
(202) 651-5000
www.gallaudet.edu

Georgetown University
(202) 687-0100
www.georgetown.edu

Germanna Community College
(540) 710-2000
www.gcc.cc.va.us

Hood College
(301) 663-3131; (800) 922-1599
www.hood.edu

Howard Community College
(410) 772-4800
www.howardcc.edu

Howard University
(202) 806-1607
www.howard.edu

Johns Hopkins University
(877) 548-9274
www.jhu.edu

Keller Graduate School of Management
(703) 415-0600; (703) 556-9669
www.keller.edu

Lord Fairfax Community College
(540) 351-1505; (800) 906-5322
www.lf.cc.va.us

Loyola College in Maryland
(410) 617-2000; (800) 221-9107
www.loyola.edu

Marymount University
(703) 284-1500
www.marymount.edu

George Mason University
(703) 993-1505
www.site.gmu.edu

Montgomery College
(301) 353-7744
www.montgomerycollege.com

Mount St. Mary's College and Seminary
(301) 447-6122
www.msmary.edu

Northern Virginia Community College
(703) 323-3000
www.nv.cc.va.us

Old Dominion University
(757) 683-4845; (800) 348-7926
web.odu.edu

Potomac College
(202) 686-0876
www.potomac.edu

Prince Georges Community College
(301) 336-6000
pgweb.pg.cc.md.us

Shenandoah University
(703) 777-7414; (800) 432-2266
www.su.edu

Southeastern University
(202) 265-5343
www.seu.edu

Stratford College
(703) 821-8570; (800) 444-0804
www.stratfordedu

Strayer University
(888) 4STRAYER
www.strayer.edu

TESST Technology Institute
(800) 488-3778

www.testcom

**University of Maryland—
College Park**
(301) 405-1000

www.maryland.umd.edu

**University of Maryland—
University College**
(301) 985-7000; (800) 283-6832

www.umuc.edu

University of Northern Virginia
(703) 536-9588; (877) 536-9588

www.unva.edu/

**University of Phoenix—
Maryland Campus**
(410) 536-7144

www.uophx.edu/maryland

**University of Virginia—
Northern Virginia Center**
(703) 536-1138

uvace.virginia.edu/northern

**Virginia Tech—Northern
Virginia Center**
(703) 538-8324

www.nvgc.vt.edu

George Washington University
(202) 994-1000

www.gwu.edu

Mary Washington College
(540) 286-8000; (888) 692-4968

www.jmc.mwc.edu/

CITY
FACT

Al Gore grew up in Washington, D.C., because his father was a U.S. Senator. But the family never actually owned a home here. Instead, they lived in the Fairfax Hotel, later called the Ritz-Carlton, now called the Fairfax Hotel in Dupont Circle.

Finding a Job

CHAPTER 11

Working in the City

People who move to Washington, D.C., in search of a job—just about any job—have come to the right place. Washington has been a stable employment center since 1996, and, according to the Bureau of Labor Statistics (BLS), it should remain so into 2010.

Where the Jobs Are

The most recent statistics put the unemployment rate in the greater Washington region at 2.3 percent, with surrounding suburban counties—Arlington, Fairfax, Montgomery, and Prince Georges—coming in at an even lower 1.9 percent.

So where are all the jobs coming from? As we mentioned earlier, government, be it federal, state, or local, has historically been the biggest source of jobs in the region. Whether the jobs were actually working within the bureaucracy or for private firms with dealings with the government, Washington, D.C., has always been very much a "company" town.

TRADITIONAL DISTRICT JOBS

Traditionally, jobs in Washington, D.C., have fallen into the following broad categories:

Federal government employee: Salaries are based on grade level and range from $28,000 to $178,000 per year.

Capitol Hill employee: Salaries are more flexible than the federal grade level, but are usually pegged to title and duties. Pay ranges from $24,000 to $130,000 per year.

Government contractor/consulting: Salaries vary wildly, depending on the job. They range from a secretary working for a defense contractor to a computer technician servicing systems in the Department of the Interior to janitorial work. The pay scale ranges from $8 to $10 per hour to executive-level annual salaries of more than $300,000.

Law: There are more than 250 law firms in downtown Washington that do some work related to government, such as lobbying or representing a client before a federal agency. There are also numerous jobs on Capitol Hill that require a law degree or legal background. In top and mid-range private practices, associate salaries are now in excess of $100,000.

Government/corporate affairs or public relations: These are nice terms for "lobbyist," a word that has taken on negative connotations in recent years. Almost every major company and industry in America has an office or representation in Washington to remind politicians and bureaucrats that they exist and are important. Salaries range from $18,000 to $36,000 for office assistants to $75,000 for writers and editors working on newsletters and publications to more than $100,000 for management positions.

Political consulting: Washington is a town of politics, and in order to stay here, politicians need to keep winning. There are more than 150 political consulting firms in D.C.; jobs include phone-bank managers, field campaign managers, speech writers, pollsters, even video specialists. Salaries vary wildly depending on experience and background, from $20,000 for office support staff members to $40,000 for speech writers to $80,000 for management positions.

Print or broadcast journalism: Journalists are a huge presence in Washington. There are more than 500 newspapers, wire services, magazines, and newsletters in the Washington area. Mix in the more than 50 broadcast services, TV and radio, and you get a sense of the possibilities. Salaries vary wildly: $18,000 for young researchers and reporters; $25,000 to $36,000 for newsletter reporters and editors; $40,000 to $50,000 for experienced reporters and editors at wire services and newspapers. There are opportunities for part-time and free-lance writers and editors, too. Journalism jobs also have opened up on the Internet. Online writing and editing salaries are competitive with the print and broadcast media pay scales.

CITY FACT

Local residents generally don't use the letter "I" when addressing mail or listing an I Street address. Rather, they spell it "Eye" Street.

Non-profit or special-interest advocacy groups: From the National Diabetes Association to People for the Ethical Treatment of Animals, there are plenty of special-interest and advocacy groups in town. If you want to make your living supporting and advancing a cause you believe in, there is probably a job in D.C. for you. Don't expect to get rich in the process, though. Salaries for this type of work are typically low, although management positions have salaries in the $80,000 range.

KEY AREAS OF FUTURE ECONOMIC EXPANSION

In downtown Washington, government employment remains the career king. But "beyond the Beltway," with the advent of the "tech" corridors in suburban Virginia and Maryland, the regional employment picture has been radically altered. Instead of people living in the suburbs and commuting into the city, more and more people are living in the city and working in the suburbs. The 'burbs are where many of the "hot jobs" are based.

High-Tech Jobs

Today, more than 350,000 people are working in the D.C. area in the fields of information technology, computer services, telecommunications, aerospace, bio-technology, and bio-science. That's more than 10 percent of the region's workforce. Labor Department estimates indicate that more than 150,000 additional jobs in the tech arena will be filled over the next three years. The BLS estimates that every working day for the next decade, an average of 150 new technology jobs may open up. And when it comes to anticipating job figures in the high-tech field, the Labor Department has historically underestimated employment growth.

According to the BLS, over the next 10 years the five fastest-growing occupations will be in the technology sector: computer engineer, computer support specialist, computer network support specialist, database administrator, and desktop publishing specialist. Washington should see more than a doubling of jobs in these areas in the coming decade.

A recent BLS survey listed the most common tech and bio-science jobs in the area, along with their average salaries. In all, about one in eight jobs in the

MOVING TIP

If you have children who are making the relocation with you, hire a baby-sitter for moving day. He or she can keep the kids out of trouble and free up the parents to concentrate on the job at hand.

Washington market is dependent on the high-tech community. The numbers break down this way:

Type of Job	Number of Jobs	Salary
Engineering, mathematical, and natural sciences managers	14,490	$69,620
Electrical and electronic engineers	13,460	$60,050
Computer engineers	15,930	$57,340
All other engineers	11,860	$60,410
Biological scientists	5,580	$55,260
Medical scientists	1,070	$62,980
All other life scientists	950	$48,960
Biological, agricultural, and food technicians and technologists	1,760	$30,430
Chemical technicians and technologists, except health	510	$29,550
All other physical and life science technicians and technologists	2,700	$32,650
System analysts, electronic data processing	40,700	$57,860
Database administrators	4,020	$48,410
Computer support specialists	15,700	$39,010
Computer programmers	28,640	$47,150
Computer programmer aides	4,650	$31,640
All other computer scientists	4,100	$58,170
Operations and systems researchers/analysts	3,550	$54,410

The state employment commissions in Virginia and Maryland estimate that over the next 10 years their high-tech communities will see an annual increase in hiring at a rate of about 8 percent. They anticipate a continual need for highly trained, computer- and technological-savvy workers.

CITY FACT

There is no "J" Street in Washington between "I" and "K" Streets. Why? Rumor has it Pierre L'Enfant hated Thomas Jefferson and refused to give a street the initial of Jefferson's last name. The more likely reason is that the letter "J" was rarely used in the English language back in the 17th century.

Internet Jobs

Another thing to consider: Many of the jobs related to Web-based businesses aren't even being taken into account in current, published Labor Department statistics. Factor in the thousands of jobs related to the Web, and the Washington region's employment picture becomes even rosier.

Recently the *Washington Post* reported on a Virginia-state survey of six heavily trafficked employment Web sites. Of the 1,821 technology positions that were available, 29 percent were for software programmers and developers, 15 percent were database administrators, developers, and programmers, 14 percent were for Web developers and graphics specialists, and 13 percent were for network administrators and engineers.

Government Jobs

When it comes to government hiring, tech jobs also remain key. But over the next 10 years, the federal government is going to need workers of all stripes and qualifications. Currently, the federal government employs more than 400,000 people in the Washington region. On average, the government fills about 40,000 new or open jobs each year.

Those positions range from janitors to White House policy advisers, from nurses working at the U.S. Naval Hospital in Bethesda to research scientists at the Department of Energy. By 2005, more than 40 percent of all current government employees will be qualified to take early retirement at almost full pension. That means over the next few years literally tens of thousands of jobs will be opening up, especially for computer- and technology-savvy people.

Employment Resources

NEWSPAPERS AND OTHER PUBLICATIONS

The Capital Source
National Journal Group
1501 M Street NW
Washington, DC 20078
(800) 356-4838

If you are a professional or recent college grad looking for job leads in such areas as legislative affairs, public relations, corporate communications, government affairs, real estate, political consulting or lobbying, law, advertising, or any form of media, you will want to purchase a copy of this quarterly publication. Put out by the *National Journal,* a glossy "inside Washington" publication, it contains more than 7,000 names, phone numbers, and e-mail addresses of major political, professional, and media outlets in the area. *The Capital Source* is one of the most indispensable resources you can purchase as you prepare to look for work in Washington. It will help you with job leads and familiarize you with the town's players. It doesn't come cheap at $46.95, but it is worth the price to buy at least one. You can also purchase the *Source* on computer disk, which would allow you, for example, to address letters to all 100 U.S. Senate offices.

The City Paper

www.washingtoncitypaper.com

Various non-congressional jobs, particularly internships, positions with advocacy groups, and jobs in the service industries (waiting tables, bartending, cashiers, etc.) are listed in the Classified section of the *City Paper*.

The Hill

www.thehillnewspaper.com

This weekly, which covers the House and Senate, has an Employment section devoted almost exclusively to congressional jobs.

Roll Call

www.rollcall.com

Another Capitol Hill weekly, it has a small Classified section that includes congressional employment opportunities

The Washington Post

www.washingtonpost.com

The newspaper has an extensive Employment section, which is also accessible online. It offers comprehensive information on the local job market, as well as lots of job listings.

INTERNET RESOURCES

Employment sites on the Internet are popping up faster than you can keep track of, and they frequently merge then re-emerge under different names and addresses. The following is a breakdown of local Washington Web sites that offer employment information and job openings.

www.ardelle.com

This is the site for AA Temps Employment, one of the more well-established temp agencies in Washington, which deal with temporary and temp-to-hire positions in accounting, finance, clerical, administrative, legal, and other professional positions.

www.dc.computerwork.com

Offers local computer job listings and technical employment resources, free résumé posting, and recruiting services for D.C., Baltimore, and surrounding areas.

www.dc-jobs.net

Another D.C. exclusive site, it features free résumé posting as well as access to a database of more than 5,000 computer, healthcare, professional, secretarial, and hospitality positions.

www.dcjobsource.com

A complete job-search site, with an emphasis on the tech corridor.

www.webjobsusa.com

This site features more than 300 jobs and internships in Washington. Positions in government affairs, legislation, print and broadcast journalism, non-profit organizations, public relations, and federal agencies are highlighted.

www.dcmetro.usjobs.com

Search thousands of jobs listed by the D.C. region's fastest-growing tech companies. Allows you to build a Web address and post your résumé.

www.dc.preferredjobs.com

One of the better Web-based job banks for Washington, D.C. It offers a résumé-posting service, a date book for job fairs, and access to a national database of jobs beyond the region. Focus is on computer, engineering, and sales jobs.

MOVING TIP

If you are being relocated to the area by your employer, check your moving contract. Almost all of them guarantee that the movers will not only pack and move the boxes to your new residence, they will also unpack all of the boxes and take the packing materials with them when they leave. Your company is paying for the service; make sure the moving company lives up to its side of the deal.

www.digitalcity.com

This is an all-purpose Washington, D.C., site, with tourist information and the like, as well as a link to several job sites. If you're relocating, it's a good site to bookmark.

www.firstmagnitude.com

This D.C.-based site features want ads for high-tech and engineering jobs exclusively. It's a good, comprehensive site.

www.hirestandard.com

A Washington-based resource for corporate and executive placement.

www.techound.com

This is a site devoted primarily to the high-tech communities in Virginia and Maryland, although there are also many postings for D.C.-based jobs. A good site, with easy access to information.

www.usajobs.opm.gov

To get a sense of just what types of jobs are available within the federal government, go to this Web site, which lists almost all job openings within the federal government, including those that are not based in the Washington area.

www.washingtonjobs.com.

Affiliated with the *Washington Post,* this is one of the best local online job-search engines.

The following Web sites are national, with regional listings for Washington. Most have extensive background information and allow you to post your résumé and create your own Web site.

www.buysellbid.com

www.careerspan.com

www.discoverme.com

www.employment911.com

www.fincareer.com

www.headhunter.net

www.hotjobs.com

www.itclassifieds.com

www.JobSafari.com

www.monster.com

www.vault.com

UNIVERSITY JOBS AND EMPLOYMENT RESOURCES

A number of local educational institutions offer career advice and information on internships and jobs available in the Washington area. While some universities require that you be a student to use these resources, others make their job placement services, want ads, and information on internship and volunteer opportunities available to the general public at no cost, often through their Web sites. The following offer employment resources.

AccuTech Business Institute
(301) 694-0211

www.accutechtraining.com

American University
(202) 885-1470; (202) 885-2514

www.american.edu

Anne Arundel Community College
(410) 647-7100

www.aacc.cc.md.us

Bowie State University
(301) 464-3000

www.bowiestate.edu

Capitol College
(301) 369-2800; (800) 950-1992

www.Capitol-College.edu

Catholic University of America
(202) 319-5000

www.cua.edu/

CITY FACT

Despite what you might have heard, all of Washington, D.C., was not swampland when planners arrived in the late 1700s—only the areas on which the Kennedy Center and the Watergate complex now stand, along with parts of lower Georgetown and other areas along the Potomac.

Charles County Community College
(800) 933-9177

www.charles.cc.md.us

MOVING TIP

Apartments built during the World War II era are prized in D.C. today. Why? The amenities. They typically feature larger living spaces, multiple closets, plenty of windows, and hardwood floors. They usually offer 24-hour security staffs and on-call repairmen, and most have installed up-to-date cable and phone lines. The minuses? Few World War II—era buildings are air-conditioned, and some get poor cable TV reception.

Columbia Union College
(301) 891-4000; (800) 835-4212

www.cuc.edu

Computer Learning Centers
(703) 823-0300

www.GetTheSkills.com

Florida Institute of Technology
(703) 751-1060

www.segs.fit.edu

Frederick Community College
(301) 846-2431

www.fcc.cc.md.us

Gallaudet University
(202) 651-5000

www.gallaudet.edu

Georgetown University
(202) 687-0100

www.georgetown.edu

George Washington University
(202) 994-1000

www.gwu.edu

Germanna Community College
(540) 710-2000

www.gcc.cc.va.us

Graduate School USDA
(202) 314-3300

www.grad.usda.gov

Hood College
(301) 663-3131; (800) 922-1599

www.hood.edu

Howard Community College
(410) 772-4800
www.howardcc.edu

Howard University
(202) 806-1607
www.howard.edu

Johns Hopkins University
(877) 548-9274
www.jhu.edu

Keller Graduate School of Management
(703) 415-0600; (703) 556-9669
www.keller.edu

Lord Fairfax Community College
(540) 351-1505; (800) 906-5322
www.lf.cc.va.us

Loyola College in Maryland
(410) 617-2000; (800) 221-9107
www.loyola.edu

Marymount University
(703) 284-1500
www.marymount.edu

George Mason University
(703) 993-1505
www.site.gmu.edu

Montgomery College
(301) 353-7744
www.montgomerycollege.com

Mount St. Mary's College and Seminary
(301) 447-6122
www.msmary.edu

Northern Virginia Community College
(703) 323-3000
www.nv.cc.va.us

Old Dominion University
(757) 683-4845; (800) 348-7926
web.odu.edu

Potomac College
(202) 686-0876
www.potomac.edu

Prince Georges Community College
(301) 336-6000
www.pg.cc.md.us

Shenandoah University
(703) 777-7414; (800) 432-2266
www.su.edu

Southeastern University
(202) 265-5343
www.seu.edu

Stratford College
(703) 821-8570; (800) 444-0804
www.stratford.edu

Strayer University
(888) 4STRAYER
www.strayer.edu

University of Maryland—College Park
(301) 405-1000
www.maryland.umd.edu

University of Maryland—University College
(301) 985-7000; (800) 283-6832
www.umuc.edu

University of Northern Virginia
(703) 536-9588; (877) 536-9588
www.unva.edu/

University of Phoenix—Maryland Campus
(410) 536-7144
www.uophx.edu/maryland

University of Virginia—Northern Virginia Center
(703) 536-1138
uvace.virginia.edu/northern

Virginia Tech—Northern Virginia Center
(703) 538-8324
www.nvgc.vt.edu

Mary Washington College
(540) 286-8000; (888) 692-4968
www.jmc.mwc.edu/

CITY FACT

The two most prestigious private clubs in Washington are the Metropolitan Club at H and 17th Streets and the Cosmos Club on Massachusetts Avenue. The Metropolitan was founded for businessmen, the Cosmos Club for intellectuals. Guess which one has more members?

TESST Technology Institute
(800) 488-3778
www.tesst.com

INTERNSHIP OPPORTUNITIES

An internship is a great way to get experience or to get a foot in the door; some lead to full-time paying jobs. There are hundreds of unpaid internships available year-round in Washington: on Capitol Hill and in the offices of newspapers, law firms, and advocacy groups. Many are filled through college programs, but many more are open to individuals. Paid internships are harder to come by; generally, they pay $6 to $8 an hour.

Following is a list of private companies, government agencies, public policy centers, museums, and other cultural outlets that have strong internship programs. Almost all offer unpaid, three- to six-month internships. Most offer internships for college credit that are primarily for juniors or seniors in college.

The Media

CBS News

Professional Advancement and
Internships, News Division
2020 M Street NW
Washington, DC 20036
(202) 331-7494
Fax: (202) 331-0275

Unpaid, for college credit only.

C-SPAN

400 North Capitol Street NW,
Suite 650
Washington, DC 20001
(202) 626-7968
Fax: (202) 737-3323

Unpaid.

The Gazette Newspapers

1200 Quince Orchard Boulevard
Gaithersburg, MD 20878
(301) 670-2031

Unpaid, college credit can be arranged.

National Public Radio

Human Resources Department
635 Massachusetts Avenue
Washington, DC 20001
(202) 414-3030
Fax: (202) 414-3047

Unpaid.

The New Republic

1220 19th Street NW, Suite 600
Washington, DC 20036
(202) 331-7494
Fax: (202) 331-0275

The NewsHour with Jim Lehrer

2700 South Quincy Street, Suite 250
Arlington, VA 22206
(703) 998-2150

Paid, college graduates only.

Roll Call

50 F Street NW, 7th floor
Washington, DC 20001
(202) 824-6834
Fax: (202) 824-0902

USA Today

Intern Coordinator
1000 Wilson Boulevard
Arlington, VA 22229

Washingtonian

Intern Coordinator
1828 L Street NW
Washington, DC 20037

Monthly general interest magazine.

The Washington Post

1150 15th Street NW
Washington, DC 20071
(202) 334-5481
Fax: (202) 334-5231

The Washington Times

3600 New York Avenue NE
Washington, DC 20002

Deadline January 31.

Museums/Performing Arts

American Symphony Orchestra League

1156 14th Street NW
Washington, DC 20005
(202) 776-0212
Fax: (202) 776-0224

Stipends available.

Arena Stage

1101 6th Street NW
Washington, DC 20024
(202) 554-9066
Fax: (202) 488-4056

Stipends available.

The John F. Kennedy Center for the Performing Arts

Washington, DC 20566
(202) 416-8807

Full-time, three- to four-month internships. Stipends and unpaid, college credit can be arranged.

National Endowment for the Arts

Office of Human Resources
1100 Pennsylvania Avenue NW
Washington, DC 20506
(202) 682-5472

Volunteer positions as well as full-time unpaid internships.

National Gallery of Art
Washington, DC 20565
(202) 842-6257
Fax: (202) 842-6935

Deadline: March

National Geographic Society
1145 17th Street NW
Washington, DC 20502
(202) 857-7000
Fax: (202) 429-5735

Three-month paid internships.

U.S. Holocaust Museum
100 Raoul Wallenberg Place SW
Washington, DC 20024
(202) 479-9738
Fax: (202) 488-6568

Paid and unpaid.

Federal Government/Public Policy

Brookings Institute
Internship Coordinator
1775 Massachusetts Avenue NW
Washington, DC 20036

Central Intelligence Agency
P.O. Box 12727, Dept. 800
Arlington, VA 22209
(800) JOBS-CIA
Fax: (703) 482-0677

Democratic National Committee
430 South Capitol Street SE
Washington, DC 20003
(202) 863-8000
Fax: (202) 863-8174

MOVING TIP

Even if it's a corporate relocation it's now customary to tip the movers. Generally, in the Washignton area, between $50 to $100 per mover is considered acceptable, and is expected, if the move has gone smoothly and without incident.

Economic Policy Institute
1660 L Street NW
Washington, DC 20036
(202) 775-8810

Environmental Protection Agency
401 M Street NW
Washington, DC 20460
(202) 260-5283

Paid.

Heritage Foundation
214 Massachusetts Avenue NE
Washington, DC 20002
(202) 546-4400
Fax: (202) 546-8328

Library of Congress
Library Services
Washington, DC 20540
(202) 707-5330
Fax: (202) 707-6269

Four-month paid internships.

National Arboretum
3501 New York Avenue NE
Washington, DC 20002
(202) 245-4523

Paid and unpaid.

National Archives and Records Administration
8601 Adelphi Road
College Park, MD 20740
(301) 713-7390, ext. 260
Fax: (301) 713-7342

National Institutes of Health
13 South Drive
Bethesda, MD 20892
(301) 496-2404

Deadline March 1, some stipends available.

National Science Foundation
4201 Wilson Boulevard, Suite 315
Arlington, VA 22230
(703) 306-1185
Fax: (703) 306-2056

Paid, rolling deadline.

Republican National Committee
310 1st Street SE
Washington, DC 20003
(202) 863-8500
Fax: (202) 863-8774

CITY FACT

Despite apparent constant road and highway expansions over the past 10 years, Washington remains the second worst city for traffic congestion in the United States.

Supreme Court of the United States
1 1st Street NE
Washington, DC 20543
(202) 479-3408
Fax: (202) 479-3484

Judicial fellowships, unpaid.

U.S. Department of State
PO Box 9317
Arlington, VA 22219

Deadlines: March 1 for fall, July 1 for spring, November 1 for summer.

The White House
Old Executive Office Building,
Room 84
1600 Pennsylvania Avenue NW
Washington, DC 20502
(202) 479-3408
Fax: (202) 479-5123

Unpaid.

EMPLOYMENT AGENCIES

Following are a few full-time employment agencies based in Washington, D.C.

The Employment Agency
1835 K Street NW, Suite 800
Washington, DC 20006
(202) 296-6606

Diana Ford Employment Agency
1660 L Street NW
Washington, DC 20036
(202) 223-8244

HV Employment Agency
1707 H Street NW
Washington, DC 20006
(202) 955-6442

Maine Employment Centers
1107 I Street
Washington, DC 20002
(202) 737-1911

Barbara Pisarra Employment
1660 L Street NW
Washington, DC 20036
(202) 223-8244

TEMP AGENCIES

There are a number of temporary employment agencies in the District, some specializing in high-tech placement.

AA Temps
1730 K Street NW #307
Washington, DC 20006
(202) 872-0900

ABC Services
3340 M Street NW
Washington, DC 20007
(202) 625-1177

Accounting Resources-Nri
1015 18th Street NW #700
Washington, DC 20036
(202) 296-0443

Accustaff Inc.
1025 Vermont Avenue NW #600
Washington, DC 20005
(202) 289-8970

919 18th Street NW #230
Washington, DC 20006
(202) 293-7770

Adecco Employment Service
1300 Connecticut Avenue NW #750
Washington, DC 20036
(202) 293-2285

Advanced Concepts Inc.
1828 L Street NW #709
Washington, DC 20036
(202) 296-9700

Advantage Resource Group
904 Pennsylvania Avenue SE
Washington, DC 20003
(202) 547-2852

Advantage Staffing Service
1101 Connecticut Avenue NW #450
Washington, DC 20036
(202) 293-0232

Alternative Business Staffing
1225 I Street NW #500
Washington, DC 20005
(202) 296-2570

Andrews Group
1900 L Street NW #300
Washington, DC 20036
(202) 331-0033

Avalon Integrated Services
1911 North Fort Myer Drive #809
Arlington, VA 22209
(703) 358-9000

Blake Hansen & Nye
1155 Connecticut Avenue NW #400
Washington, DC 20036
(202) 429-6611

Bloomfield & Co.
910 17th Street NW #400
Washington, DC 20006
(202) 293-7600

City Staff
1725 K Street NW
Washington, DC 20006
(202) 861-4200

Counsel Temps Inc.
1200 G Street NW #800
Washington, DC 20005
(202) 244-2517

Endeavor Business Services
1250 I Street NW #703
Washington, DC 20005
(202) 289-1435

Georgetown Technology Partners
2457 P Street NW
Washington, DC 20007
(202) 339-0000

Graphic Mac Specialists
1301 Connecticut Avenue NW #Ll
Washington, DC 20036
(202) 785-1333

Help Unlimited Temps
1634 I Street
Washington, DC 20006
(202) 296-0200

Hill Employment
141 Kennedy Street NW
Washington, DC 20011
(202) 829-4040

Interim Personnel
1025 Connecticut Avenue NW
#214
Washington, DC 20036
(202) 293-9370

CITY FACT

If you have friends who work in the House or Senate and are wondering if they are working late, just check out the dome of the Capitol building. There, you will see two lights, if they are on, it indicates that the House and/or Senate remain in late session. At budget times, the lights can be lit well past midnight.

Mayfair Associates Inc.
1828 L Street NW
Washington, DC 20036
(202) 872-0112

McPherson Square Associates, Inc.
1025 Connecticut Avenue NW
#1012
Washington, DC 20036
(202) 737-8777

MEC Resource Group
1029 Vermont Avenue NW #720
Washington, DC 20005
(202) 861-7775

Norell Services Inc.
4401 Connecticut Avenue #604
Washington, DC 20008
(202) 686-1199

PoliTemps
1301 Connecticut Avenue NW
#905
Washington, DC 20036
(202) 785-8500

Don Richard Associates of Washington
1020 19th Street NW #650
Washington, DC 20036
(202) 463-7210

Snelling Personnel Service
1000 16th Street NW #805
Washington, DC 20036
(202) 223-3540

Source Services
1111 19th Street NW #620
Washington, DC 20036
(202) 822-0100

TeleSec Staffing Services
1725 K Street NW #1205
Washington, DC 20006
(202) 223-4900

Temp-Placements Inc.
1120 Connecticut Avenue NW
#450
Washington, DC 20036
(202) 223-8844

Temps & Co.
655 15th Street NW
Washington, DC 20005
(202) 463-8686

MOVING TIP

Don't forget: almost all mileage on your cars from a move is tax-deductible. Save gas receipts and odometer information for filing.

Volt Services Group
1211 Connecticut Avenue NW
#805
Washington, DC 20036
(202) 429-8600

Woodside Employment Consultant
1225 I Street NW #401
Washington, DC 20005
(202) 857-0150

JOB BANKS

Jubilee Jobs
2712 Ontario Road NW
Washington, DC 20009
(202) 667-7390

Potomac Job Corps Center
1 DC Village Lane SW
Washington, DC 20032
(202) 561-6162

Operation Job Match
2021 K Street NW #715
Washington, DC 20006
(202) 887-0136

U.S. Job Corps
200 Constitution Avenue NW
Washington, DC
(202) 219-8550

INDEX

Recreation departments, 256
Registry, online apartment service,
  124
Rehoboth Beach, Delaware, 281
Remax Web site, 143
Rental search, 109–130
Rentals, houses, 130
Rent.com, 124
Renter's insurance, 129
Renwick Gallery, 233
Republic Gardens, 224
Resources Pharmacy, 304
Restaurant at the Jefferson, 248
Restaurants, 241–251
  Woodley Park, 20–21
Reston, 76–79
  housing and rental costs, 78
  key places, 78–79
Reston Community Center Theatre,
  235
Reston Hospital Center, 79
Reston Town Center, 77
Results gym, 220
Richmond, 277–278
Rite Aid, 304
River Club, 249
Riverdale, 98–99
Robinsons Pharmacy, 304
Rock Creek International School,
  340
Rock Creek Park, 8, 20, 137, 141,
  265
Rock Creek Park Horse Centre, 258
Rocklands-Washington's Barbeque
  & Grilling Co., 249
Rockville, 89–91
  housing and rental costs, 90
Rockville Pike, 80, 83
Rodmans Discount Drug, 304
Roll Call
  apartment listings, 122

job listings, 366
Roman Catholic churches, 311
Roommate Assistant online service,
  125
Roommate Locator online service,
  125
Roommates
  for college students, 125
  finder services, 125–126
  online services, 125–126
  pros and cons, 124–125
Roommates Preferred online and
  offline service, 126
Rosecroft Raceway, 255
Rosslyn, Virginia, 47
Round House Theatre, 234
Rouse Co., 107
Royalle Video, 240
Russian Orthodox churches, 310
Ruth's Chris Steak House, 249

S

Sackler Gallery, 233
Safeway stores, 301–302
Saks Fifth Avenue, 317
Salvation Army, 285
Sam & Harry's, 249
Sanitation, useful D.C. area phone
  numbers, 209
Sbarro, 249
SCENA theatre, 235
Schools
  District 1, 323–324
  District 2, 325–326
  District 3, 326–327
  District 4, 327–328
  District 5, 328–330
  District 6, 330–332
  District 7, 332–334
  District 8, 334–335
  enrollment policies, 320–322

About

 **monstermoving.com**

Because moving affects almost *every aspect* of a person's life, Monstermoving.com is committed to improving the way people move. Focusing on an individual's needs, timing, and dreams, the site provides everything for the entire lifestyle transition and every stage of the move. Free service provider content, interactive products, and resources give consumers more control, saving them time and money, and reducing stress. Site features include cost-of-living comparisons, home and apartment searches, mortgage calculators and services, an interactive move-planning application, an address change service, relocation tax advice, and virtual city tours. Monstermoving.com is committed to remaining the most effective, comprehensive, and lifestyle-centric point of service for everyone involved in moving.

Monstermoving.com is part of the Interactive Division of TMP Worldwide (NASDAQ: "TMPW;" ASX: "TMP"). For information, visit *www.monstermoving.com* or call (800) 567-7952.

Bekins is pleased to offer you the following extra value services and cost savings on your next out of state move.

You will receive:

- A minimum discount of 52% off a move between 5,000–7,999 lbs., or a minimum discount of 55% off a move 8,000 lbs. and over.
- Free First Day Service – Bekins will unpack up to 5 cartons of essential items that you will need upon arriving at your new home.
- The FAS-Hotline – Instant access to a powerful collection of relocation assistance services such as a preferred mortgage program, cost of living reports and much more.
- Firm Pick-Up and Delivery Dates on shipments greater than 5,000 lbs.

To find the participating agent nearest you, please use our agent locator at www.bekinsagent.com, or look in the yellow pages under the "movers" heading.

Terms & Conditions

You must have a minimum weight of 5,000 lbs. within the continental U.S. to qualify for the discounts. The rules and restrictions of all programs are described in and governed by HGB 400-M tariff and section 13 of the HGB 104-F tariff, or as amended or reissued.

Coupon must be presented at the time of the estimate, must accompany your moving documents, has no cash value, is void where prohibited, may not be combined with any other discount and is subject to service availability. Coupon sets forth minimum discount level; final discount offer may be affected by prevailing market conditions. Offer is valid at participating Bekins agents only and cannot be used if estimate has already been performed. Offer is not valid for local or intrastate moves. DOT52793. Shipment must be registered using corporate code number 31402.

$10 Off an Avis Weekend Rental

Rent an Avis car for a minimum of two consecutive weekend days and you can save $10 off your rental.
For reservations and information, call your travel consultant or Avis toll free at: 1-800-831-8000.

- Rental must begin by December 31, 2001.
- Valid on an Intermediate through Full Size four-door car.
- Valid at participating locations in the contiguous U.S.
- Subject to complete Terms and Conditions on reverse side.
- An advance reservation is required
- Visit Avis Online at www.avis.com

AVIS
We try harder.

Coupon # **MUWA014**

Bekins is pleased to offer you the following extra value services and cost savings on your next out of state move.

You will receive:

- A minimum discount of 52% off a move between 5,000–7,999 lbs., or a minimum discount of 55% off a move 8,000 lbs. and over.
- Free First Day Service – Bekins will unpack up to 5 cartons of essential items that you will need upon arriving at your new home.
- The FAS-Hotline – Instant access to a powerful collection of relocation assistance services such as a preferred mortgage program, cost of living reports and much more.
- Firm Pick-Up and Delivery Dates on shipments greater than 5,000 lbs.

To find the participating agent nearest you, please use our agent locator at www.bekinsagent.com, or look in the yellow pages under the "movers" heading.